COMMON LEARNINGS:
Core and Interdisciplinary
Team Approaches

COMMON LEARNINGS:
Core and Interdisciplinary Team Approaches

Edited by

GORDON F. VARS

Professor of Education
Kent State University

INTERNATIONAL TEXTBOOK COMPANY
Scranton, Pennsylvania

Preface

Common learnings are those that are considered essential for any citizen, regardless of his occupation or station in life. These fundamental concepts, skills, and values bind a society together, making communication and cooperative action possible. Examples include knowledge of how our government operates, skill in reading, and respect for the worth and dignity of the individual. This "general education" contrasts with the "specialized education" that is designed to promote the uniqueness of each individual. Elective courses in foreign language and specific vocational preparation would fall in the latter category.

Schools ordinarily provide common learnings by requiring all students to study certain subjects. Elementary education consists almost entirely of common learnings, with heavy emphasis on the basic skills of reading, writing, and arithmetic. Most often required at the secondary level are courses in English, social studies, science, mathematics, and physical education. At the junior high or middle school level, brief exposure to art, music, home economics, industrial arts, and perhaps foreign language also may be required.

The separate-subjects approach to common learnings has long been criticized as fragmented and compartmentalized, making it difficult for the learner to see life whole. The core curriculum is an attempt to bring more unity and coherence into this phase of education. Core classes bear a variety of labels and may be taught by one teacher or by an interdisciplinary team.

Since concepts like team teaching, nongrading, individualized instruction, and flexible scheduling now dominate popular discussion in education, many educators ask: What ever became of the core curriculum? Has it, like spats and the hula hoop, passed from the scene after a brief spasm of popularity? Was it such a tender educational idea that it could bloom only in the special climate of the "Progressive Education" era, or does it continue to grow and prosper today? How does the core curriculum of the 1960's and 70's differ from that which was so prominent in the 1940's and 50's? How does core relate to currently popular ideas such as team teaching, independent study, nongraded programs, the middle school, discovery, and the conceptual structure of the disciplines? How can a school develop and maintain a truly modern core curriculum?

In this book, answers to these questions are suggested by a group of educators who are both conversant with the core idea and actively engaged in the current educational enterprise. Chapters have been contributed by four classroom teachers, two principals, three supervisors, and four college professors, one of whom also teaches a middle school core class. In addition, school personnel from many parts of the country have contributed up-to-the-minute descriptions of their programs. The result is a compendium of practical suggestions on how to utilize the core idea in a modern educational program, all based on careful theoretical analysis of core and other innovations in education.

It is hoped that educators at all levels and in all types of schools will find here both food for thought and spurs to action. Those preparing for service in the profession also should benefit from consideration of core and interdisciplinary team approaches to common learnings.

In Chapter 1 the editor traces the evolution of the core concept, defines its four major variations, cites its advantages and disadvantages, and summarizes research to date on its status and effectiveness. In Chapter 2 Rosalind Zapf Pickard describes a multitude of teaching procedures appropriate for block-time and core programs, with emphasis on problem-solving methods. Wayne Jennings, in Chapter 3, emphasizes the core teacher's responsibility for helping students develop as citizens and individuals.

Chapters 4, 5, and 6 examine the implications of team teaching for the core curriculum. Loren Tompkins analyzes the theoretical relationships between the two ideas in Chapter 4 and then describes how a core staff has utilized team teaching. In Chapter 5, H. Edgar Pray explains how common learnings may be provided in a carefully conceived interdisciplinary team teaching program. Team teaching programs that emphasize the humanities are described in Chapter 6 by Parker LaBach and Mary Jane Rodabaugh.

Chapters 7 through 10 examine relationships between core and four current innovations or concerns in education. James D. Wells relates core and the concept of independent study in Chapter 7. The editor considers the relationships between core and the nongraded curriculum in Chapter 8, then joins with Kilmer D. Rivera in Chapter 9 to consider the place of core in the middle school. In Chapter 10, Morrel J. Clute examines the value of the core idea in the education of culturally disadvantaged students and describes how teachers may be prepared for this kind of teaching.

Chapters 11 and 12 are addressed specifically to school leaders. The role in core program development of central office personnel, such as curriculum directors or supervisors, is set forth in Chapter 11 by Robert C. Hanes. The school principal's responsibilities are elaborated in Chapter 12 by Ralph E. Chalender. In Chapter 13 the editor argues the value of the core approach to common learnings for the decades ahead.

Next come brief reports from the field, written by teachers, principals, and other school staff members. These describe many different types of core and block-time programs that are currently in operation in various parts of the United States. A selected bibliography and an appendix bring the book to a close.

At a time when the curriculum field is a chaos of divergent and often conflicting proposals, it is essential that the core curriculum concept be given a thorough examination. It is the conviction of the writers that a well-conceived core curriculum may provide an unsurpassed vehicle for helping young people make sense out of the complex world in which they live. It is hoped that this book will help educators make effective use of this vital concept.

GORDON F. VARS

Kent, Ohio
September 1969

Acknowledgments

The editor wishes first to express his personal indebtedness to Hilda W. Hughes, former professor of education at Antioch College, who sparked an interest in the core idea. At Ohio State University the editor came under the stimulating influence of Harold Alberty and had an opportunity to observe dedicated core teachers at work in the Ohio State University School. William Van Til, then at George Peabody College for Teachers, encouraged the editor to write his doctoral dissertation on the core curriculum and contributed invaluable insights into curriculum foundations. Not to be overlooked are the lessons he has learned from his students during more than twelve years of teaching block-time and core classes in Maryland, Tennessee, New York, and Ohio. Many thanks also are due to the college students, teachers, administrators, and other professionals with whom he has worked as a curriculum consultant and teacher of teachers for the junior high and middle school grades. As Executive Secretary-Treasurer of the National Association for Core Curriculum it has been his privilege to associate with many of the leaders in the core movement.

It goes without saying that a book of this type would be impossible without the generous cooperation of many people. Contributors were warned that their manuscripts would be edited "to the degree necessary to avoid repetition and to achieve as much unity of style as possible." The editor hopes that no major misconceptions crept in during the process, but if they have, he accepts full responsibility. Whether unity of style has been achieved must be judged by the reader. Unfortunately it was not possible to use all the descriptions of current programs that were submitted. Here, again, the editor selected those that were reported.

To these and numerous others who have assisted in this endeavor, many thanks.

G. F. V.

Contents

Part I

APPROACHES TO COMMON LEARNINGS

Part II

CURRENT BLOCK-TIME, CORE, AND INTERDISCIPLINARY TEAM PROGRAMS

Part I

Unit   I

The Core Curriculum

Chapter 1

A Contemporary View
of the Core Curriculum

by Gordon F. Vars

Gordon F. Vars is currently Professor of Secondary Education at Kent State University in Ohio, where he teaches a middle school core class in addition to graduate and undergraduate courses in curriculum and instruction.

The long-range goals of education in the United States are: (1) to prepare citizens who can function effectively in a democratic society, and (2) to help each person become a fully functioning individual. Since these are goals of the entire society, many institutions share responsibility for their attainment—the home, the school, the church, the mass media, and voluntary youth agencies.

How can the schools best carry out their part of this momentous task? From time immemorial the assumption has been that knowledge, passed on from one generation to the next, would suffice. Because scholars find it easier to generate new knowledge if they specialize in a particular discipline, it has been assumed that subject areas derived from these disciplines would be effective vehicles for transmitting knowledge to youth. It was further assumed that students would acquire essential common learnings by studying a specified set of subjects or courses.

During the past decade, vast quantities of time, energy, and money have been spent in updating and reorganizing the school subjects. Yet many educators, including some who are themselves engaged in revamping the curriculum of one field or another, question how everything will fit together. They ask, is exposure to discrete subject areas, even if each is "the newest," the best way to develop effective citizens and fully functioning individuals in today's incredibly complex society?

Mankind today is literally reaching for the stars. At the same time his civilization faces catastrophe unless he can solve such critical problems as the massive pollution of the natural environment, the population growth that is rapidly outstripping the food supply, and the world-wide ideological conflict, characterized by proliferation of nuclear weapons and escalating brush-fire wars.

Meanwhile, American youth distress their elders by their desire to escape from reality via LSD, their motorcycle gangs openly espousing an odious Nazi ideology, their resort to riot and the molotov cocktail as means of social protest, and their general alienation from the social goals once taken for granted. In times like these it behooves educators to take a fresh look at the core curriculum, a major departure from conventional schooling that is designed to provide common learnings through direct confrontation with contemporary problems.

Some Definitions

The core curriculum evolved during the late 1920's and early 1930's as part of the Progressive Education Movement. Elementary education was being transformed under such banners as the "activity movement," the "project method," and "the experience curriculum" and a special name was needed for the various programs that attempted to apply similar ideas in the high school. "Core" was a term used frequently, but others included "general education," "common learnings," "basic education," "unified studies," and, more recently, "block-time."

Frequently core appeared in the high school schedule as a specific course, often meeting for longer than the usual class period. The course might be taught by one teacher who was knowledgeable in several disciplines or by a team consisting, for example, of an English teacher, a social studies teacher, and a science teacher. Sometimes the "core curriculum" was a group of required courses bearing conventional subject labels but focused on some broad problem or theme developed cooperatively by the teachers. Some core classes had almost complete free rein to study any problem or topic, while others worked within limits carefully set by the school staff. Little wonder that there has been confusion and disagreement about the meaning of the term core, not unlike the contemporary problem of defining such concepts as "team teaching," "non-graded program," and "structure of a discipline."

One source of difficulty is that the term *core* has both a generic and a specific meaning. As a generic term, core curriculum may mean approximately the same thing as common learnings or general education. Using a broad definition of the term, Alberty identified five different types of core programs, ranging from a set of specified courses required of all students to a single course in which a teacher and his class were given a large block of time to carry out whatever learning experiences they judged to be worthwhile.[1] Curriculum specialists sometimes use such phrases as "Alberty, Type V" or "Alberty, Type III" to categorize core programs.

In her surveys for the U.S. Office of Education, Wright limited the term to that portion of the common learnings in which content of two or more subject

---

[1]Harold B. and Elsie J. Alberty, *Reorganizing the High-School Curriculum.* 3rd ed. (New York: Macmillan, 1962), pp. 203–229.

areas is combined or fused in some way.[2] Van Til et al. restrict the term still further, limiting it to a program with a specified form of content organization.[3] Although absolute consistency cannot be maintained in a book of this nature, the following terminology, based on Van Til, will be employed.

A *block-time* class is one which a teacher or a team meets for a block of time of two or more class periods and which combines or replaces two or more subject areas that are required of all pupils and ordinarily taught separately. The subject areas most often combined or replaced are English and social studies, although occasionally science and mathematics are included. Some schools have two blocks, one replacing English and social studies and the other replacing science and mathematics. Common learnings not included in the block-time class are provided in separate required courses, such as physical education, and there are the usual electives and student activities.

Most contemporary programs called core might more properly be labeled block-time. Notice that this definition is based primarily upon the way students and teachers are scheduled. The four specific types described below differ according to how content is organized *within* the block-time class.

In the *subject-area block* class each subject area retains its identity and is taught separately, with or without consciously planned correlation. In such a program, for example, words from the history text might appear in the class spelling list, or the teacher might use a literary selection like Esther Forbes' *Johnny Tremain* to reinforce the learning of United States history. Time needed to complete an activity in one subject, such as a debate, might be "borrowed" from another subject included in the block, to be "paid back" some other day. Improved guidance may result as students become better known to their teachers because of their extended time together, but the main focus is on the teaching of English as English, or social studies as social studies.

A *unified studies* course moves a step beyond correlation of separate subject areas. Here subject matter is fused or merged, usually around the basic structure of whatever social studies or science course is replaced by this type of block-time class. Language arts and mathematics are taught largely within the context of social studies or science units, although additional time ordinarily is set aside for specific attention to skills, recreational reading, creative writing, and the like. Regardless of the degree of fusion, however, teaching subject matter is still the main concern in unified studies.

A *core* class is a full and important step removed from either unified studies or the subject-area block class. Here there is reduced emphasis upon mastery of

[2]Grace S. Wright, U.S. Office of Education, *Block-Time Classes and the Core Program in the Junior High School,* Bulletin 1958, No. 6 (Washington, D.C.: Government Printing Office, 1958), pp. 9–19.

[3]William Van Til, Gordon F. Vars, and John H. Lounsbury, *Modern Education for the Junior High School Years.* 2nd ed. (Indianapolis: Bobbs-Merrill, 1967), pp. 181–192.

subject matter, and first priority is given to helping students work toward solving problems that have meaning to them. Subject matter from any area may be utilized, but no content is regarded as sacred, something that *must* be taught no matter what.

In *structured core* the students explore broad "problem areas" or "centers of experience" that are specified in advance by the staff. These areas or centers are categories of human experience that embrace both the personal problems, interests, and needs of students and the problems confronting contemporary society. In emphasis they range from those heavily weighted with adolescent concerns, such as "Personality Development" or "Problems of Family Living," to those that emphasize broader social issues, such as "Intercultural Relations" or "Problems of World Peace." Within these areas, students and teachers cooperatively develop learning units focused on specific problems identified by members of that particular class. The problem areas and illustrative learning units below were developed by Jean V. Marani, supervisor of interns in the public schools of Sarasota, Florida.

Suggested Problem Areas for a Junior High School Core Program That Replaces English and Social Studies

Problem Area	Illustrative Learning Units
Grade Seven	
1. Education and School Living	Orientation to Junior High School
	What Are My Talents?
2. Self-Understanding	Growing Up
	How to Make Wise Decisions
3. Living in the Community	The Outlook for Teenagers in Sarasota
	How Florida Meets the Problems of a Growing State
4. Economic Understanding	How Our Natural Resources Are Utilized
	Business Around the World
5. Intercultural Understanding	Teenagers Around the World
	Understanding Our Asian Neighbors
Grade Eight	
1. Education and School Living	Orientation
	How to Study
2. Personal-Social Relations	Achieving Maturity
	Boy Meets Girl

Problem Area	*Illustrative Learning Units*
3. Democratic Government	Documents of Democracy
	Our Old World Heritage
	The Beliefs of a Democratic
	People
4. Vocational Preparation	Planning for High School
	Vocational Orientation
5. Relationships with Minority	The Negro's Role in Our Society
Groups	Religions of the World
6. Intercultural Understanding	Men and Achievements of the 20th
	Century
	The U.S.'s Rise to World Leadership

Grade Nine

1. Education and School Living	Assessing My Potential
	Our Educational Future
2. Personal-Social Relations	How to Deal with Juvenile
	Delinquency
	Youth's Status
3. Healthful Living	The Community Health Program
	Healthful Products
4. Economic Understanding	My Role as a Consumer-
	Producer
	Money Management
	World Economic Systems
5. Democratic Government	Comparative Governments
	The Citizen's Role in Policy
	Making
6. Intercultural Understanding	The World's Resources
	Ways of Achieving Peace

To aid in teacher-student planning, many schools provide resource units or guides that explore the ramifications of a problem area, suggest objectives, list possible learning activities and instructional materials. From these a teacher and his students can select or develop learning experiences they deem most appropriate. In preparing resource units, staff members may be joined by parents, students, university consultants, and other knowledgeable people.

In *unstructured core*, students and teachers are free to study any problem that they consider worthwhile. To be sure, classes usually rule out topics that they have studied before, that interest only a minority of the students, or for which the school and community provide insufficient learning resources. In some cases criteria such as these are defined in advance by the staff; at other times they are developed cooperatively by teachers and students.

Units studied in unstructured core may fall within the same problem areas or centers of experience as those of a structured core program. Often as not, however, they may cut across or combine several areas. Consider, for example, the class that started out to study boy-girl relations, became concerned with the problem of juvenile delinquency in the local community, and ended up spearheading a community-wide effort to provide wholesome recreation for young people.

In addition to work on broad problems or topics, students in all types of block-time classes spend a good deal of time developing their communication skills, reading for enjoyment, carrying out homeroom-type activities, discussing current affairs, solving problems of interpersonal relations, and the like. The problem-centered unit provides the central focus of instruction, but in some cases it may actually involve as little as one-third of the class time.

It may be seen that the four types of block-time classes fall along a continuum, with each succeeding type departing further from commitment to predetermined subject matter. Some curriculum planners see the subject-area block class as merely the first step in a process of curriculum development and staff improvement leading ultimately to full-fledged core teaching in every classroom. However, differences in philosophy and background make it unlikely that all teachers, even those in the same school, will arrive at the same point, even if they accept core as the ideal toward which they aspire.

The overall pattern or design of the curriculum within the core classes of a particular school or district may be referred to as the *core program*. Thus the core program in one district may be defined by a series of preplanned problem areas, whereas in another the core program may be bounded only by a statement of objectives and some criteria to be used in guiding teacher-student selection of problems for study.

A school that utilizes some kind of core class to provide a major portion of students' common learnings is said to have a *core curriculum*. Ideally, other courses, activities, and services are coordinated with and contribute to the learning experiences provided in the core class. For example, specialists from various subject fields may help to plan the core course and serve as special resource people for certain activities. Students carrying out core projects may work in home economics, art, or industrial arts laboratories. Guidance specialists may work in and through the core classes. Thus the core program may become the hub around which revolve activities that contribute to both general and specialized education.

Advantages and Disadvantages

New Jersey secondary school principals identified the following as advantages of block-time when compared with a conventional program of separate subjects.

Advantages of Block-Time Classes[4]

1. Teachers have fewer pupils for a longer period of time.
   (a) They get to know individual pupils better.
   (b) The guidance function is more readily achieved.
   (c) There is greater opportunity to provide for individual differences.
   (d) Earlier identification of exceptional pupils is possible.
   (e) There can be more attention to continuous growth of the total individual.
2. Pupils meet fewer teachers.
   (a) This provides a gradual transition from the self-contained elementary to the departmentalized secondary program.
   (b) There can be more effective orientation and adjustment to the new environment.
   (c) There is greater security for the pupil since he is well acquainted with at least one teacher.
3. The same teacher teaches one group of pupils two or more subject areas.
   (a) More effective correlation and integration by both pupils and teachers is possible.
   (b) There are greater opportunities for application of knowledge and skills.
   (c) There is more efficient use of time as a result of reduced instructional duplication.
4. Pupils and teachers are together for continuous periods of time greater than a single period.
   (a) Greater flexibility and variety of learning activities are possible.
   (b) Greater continuity of learning experiences is possible because of reduced emphasis on fixed time allotments and period changes.
   (c) There are better opportunities for teacher-pupil planning and cooperative evaluation.
   (d) It is easier to schedule field trips and the use of other resources outside the classroom.
   (e) The class can deal with topics of value to early adolescents whether or not they "fit" a particular subject area.

Core, as a special variant of block-time, exhibits all these advantages and more. For example, the content studied in core tends to have immediate appeal to students. Whether the program is structured or unstructured, the focus is on the needs of young people growing up in contemporary society, as well as upon

---

[4]Adapted from "Block-Time Programs in Junior High Schools and Six-Year High Schools in New Jersey," *Secondary School Bulletin of the New Jersey State Department of Education*, No. 2 (March 1960), pp. 2–3.

current social problems. Through teacher-student planning this content is brought even closer to the lives of a particular group of students. Under these circumstances a student's school experiences are much more likely to result in changed perceptions, values, and behavior.

Organizing content around problems further enhances learning. Students become actively involved when examining genuine controversial issues. This is not to suggest that all learning in a core class is problem-centered, or that students are expected to "solve" complex social problems. Examination of issues provides the motivation for whatever additional systematic study proves to be desirable, and, in the process, students learn useful strategies for attacking problems.

Core content also enhances the guidance advantages inherent in any block-time class. Concern for guidance infuses the entire core curriculum. Problem areas include direct attention to many of the needs and developmental tasks of the learner that are the usual concern of a guidance department. Teacher-student planning focuses attention even more sharply on specific concerns of the students in the class. Personal conferences with the teacher grow naturally out of study of such units as "Getting Along with Others," "Planning My Career," or "Finding Values by Which to Live." These informal interviews in turn may lead the teacher to refer the student to guidance specialists for further, in-depth counseling, if needed. In a core program, curriculum, methods, and personal counseling may be focused on guidance objectives, hopefully with the coordination and support of well-trained guidance specialists.

The following are the disadvantages of block-time that are sometimes cited. Note that many of them reflect the point of view that subject-matter mastery is the desired outcome of education.

Disadvantages of Block-Time Classes

1. Curriculum Difficulties
   (a) Combining subject areas may blur the distinctive nature of the disciplines involved.
   (b) Effective sequence in one subject area may be distorted in an attempt to correlate it with another.
2. Teaching Difficulties
   (a) If the teacher is ineffective, the student will have poor teaching in two subjects instead of one.
   (b) The longer period of time together may aggravate a personality clash between teacher and student.
   (c) The extended period may prove tiresome and boring to students if the teacher does not use varied learning activities.
   (d) The teacher may stress one subject and neglect the other.
3. Guidance Difficulties
   (a) The teacher may lack interest in or preparation for teacher-counseling.

(b) The teacher may be tempted to go beyond his depth in counseling with students.

(c) The teacher may experience role conflict in trying to combine teaching and counseling.

(d) Exclusive reliance on teachers to provide guidance may deny students access to highly trained and impartial counselors.

4. Administrative Difficulties

(a) Continuous in-service education of block-time teachers is necessary to realize the full benefits of the program.

(b) The block-time program must continually be interpreted to students, parents, other teachers, and the public.

(c) The double period may introduce some rigidity into the daily schedule.

(d) A common planning period for block-time teachers is desirable but difficult to schedule.

5. Resource Difficulties

(a) Instructional materials are seldom designed to capitalize on correlation of subjects.

6. Certification Difficulties

(a) Teachers fully qualified in two secondary teaching fields are relatively rare.

(b) Available teachers may be trained in the same field, reducing the possibility of exchanging classes and learning from one another.

When applied specifically to a core curriculum, several of the above disadvantages become irrelevant. Core is based on the premise that the distinctive nature of the disciplines should *not* be preserved, and that sequence is to be found not in the structure of a discipline but in the problem-solving process. Direct study of a discipline, as a discipline, may be appropriate elsewhere in the school program, but not in core. It is interesting to note that some curriculum experts advocate a program that consists of a core class *and* separate courses in the disciplines usually replaced by core. To date this idea has had very limited trial in the schools.[5]

Inadequate teachers hamper any program, and many of the criticisms of block-time are essentially criticisms of bad teaching. It is ironic that when students receive poor instruction in English, the teacher may be replaced, whereas poor instruction in core may lead the school to scrap the entire program. Preservice teacher preparation for core is hampered by the fact that even when colleges offer special preparation for core teachers, few students enroll because the course they are preparing to teach is found in only a minority of secondary schools. Continuous in-service education is necessary to launch and maintain any curriculum innovation; core is no exception.

[5]Van Til et al., pp. 193–194.

Inadequate financial support lies behind a number of the disadvantages listed; this, too, is not peculiar to core. In the long run, however, the real key to the success of an educational program appears to be the administrator. An effective educational leader can muster community support, provide the needed in-service programs, and solve many of the adminstrative problems inherent in any curricular innovation.[6]

Research

To what extent have schools been able to capitalize on the advantages and minimize the disadvantages listed above? A recent bibliography listed more than fifty studies designed to test the effectiveness of all types of block-time programs.[7] In general, the preponderance of evidence is that students in block-time programs learn conventional subject matter and skills as well as or better than those in separate-subject programs. Moreover, the teachers, pupils, and parents involved usually favor the program.

Unfortunately, researchers do not always indicate precisely what kind of block-time program is being evaluated, and teachers' differences in approach are obscured. Many studies were made before a clear-cut typology of block-time programs was available, and even the more recent studies rarely utilize newly developed techniques such as interaction analysis to get at specific teacher behavior in the classroom. In other words, while the amount of research on this question is impressive, measures have been too coarse to detect more subtle differences, such as those between structured and unstructured core.

Core research also is hampered by the difficulty of measuring such outcomes as critical thinking ability, personal and social adjustment, and democratic attitudes. Many of the pioneering instruments and procedures developed for the Eight Year Study[8] failed to gain widespread acceptance, largely because scoring was complicated and time-consuming. It is to be hoped that modern data-processing equipment will make it easier to assess some of the less tangible outcomes of education. In the meantime, educators must do the best they can with rating scales, inventories, observation, and other informal evaluation procedures.[9]

A number of research studies show the expected superiority of core over conventional programs, but differences are not as large as predicted. After examining research reported over a sixteen-year period, Wright pointed out the

---

[6]See Henry M. Brickell, *Organizing New York State for Educational Change.* (Albany: New York State Education Department, 1961), pp. 22–24; Gordon F. Vars, "Administrative Leadership–Key to Core Program Development," *Bulletin of the National Association of Secondary-School Principals,* Vol. 46 (February 1962), pp. 91–103.

[7]Gordon F. Vars, "A Bibliography of Research on the Effectiveness of Block-Time Programs" (Department of Secondary Education, Kent State University, 1967).

[8]Eugene R. Smith, Ralph W. Tyler, and others, *Appraising and Recording Student Progress* (New York: Harper & Brothers, 1942).

[9]See, for example, Merle E. Bonney and Richard S. Hampleman, *Personal–Social Evaluation Techniques* (New York: Center for Applied Research in Education, 1962).

following difficulties in judging the effectiveness of core on the basis of existing studies:

1. Too few of the studies reported may have actually been the type of program which uses the problem-solving approach in real problem situations. In other words, the class or classes tested may have been English-social studies fusions, providing little opportunity for pupils to work on problems of concern to them, to engage in teacher-pupil planning, and generally to be part of a democratic social-living situation. Unless the situations tested are genuine core situations with stated core objectives, the core program cannot be judged by the results of the studies.

2. Too frequently teachers are not adequately prepared for core teaching. When such teachers attempt to use certain core techniques, they may lack the necessary understanding to make these techniques effective in pushing the class towards the attainment of the desired behavioral goals.

3. Behavioral goals are not readily tested objectively. It has always proven difficult to find valid and reliable instruments with which to measure growth toward a wider range of educational values than is encompassed by subject achievement.[10]

Any one who contemplates introducing any kind of block-time program in his school should familarize himself with the research, at least to the extent of studying some of the summaries listed in the bibliography. This will provide him with data to use in reassuring teachers, parents, and students that they need fear no loss of achievement in the new program. Moreover, the better studies may provide models of the kind of continuous evaluation desirable. Carefully conducted research studies are especially needed when the schools are undergoing widespread critical examination from both within and without the profession.

Status

Although popularity is by no means an adequate measure of the worth of an idea, numerous studies have been made of the proportion of schools that have block-time programs. These suffer from the usual weaknesses of sampling surveys, plus the added difficulty of definition of terms. The more detailed studies, such as those conducted by Wright for the U.S. Office of Education, are particularly helpful because they describe how programs have been initiated and developed in various parts of the country.

Block-time has been especially well received at the junior high school level. The block-time class is seen as a desirable transition between the single-teacher self-contained classroom of the elementary school and the complete departmentalization of the high school. The guidance emphasis also is important for

[10]Grace S. Wright, U.S. Office of Education, *The Core Program: Unpublished Research, 1956-1962,* Circular 713 (Washington, D.C.: Government Printing Office, 1963), p. 11.

youngsters going through the stresses and strains of adolescence. U.S. Office of Education surveys have revealed the following percent of junior and junior-senior high schools having at least some block-time classes:[11]

Type of School	Percent of Schools		
	1948–49	1956–57	1959–60
Junior high schools	15.8	31.4	40.0
Junior-senior high schools	6.4	12.1	16.4

Fifty percent of the junior high schools studied by Lounsbury in 1964 had block-time,[12] while Gruhn found an incidence of 46 percent in his 1965 survey of schools enrolling 300 or more pupils in grades 7, 8, and 9.[13] Wide variations from state to state have been noted in more localized block-time surveys. In all studies the incidence of genuine core appears limited. Nevertheless, the outward form of core—the block-time class—remains prominent in junior high schools.

A number of the early core experiments were conducted at the senior high school level. In 1956 Bossing sampled 1,000 upper secondary schools and found block-time in 9.3 percent of the junior-senior high schools, 5.8 percent of the four-year high schools, and 6.6 percent of the senior high schools.[14] Note that the figure for senior high schools is less than one-fourth the percentage Wright found that same year in junior high schools. In the absence of more recent studies one may only hazard the guess that few block-time or core programs exist in grades 10 through 12, with the possible exception of the team-taught humanities courses discussed in later chapters.

At both junior and senior high levels, schools otherwise completely departmentalized may have block-time or self-contained classes for students with learning difficulties. An extended period of time with one teacher is often recommended for the mentally retarded, the slow learner, the emotionally disturbed, and the culturally disadvantaged. New York City's XG program for slow learners, for example, was introduced in 1948, and Cleveland's first Transition Class for culturally disadvantaged students began in 1960. Unfortunately, surveys seldom differentiate between these special classes and block-time programs required of all students.

Trends

To estimate where the core movement may be headed today it is necessary

[11] Grace S. Wright and Edith S. Greer, U.S. Office of Education, *The Junior High School: A Survey of Grades 7-8-9 in Junior and Junior-Senior High Schools, 1959–60,* Bulletin 1963, No. 32 (Washington, D.C.: Government Printing Office, 1963), p. 20.

[12] John H. Lounsbury and Harl R. Douglass, "Recent Trends in Junior High School Practices, 1954–1964," *Bulletin of the National Association of Secondary-School Principals,* Vol. 49 (September 1965), p. 92.

[13] William T. Gruhn and Harl R. Douglass, unpublished study of block-time and core programs, 1965. (Used with permission.)

[14] Nelson L. Bossing, "Development of the Core Curriculum in The Senior High School," *School Review,* Vol. 44 (May 1956), p. 224.

to look briefly at where it has been. The roots of the core idea may be traced as far back as the writings of Spencer and Herbart in the 1800's, but school programs bearing the core label first appeared in the 1920's. Core programs were prominent in many of the high schools that participated in the Eight Year Study of the Progressive Education Association between 1932 and 1940. In the 1940 edition of his book, *The Emerging High School Curriculum and Its Direction*, Harold Spears remarked at the popularity of the core curriculum and predicted its widespread acceptance. A common learnings course was a salient feature of the ideal schools depicted by the Education Policies Commission in its influential reports, *Education For All American Youth*, 1944, and the 1952 sequel, ...*A Further Look*. The year 1953 marked the first meeting of what was to become the National Association for Core Curriculum, an organization that continues to hold annual conventions in various parts of the country and to publish a quarterly newsletter, *The Core Teacher*. Throughout this period, core was the subject of numerous magazine articles and discussions at educators' meetings.

Developing the Core Curriculum, a definitive text by Faunce and Bossing, was first published in 1951 and revised in 1958. General procedures for *Developing a High School Core Program* were set forth in 1957 by Lurry and Alberty. Two books on teacher-pupil planning, one by Giles in 1941 and another by Parrish and Waskin in 1958, reflected a persistent emphasis on that process by core educators. The first comprehensive methods textbook emphasizing procedures especially appropriate for core classes was Zapf', *Democratic Processes in the Secondary Classroom*, published in 1959. Methods also received extensive treatment in *The General Education Class in the Secondary School*, a 1960 publication by Hock and Hill, and in both the 1961 and 1967 editions of *Modern Education for the Junior High School Years*, by Van Til, Vars, and Lounsbury.

Popular discussion of the core idea reached its peak in the 1940's and early 1950's. It was overshadowed in the late 1950's and 1960's by the post-sputnik demand for more rigorous instruction in science and mathematics, followed by widespread efforts to revise programs in most subject areas.

Since to many people, "out of sight means out of mind," some observers have jumped to the conclusion that the core curriculum has passed from the scene. Introducing Harvey Overton's article on "The Rise and Fall of the Core Curriculum," the editor of *Clearing House* proclaimed:

The growing rejection of the core has shaken the foundations of education; it has caused a severe rent in the solid wall which for years encased the curriculum. Who will weep over the demise of core? Let the diehards carry on with the laments. As for me, it represents significant educational progress.[15]

[15] Harvey Overton, "The Rise and Fall of the Core Curriculum," *Clearing House*, Vol. 40 (May 1966), p. 532.

Even the staunchest core advocate would be dumbfounded by the suggestion that core has been so deeply entrenched that its "demise" shakes education to its foundations. The "solid wall" metaphor would leave him completely perplexed. As shown above, core has never been the dominant pattern in secondary education, even at the junior high school level, and one of its main purposes has been to break down the "walls" between subjects. The editor's rhetoric is yet another example of the emotional fervor frequently brought forth by the core idea in both its opponents and its supporters.

Asserting that the core curriculum has "fallen," Overton blames educators' failure to arrive at common definitions of terms, the lack of experimental support of the core idea, the demise of the experimentalism, and zeal for social reform that motivated the Progressive Education Movement. Yet he admits that "the problems of American education to which the pioneers of core addressed themselves are still with us, magnified and more unmanageable than before."[16]

Conclusion

Despite premature efforts to bury it, core remains remarkable lively today.[17] In classrooms throughout the nation, teachers of block-time classes strive to approach the core ideal as closely as they can under the circumstances in which they teach. Others seek similar results through a variety of team teaching programs, often under such labels as humanities or American studies. Independent study programs in many schools represent a formalization of the kind of individualized instruction usually associated with core. Core ideas and ideals also are manifest in many of the modified self-contained programs in the burgeoning middle schools, not to mention numerous special educational programs for the disadvantaged. Each of these modern-day transformations of core is examined in detail in subsequent chapters of this book. Taken together they testify to the vitality of the concept and suggest that, in one form or another, the core curriculum will be with us for some time to come.

[16]*Ibid*, p. 536.
[17]See Gordon F. Vars, "Core Curriculum: Lively Corpse," *Clearing House*, Vol. 42 (May 1968), pp. 515–519.

Chapter 2

Teaching and Learning

in a Core Class

by Rosalind Zapf Pickard

Unique teaching methods are not implicit in the core concept. Yet teaching a core class calls into play a number of techniques and procedures that are less frequently used in conventional classes. These are elaborated here by an experienced core teacher, author of Democratic Processes in the Secondary Classroom (Prentice-Hall, 1959). Until recently Dr. Pickard served as Supervisor of Program for Early Adolescents in the Detroit Public Schools.

Whether a program is listed as block-time, unified studies, structured core, or unstructured core, the general procedures for classroom operation are quite similar. The differences lie largely in the areas considered for study rather than in procedure. In all four approaches the following characteristics can be distinguished in the daily operation of a class:

1. The use of the problem-solving approach to relatively large units of work which cut across subject-matter lines, rather than a page-by-page use of a single textbook.
2. Pupil-teacher planning of many classroom activities.
3. Frequent small-group work.

Problem-Solving Methods

Problem-solving methods of operation can be used best when course content is broken into units larger than a single topical chapter in a text. An overall question or problem to be considered is decided upon by the teacher, as often as possible in consultation with the class. Then subproblems are selected and studied by small groups. Techniques of research, such as use of resources and note-taking, are taught as pupils use a wide variety of materials—reference books, textbooks, magazines, newspapers, transparencies, films, filmstrips, and the like. Information gleaned by individuals from these and other sources is shared with the other members of the small group and later presented by the group to the entire class.

19

The amount of pupil-teacher planning which a teacher does depends both upon his experience and the degree to which a class can handle it. However, it is important to use pupil-teacher planning as frequently as possible, using at first simple situations in which pupils may assist in reaching decisions, followed by more difficult ones as they show success. A problem which pupils have helped both to select and to plan has more interest and meaning to them than one selected and planned solely by the teacher. Because of their involvement, pupils feel more responsibility for the problem's solution. Thus pupil-teacher planning supplies motivation toward the class work in addition to helping pupils learn how to plan.

Of course, small groups are not used for every aspect of core work. Whenever it is important to involve pupils in sharing their ideas or when a division of labor will help in solving a problem, the small-group method should be used. Small groups are usually used, for example, in working on the major units throughout the year.

A part of the content of a year's work in a core or block-time class includes the development of the skills and techniques of democratic operation. At a time such as the present, when the free world, our own country included, is threatened as never before, we must recognize and accept the responsibility for helping youth to understand the meaning of democracy and to develop the skills and techniques needed for moving into adult life as informed, skilled citizens in a democracy. The skills needed include the ability to think and work with others in small groups and in large groups, as well as the ability to think critically as an individual.

Neither the skills of working with others, nor those of problem solving, come automatically. Working in small groups, learning to plan a unit, learning to use the facilities of a library to best advantage, all of these must be taught. They are, therefore, a part of the content of a core course.

Guidance

Since a teacher in a block-time class has contact with his pupils for two periods each day instead of the usual single period, considerable attention is given to the educational and personal guidance of the boys and girls. Guidance is an integral part of all classroom activities. The assumption is made that the teacher cannot avoid "guiding," and that he influences in one way or another the attitudes children develop toward learning, toward achievement, toward themselves. He does this by the way he lives in the classroom—his words, his relationship to the pupils, his arrangement of the room, his methods of operation—in short, by everything he says or does. There will be occasions, of course, when considerable time needs to be spent on some particular aspect of group or individual guidance. Such specific guidance activities are not included in this chapter, since they are treated extensively in books on guidance, especially those that stress the teacher's role in the process.

How to Use the "Guide to Teaching a Block-Time Class"

Detailed suggestions are offered in the following "Guide to Teaching a Block-Time Class." It is designed for a two-period subject area block-time program that combines English, social studies, and guidance. In some classroom activities the elements of English and social studies are identical. Teaching the two subjects together thus saves a great deal of time. For example, learning how to use library resources is as important to social studies learning as it is to English. There are also activities in either the English or social studies field for which no reference is made to the other field. Examples might be developmental reading in the language arts area or the practice of map reading in social studies.

The techniques described should, of course, be modified to fit the particular school and classroom situation in which they are to be used. The list of suggested activities is far from complete. Nor should the guide be considered as a course of study, such that all the items included are to be accomplished. Rather, the core teacher should use it as a point of departure in planning his own program.

Two phases of a block-time program are considered: (1) *Orientation and Organization of a Block-Time Class,* and (2) *Working on a Unit.* As the title indicates, the first suggests ways in which a teacher and his class can get acquainted at the beginning of the year and how they can establish the goals and procedures necessary if they are to function as a democratic group. The second includes references to history or geography topics for the benefit of teachers who feel some obligation to cover conventional subject matter. The procedures suggested, however, are easily adaptable to any unit of study in any type of block-time program.

For each item listed in the column headed *Purpose,* a number of activities are enumerated in the column headed *Possible Activities.* Reading horizontally across the page, various aspects of social studies, English, and guidance are indicated for each activity. The dotted lines separate the materials referring to one activity from those referring to another activity. At the conclusion of the material related to an item listed in the *Purpose* column, a heavy ruled line has been drawn. The sequential development of a unit may be inferred by reading down the page, but teachers should not feel bound to follow these steps exactly.

A Guide to Teaching a Block-Time Class*

I. Orientation and Organization of a Block-Time Class

Purpose	Possible Activities	Social Studies Aspects	English Aspects	Guidance Aspects
A. To help pupils become acquainted with one another. (All of the activities listed would probably not be used.)	1. Howdy Tags may be used.[1] This is a 15–20 minute activity. Each tag, approximately 5" X 8" in size, has a narrow space at the top for the pupil's name. This part can be torn off and worn. Class members move about the room asking fellow pupils to sign their names on the larger section of the tag. Both pupils and teacher participate.			a. The teacher has an opportunity to speak to each pupil individually and each pupil has a moment of special attention from the teacher. b. The teacher watches for nonparticipants, for aggressive individuals, etc.
	2. Paired interviews help pupils become acquainted. The class is divided into pairs. Each child interviews the other member of his pair and later introduces him to the class. Some things which might be reported are: • former school attended • hobbies or interests		a. As the children introduce one another the teacher listens for and records for later use the names of pupils who: • mumble • lisp • stutter • vocalize a pause (a-uh) • transfer one sound for another	The teacher watches for and records the names of pupils who seem to be shy and have difficulty speaking before the group as well as those with speech difficulties. He also records the names of those who speak easily and well before the group.

- brothers and sisters
- an interesting place visited
- omit parts of words

3. A *Who's Who* bulletin board always interests pupils.[2] Each pupil (and the teacher) makes a *Who's Who* card on a 5" X 8" sheet of colored paper or index card. Photographs, drawings, magazine cut-outs, or stick figures, may be used to illustrate the items included on the *Who's Who* card. Types of items to be included, such as family, pets, hobbies, and the like, are pupil-teacher planned. The cards are exhibited on the bulletin board.	a. Time should be set aside in class for planning the cards. The teacher should assist where needed: spelling of unusual words, suggestions for items to include, ways to illustrate, etc. b. Discuss interesting headings for cards as well as interesting titles for items included.	a. The teacher becomes aware of pupils' interests and family backgrounds. Their creative possibilities and the ability to organize materials are also shown to some extent through this activity.
4. A Nationality Tree is another possible activity. Where many nationali-	a. The countries are located on a world map. b. Facts about these coun-	a. The spelling of the names of the countries is considered.
		a. The teacher's interest in stories about *all* the countries represented

*Adapted from *Combining English, Social Studies, and Guidance in a Block-of-Time Class.* Copyright 1965 by the Detroit Public Schools.

[1] Rosalind Zapf, *Democratic Processes in the Secondary Classroom* (Englewood Cliffs, N.J.: Prentice-Hall, Inc., 1959), pp. 27–28.

[2] *Ibid.,* pp. 33–34.

Purpose	Possible Activities	Social Studies Aspects	English Aspects	Guidance Aspects
	ties are represented, a tree can be drawn on a large sheet of paper. Each limb is marked with the name of a different country. Each pupil writes his name on a leaf and attaches it to the branch which represents his nationality or that of his ancestors.	tries and interesting customs that differ from our own are told by the pupils during the discussion. c. Surnames which indicate nationality background can be discussed, such as: Kelly, Olsen, Schmidt.	b. Pupils are urged to ask questions and to talk about the things they know concerning these countries. c. A paragraph may be written, entitled: • My Grandfather Told Me • My Leaf on the Tree • My Grandmother Told Me d. The teacher records, for future use, the types of writing errors made.	helps in setting the tone of respect for people with widely differing backgrounds. b. Knowledge of the cultural background of the pupils is provided for the teacher.
B. To help pupils adjust to a school new to them.	1. A tour of the school plant can be led by the teacher or by members of an older class of pupils.	a. Floor plans in the school handbook may be followed during the tour. b. Simple unlabeled floor plans may be duplicated. Pupils label the plans as the tour proceeds. c. Pupils draw a map of the school grounds with N, S, E, W directions indicated.	a. Pupils write a paragraph on one of the following: • On My Way to School • My First Day • The People in This School • What I Like About This School • What I Don't Like About This School b. The teacher records for future use the types of writing errors made.	a. Behavior rules should be pupil-teacher planned before taking the trip. Consideration for the classes in session during tour time, for property, and for one another should be stressed. b. The reaction each child has to his new school home often gives the teacher clues as to which pupils need special help

			in adjusting to the new situation. These might well be the pupils with whom the teacher has the *first* individual conferences. There should be a conference with every child, however, as soon as possible.
2. The school boundaries can be drawn on a city map. The location of each child's home can be marked with a crayon.	Directions N, S, E, W, etc., may be discussed and the direction each child travels in coming to school.		
3. A visit to the school library is an important part of the orientation to the school. If possible the Librarian should set a time when he can work with the class to acquaint the pupils with the location and use of the library resources. Rules for the withdrawal and return of books should be clarified.	The locations and use of various resources of the school library should be pointed out such as: • maps • atlas • dictionary • history and geography book section • encyclopedia • almanac • card catalog • picture file • clipping file • *Readers' Guide to Periodical Literature*	a. Same as for *Social Studies Aspects* plus: • fiction book section • poetry book section • drama book section b. As an outgrowth of the introduction to the library a beginning can be made in the reading of fiction books.	The teacher cannot assume that because pupils have been exposed to such an orientation to the library that they will now be able to use the resources fully. Such ability is of slow growth requiring an infinite amount of assistance and endless patience on the part of both the teacher and the librarian.

Purpose	Possible Activities	Social Studies Aspects	English Aspects	Guidance Aspects
	4. A member from each of a number of school clubs may be invited to visit the class and tell of the club's activities. Each club may also be invited to prepare a one-page notice for the classroom bulletin board aimed to attract pupils to membership.		a. Letters of invitation may be written. Thank-you letters should follow the visits. • Use English text as a reference book. b. Emphasis should be placed on the listening skills: • listening for main ideas • listening for important details • listening for interesting details • listening in order to question • listening in order to add information c. Visits should be followed with discussion of what interested pupils most about the clubs.	a. Pupil behavior toward the guests should be discussed before the visit. Some pupils may be selected to act as hosts or hostesses to introduce the guests to the class. b. [see below] c. The teacher should urge pupils to take part in school activities in order to enlarge their fields of exploration and their interests. d. The consideration of what should be said in a letter of invitation and in a thank-you letter to the guest is a guidance activity as well as an English activity.
	5. Members of the staff with whom pupils should be acquainted may be invited		a. Letters of invitation and thank-you letters need to be written.	a. The teacher should help the pupils to feel at ease with the visitors.

to visit the class—the principal, assistant principal, counselors, nurse.		• Use English text as a reference book. b. Listening is emphasized. c. The visits are followed with discussions or writing about how and when these people can be of help to the pupils.	b. Pupils should be helped to understand how these people can be of service to them and that each is deeply concerned with the welfare of the boys and girls of the school.
C. To help pupils become acquainted with the teacher. 1. Since the teacher urges pupils to tell about themselves, he too should take time to tell about himself—his family, hobbies, and interests.	If the teacher has lived in other places or has traveled widely he can point out the places he tells about on a map. Bringing in items collected on a trip is especially interesting to pupils.	a. The teacher should help pupils to feel free to ask reasonable questions. b. The initial discussion might be followed with a written paper on: What My Teacher Seems to be Like.	If not overdone, this introduction of the teacher to the pupils serves to build a bridge between the two.
2. Much of the orientation of the pupils to the teacher takes place in the few minutes before or after class throughout the semester. The teacher makes himself available to pupils and lets them see him as a person and not just as a teacher figure.			

Purpose	Possible Activities	Social Studies Aspects	English Aspects	Guidance Aspects
D. To help the teacher become acquainted with the pupils.	1. After some weeks have gone by, each pupil can be asked to write an autobiography of himself. The general contents of this should be decided by pupils and teacher together. It should be made clear that the personal contents of the autobiography will be kept strictly in confidence and that these papers will not be graded.	a. If pupils indicate that they have taken trips or have lived in other places, the teacher might suggest that each point out on a map where he has formerly lived or visited, and to tell what he found of interest in these places.	a. The autobiography or time line should not be corrected and graded but kept in the pupil's confidential file for future reference. b. Writing autobiographies can serve as an introduction to the reading of autobiographies of famous people.	a. Data from an autobiography or time line provide much needed information to the teacher. This includes the "tone" of the paper, the feelings and attitudes expressed, as well as the information given. Items from a biography often furnish material for initial conversation in a pupil-teacher conference.
	2. An individual time line in place of written autobiography might be made. It would show the important events in a pupil's life in a time sequence.	The idea of chronological happening of events may be developed (or reviewed) from this.		
	3. An individual pupil file of all materials of a confidential nature may also contain papers on such topics as: ● When I Grow Up ● Myself as I See Myself		Such papers are not to be corrected and graded and their contents are strictly confidential.	Items from such papers are excellent topics for starting discussion in personal interviews. They also serve as a means of identifying areas in which group guidance would be helpful. For ex-

Objectives and Activities	Suggested Procedures	Comments
• Three Things I Wish For Most • What I Like to Do in My Spare Time At the end of the semester or year, dated additions may be made by the pupils to each paper, thus bringing them up to date. ———— 4. Four or five weeks after the beginning of a semester a sociogram should be prepared in order to see more clearly the social pattern of the class.		ample, they might indicate a need for a unit on vocations or one on getting along with other people. ———— A sociogram indicates which pupils are establishing good personal relationships with classmates and which are not. This device frequently assists the teacher in determining how to group pupils.
E. To set class goals and make class rules. 1. Through pupil-teacher planning, chiefly by means of class discussion, a set of goals is established which the class hopes to achieve. The rules by which a class will operate should also be pupil-teacher planned.	a. Class and school rules can be compared with city and state traffic laws, laws for rubbish and garbage disposal, and the like. b. The meanings of terms such as democracy, dictatorship, anarchy are discussed.	a. Emphasis in the discussion should be on: • expressing ideas clearly • enlarging on an expressed idea • questioning ideas • presenting reasons for ideas a. Involvement of pupils in these activities makes both the goals and the rules important to the pupils. The guide lines are of their own making and there is a feeling of responsibility for carrying them out.

Purpose	Possible Activities	Social Studies Aspects	English Aspects	Guidance Aspects
			• respecting the ideas of others • listening b. Both class goals and class rules may be copied by each pupil into his notebook for future reference.	b. The teacher makes every effort to help pupils to see, understand and express their own real purposes in order to better understand themselves. The teacher guides the discussion, asking such questions as: • "Why do you think this is important?" • "How do you feel about this?" • "What do you think of John's idea?" • "What could you add to this idea?" c. d. The teacher should show a friendly willingness to wait while a pupil tries to express himself. Consideration for the individual pupil when he has difficulty expressing himself or helping an individual to think his idea through makes him feel that his ideas are important. This

F. To involve pupils in class management.	1. The class elects officers. Discussion before the election includes: ● what officers are needed ● the functions of each office ● method of election Use English or speech text as reference. Class officers should be changed several times each semester in order to give many pupils the opportunity for practice in leadership positions.	a. The meaning of words such as these should be developed: ● election ● nomination ● majority ● minority ● consensus ● voting ● unanimous ● motion ● minutes b. Class elections can be compared with city or state elections.	a. A simple but correct method of selecting officers should be used. Use English or speech text as reference. b. Pupils should be urged to give reasons for nominations made. c. Oral skills as under 1–E–*English Aspects* should be stressed. d. Words listed may be used as spelling words.	helps each pupil to build a better self image. a. The teacher promotes a feeling of the importance of the elections by showing interest and giving full attention to the election procedures. He emphasizes consideration for the feelings of all class members. b. The approach as listed under 1–E–*Guidance Aspects* is continued.
	2. Class officers should function each day. The chairman starts the class and the secretary reads his report of the previous day's activities.	a. A copy of the *Congressional Record* may be obtained for the class members to examine. b. A group can find out how a bill is passed in Congress. c. *Robert's Rules of Order* are examined and simple rules for conducting daily class meetings are decided upon.	a. A simple but correct method of daily operation is used. b. For one week all pupils write minutes. These are compared as to content and form. c. The secretary's minutes are posted on a bulletin board each day. The report is then placed in the class "Minutes" form.	New officers should be assisted but the teacher should not take over their work, thereby dismissing them from a responsibility they have accepted.

Purpose	Possible Activities	Social Studies Aspects	English Aspects	Guidance Aspects
			book for reference. d. Consistent help is given to pupils in developing skills of oral communication in discussions. Use English or speech text as reference. e. Listening skills are stressed. See I–B–4 English Aspects.	
	3. Pupils assist in planning the week's work. At the beginning of the semester, pupils and teacher plan the next day's work at the end of each day. Later a week's general plan may be established. A planning committee may be established for this purpose. The teacher works with this committee.	Such pupil-teacher planning of classroom activities develops a sense of: • continuity of classroom activities • time (and time limits) for accomplishing activities • immediate needs in terms of present difficulties • future needs in terms of class goals • future needs in terms of pupils' evaluation of successes and failures	Same as for Social Studies Aspects with emphasis on communication skills during the planning period. See I–B–4 English Aspects and I–E–English Aspects.	Pupils should not be led to believe that they will make all decisions but that they and the teacher together will decide some of the many things that need to be done in the classroom. When pupil-teacher planning is used, however, the teacher should consider pupil suggestions carefully. He should not attempt to draw pupils on until they express the idea that the teacher wants them to express. When this is done pupils will only try to guess what the teacher wants.

II. Working on a Unit

Purpose	Possible Activities	Social Studies Aspects	English Aspects	Guidance Aspects
A. To introduce a unit for study. (All of the activities listed would probably not be used.)	1. A film or filmstrip may be used. The showing should be followed by class discussion of the film.	a. The stage should be set by asking pupils to watch for and jot down 4 or 5 main points during the showing of the film or filmstrip. These are discussed after the film showing. b. Pupils should be urged to raise questions and a list of the questions should be kept for later consideration.	a. Continued emphasis should be given to oral skill development as under 1-E-*English Aspects*. b. A few of the special words in the film may be used for vocabulary. Flash cards can be made each time new words are added. Meanings and usage can be reviewed with the cards in spare minutes.	a. As in all discussion sessions pupils need help in learning to show respect for the opinions of others. The teacher stands as an example for them in the way *he* accepts *their* ideas and opinions. b. As many pupils as possible should be drawn into the discussion.
	2. Pictures on the subject can be examined and discussed. To develop ability to use pictures as sources of data, pupils can cover the captions of pictures in the textbook and describe what the pictures tell. Larger individual pictures can also be used.	a. Pupils should be helped to see that information can be obtained from pictures. b. Pupils should learn to draw inferences from pictures. Example: 'From this picture what can you say about the climate in this part of the country?"	Same as for *Social Studies Aspects*.	

Purpose	Possible Activities	Social Studies Aspects	English Aspects	Guidance Aspects
		c. Pupils should be urged to ask questions and a list of these should be kept. d. At the end of the discussion the ideas can be summarized by different children.		c. The guidance approach as indicated under I–E *Guidance Aspects* should be continued.
	3. An exhibit of objects related to the subject may be used. If possible pupils should have an opportunity to handle these. There should be time for pupils to talk about them. The local museum or the school materials center may be good sources of exhibit material.	a. Pupils should be helped to see that information can be obtained from objects. b. They can "guess" what some of the objects were used for. Later they can check their guesses. c. Pupils should be urged to ask questions. d. Pupils should be helped to draw inferences from the materials. e. At the end of the discussion the ideas should be summarized.	Same as for *Social Studies Aspects*.	
	4. Books dealing with the subject can be brought into the classroom. Some time	a. A review lesson may be needed on the parts of a book and how each is used:	a. Same as for *Social Studies Aspects*. b. The various kinds of writing from which in-	

spent in browsing gives pupils new ideas concerning the area for study.	• index • table of contents • author • copyright date • glossary b. Pupils can practice skim reading for browsing purposes. c. Questions should be listed.	formation may be obtained should be considered—reference, novel, essay, short story, biography, autobiography, poetry, and the like.	
5. Pupils can write a "What do you think?" paragraph. Example: If the subject area were Mexico: "What do you think a Mexican house looks like? or a school? a town? a Mexican boy or girl?" If the subject area were the colonial period: "What do you think a trip from New York City to Boston was like in 1775?"	a. Discussion of these papers shows pupils that there are many different ideas. This can lead to a consideration of sources for determining which ideas are correct. b. Papers can be saved until the end of the unit at which time pupils again write on the same subject and compare their "before" and "after" papers for accuracy of information.	a. Pupils can exchange papers before writing the final draft and check for errors—spelling, punctuation, capitalization. This is a lesson in proofreading. b. The correction of the final papers by the teacher leads to a lesson—or several—on the errors made. The grammar text is used as a reference in this study.	a. The teacher does not say "Right" or "Wrong" to any of the ideas expressed. He shows interest, however, in all ideas. b. Writing papers in class gives the teacher an opportunity to give individual assistance at the time it is needed.
6. Pupils examine either a wall map or a map in the textbook and make a list of	a. Determining facts about the topography of the country—rivers, lakes,	New words are added to the vocabulary list.	

Purpose	Possible Activities	Social Studies Aspects	English Aspects	Guidance Aspects
	the facts that can be determined about the country from the map.	mountains, size of the country, neighboring countries, elevation, location of cities—may serve as an introductory overview. b. If it is found that pupils cannot read a map, time must be taken for working on this difficulty. c. Questions should be listed.		
	7. A story with the setting in the country or period of history to be studied can be read.	a. Through discussion, the class may identify the ideas that are given in the story about the country, perhaps something of its size, its population, customs, climate, topography or occupations of its people. b. Questions should be listed.	a. To set the stage for listening to the story, pupils are asked to watch for certain things and to jot them down. (These will depend on the story selected.) b. The people in the story can be compared either orally or in writing with people the pupils know in their own country— their appearance, their characteristics, their way of living.	Pupils should be helped to see that all people are both different and alike, not better or worse. They are different because of their experiences and their opportunities. In basic things—in feelings, desire for success and happiness—they are alike.

8. Starting a week or two before the unit begins news items on the country or problem to be studied can be collected both by the pupils and the teacher.	a. Discussion of the news items when work on the unit begins will bring many questions to light. b. The places named should be located on the map. c. People should be identified. d. Questions should be listed.	A good method of preparing news items for use is as follows: The news clipping is pasted on a sheet of notebook paper. Next to it (or below it) the pupil writes a paragraph in his own words. This tells *who* the article is about; *where* it took place; *when* it took place; the main points of *what* happened. **Below this he writes his own** reaction to the article, his feelings about what took place or any questions he may have. Such a method serves well as a basis for discussion.	As children respond during the discussion to the reactions of other individuals, continued emphasis must be given to consideration and respect for the opinions of others. **Pupils should not** be expected to accept these blindly but should be helped to determine the bases for opinions and feelings. Discussion should develop better judgment.
B. To select the overall class problem. Out of the introductory activities should grow some broad questions that can be considered as possible class problems for the unit. For example:	1. Criteria for choice of an overall question should be established with the pupils. For example: ● Will it help us to better understand the world around us? ● Is it broad enough so that all of us may work on it?	The criteria should include more than items which will indicate pupils' interest.	a. Discussion and listening skills as described under I–B–4 and I–E–*English Aspects* should continue to be emphasized. b. The list of criteria may be copied by each pupil into his notebook for future use.

There should be continued consideration for the individual pupil who has difficulty expressing himself.

Purpose	Possible Activities	Social Studies Aspects	English Aspects	Guidance Aspects
What is Mexico's part in the world picture? or How is life in Mexico different from life in our community? or ?	● Is it one we want to find out about? ● Is there enough material on it? ● Is it an important question? 2. The questions suggested by class members should be discussed in terms of the criteria agreed upon. 3. The class votes for its choice of a class problem after careful discussion.	Questions raised during introductory activities should be reviewed. The class should add other possible questions. Correct voting procedure should be used in making the final selection.	Same as for *Social Studies Aspects*.	a. The teacher should urge that criteria be considered carefully in order that pupils may continue to learn to use good judgment in making decisions. b. See also I–E and II–A *Guidance Aspects*. c. As many pupils as possible should be drawn into the discussion.
C. To determine subtopics of the overall class problem.	1. A list is made on the board of all the things the class members (and the teacher) feel they ought to find out in order to solve the class problem that has been selected. ● This may be developed	Questions raised during introductory activities are reviewed as possible sources of ideas for this phase of the work.	Discussion and listening skills should be stressed as described under I–B–4 and I–E–*English Aspects*.	Same as described under I–E and II–A–*Guidance Aspects*.

from lists originally prepared by small groups of 2 or 3 pupils.
- It may be developed from lists prepared by individuals.
- It may be done orally directly from ideas suggested by the entire class.

---

2. The list of suggestions (possibly 25–30) is organized under major headings, which fit the particular items listed. Example:

- Geography
- History
- Products and trade
- Government
- Customs
- How the people live
- How the people work
- Foreign relations

Such headings should grow out of the discussion.

Each heading becomes a topic for investigation by a small group. There should

Pupils should be helped to see relationships between the various items on the list, thus determining which items fit together under a common heading.

Simple outlining may be taught at this point. Use English text as a reference.

Purpose	Possible Activities	Social Studies Aspects	English Aspects	Guidance Aspects
be enough headings so that each group will have no more than 4 or 5 pupils in it. D. To divide the class into small groups, each responsible for working on a subtopic of the overall class problem.	There are many ways to divide the class into small working groups, but one that has been found to be very satisfactory is as follows: Each child lists on a sheet of paper his first three choices of topics in order of preference. These are collected and the teacher arranges the groups using the lists of preference as his guide.	Individual choice of a topic for investigation is made on the basis of a consideration of the possible content of each subtopic and its importance in the solution of the overall class problem.	Even in this simple task pupils should be reminded to write neatly and to spell correctly.	a. Every effort should be made to keep group size to a maximum of 5 pupils, preferably 3 or 4 in the early attempts at group work. This makes it possible for pupils to keep track of the work being done and leads to more pupil satisfaction and success. b. In forming groups from the preference lists, attention should be given to the personal relationships of pupils with one another, keeping in mind the social needs of individual pupils. The sociogram made earlier is helpful at this point.

E. To prepare small group plans of operation.	1. Each group selects its own chairman and recorder. 2. A plan of operation should be decided upon by the members of each group and a copy made by each member. An additional copy should be made for the teacher by each group secretary. A plan should contain: • the problem or topic • what the group feels it needs to find out • who is responsible for doing what • where the group thinks it can get information	The responsibilities of a chairman and a recorder as well as other members of a group are reviewed. a. Each small group should make plans to cover the various aspects of its area for study as completely as possible. The depth to which a group can probe will depend upon the abilities of its members, the resources available and the sensitivity of the teacher to the potentials of the pupils. b. Social studies and literary sources that are little known to pupils may be suggested by the teacher.	Same as for *Social Studies Aspects*. a. The plan sheet should be neatly written and statements should be clearly stated. b. The teacher copy is checked for the above, for misunderstandings, and for gaps pupils may have left. c. The final teacher copy is kept by the teacher to assist him in following a group's work. d. If the plan is satisfactory the group moves ahead. Any group having trouble in preparing a plan meets with the teacher for assistance.	The importance of the jobs of chairing a group and of keeping its records as well as the importance of all group members working together should be considered. a. The teacher should consider each group's plan carefully to see that the work assigned each individual fits his particular abilities. One child may need to be urged to try a more difficult task than he has been assigned, or another may have been given a job that he cannot possibly carry out because of its difficulty. b. The teacher moves from group to group, being available to give assistance but trying not to make the decisions.
F. To collect data for the solution of the small group problems.	1. Pupils learn to take notes.	a. A simple form on 3" X 5" cards is desirable. Included should be the	Same as for *Social Studies Aspects* plus emphasis on spelling and care in writing.	a. Patient and continued assistance will be needed. It may be neces-

Purpose	Possible Activities	Social Studies Aspects	English Aspects	Guidance Aspects
(As many sources as possible are used in addition to the textbook.)		name of the book, the author, a title of the note (what the particular note is about), the note, written in phrases in the pupil's own words, and the page on which the note was found. b. A practice period spent in identifying the main ideas in passages is helpful. The need for accuracy is emphasized. c. Each pupil can practice note taking on 2 or 3 index cards using textbook material before starting work on the unit.		sary to give repeated special help to individuals or small groups of pupils who have difficulties in certain phases of note taking. b. The entire two period block-of-time should not be devoted to research unless interest is very high. The class period should contain a variety of activities.
	2. All pupils are expected to read the textbook material covering the unit.	a. This should give an overview of the place or period being studied. b. The meaning of the word "textbook" should be explained together with the need for further	Words that pupils will need to know for understanding should be indicated and explained.	

depth study beyond the textbook for understanding.			
3. Data are collected from many sources: supplementary texts, reference books, fiction, poems, magazines, newspapers, pamphlets, etc. Make use of any that are available such as: • Language Arts kits • Block-of-time kits • Public Library kits	a. The parts of a book are reviewed: index, table of contents, appendix, author, glossary, copyright date, use of boldface or italicized headings, chapter titles, and subheadings. b. Library skills are developed: use of such tools as the card catalog, atlas, almanac, encyclopedia and for advanced pupils, the *Readers' Guide to Periodical Literature.* c. Pupils must learn to be selective in their note taking, recording those data that specifically apply to their problems.	a. Same as for *Social Studies Aspects.* b. A large crossword puzzle based on words from the unit can be put on the bulletin board for pupils to solve. c. Fiction that relates to the period should be read. Pupils should be helped to see how fiction aids in understanding the place or period and the people they are studying. d. The use of the dictionary should be emphasized but pupils also need to develop the ability to determine word meaning from the context.	a. In assembling books for class use there should be books suitable for the good readers and for the slow readers. b. At the end of several days of note taking, note cards should be collected and checked to find difficulties pupils are encountering. Those pupils showing serious lack of understanding should be taken aside and worked with on their particular problems.
4. People who can give assistance can be interviewed. An individual may be	a. There is need to help pupils understand that information can be ob-	a. If a letter of invitation or a letter requesting an interview is sent, time	a. The place of courtesy in people's relationships with other people is con-

Purpose	Possible Activities	Social Studies Aspects	English Aspects	Guidance Aspects
	invited to speak to the entire class, or a small group of pupils or an individual pupil may go to the person for an interview.	tained from "people who know" as well as from books. b. Pupils should decide on the questions to be asked of such individuals in order to obtain the information that will be most useful to them. c. Such an interview may well lead to a consideration of the difference between fact and opinion and how to tell them apart.	should be taken to review how to write such a letter. b. A thank-you letter should be written to the person interviewed. c. If the arrangements are made by telephone, the skills of telephone usage should be considered. Telephoning a person to be interviewed may be role-played by different pairs of pupils previous to the official call. Use English or speech text as a reference. d. The skills of interviewing—the introduction of oneself to the person being interviewed, the type of questions to be asked, how to conclude an interview—may be role-played by different small groups in the class. e. Practice may be needed	sidered both before the interview and in the evaluation of the experience. If a speaker is brought into the classroom, a host or hostess may be selected to greet the guest and to introduce him to the class. b. In responding to or in making telephone calls from the classroom on an interroom phone, the teacher should be careful to fulfill the rules of good telephone manners at all times. c. In class discussions the teacher should frequently question whether a statement is opinion or fact. In his own speech he should be careful to differentiate between these.

		in order to learn how to take notes from the material offered as a person is interviewed.	
5. A field trip is frequently a source of information.	a. Preplanning should be done with the pupils in terms of what will be seen on the trip.	a. Telephone and letter writing skills are stressed as above in II–F–4 *English Aspects*.	a. Planning should include a discussion of behavior. How pupils should act on the field trip should be pupil-teacher planned.
	b. Following the trip pupils can exchange notes in order to check accuracy.	b. New terms which pupils will need to know should be considered before the trip.	b. A method for keeping track of all members of the group should be pupil-teacher planned.
	c. Discussion after the trip should review the information that has been obtained and the relationship of facts learned to things previously learned or possibly to other problems.	c. Notes are taken during the trip.	c. During the discussion the approach as listed under I–E–*Guidance Aspects* is continued.
	d. Data especially pertinent to the topic being studied by an individual should be transferred from the notes taken on the trip to the note cards on the topic.	d. Discussion after the trip involves points made under I–E–English Aspects.	
	e. The class should evaluate the trip in terms of its worthwhileness toward solving the class problem.	e. Each pupil writes a report of the trip. Introductory sentence, closing sentence, order of activities, title, as well as grammatical accuracy, punctuation and spelling should be considered.	
		f. Lessons should follow in those aspects in which pupils made most errors on their written papers.	

Purpose	Possible Activities	Social Studies Aspects	English Aspects	Guidance Aspects
	6. There are many sources of free and inexpensive materials which may be sent for and used in the search for data. Such a project needs to be carried out long enough before work is to start on the unit to allow time for the material to arrive.	When the material arrives it needs to be sorted and filed in an easily accessible place. Valuable material needs to be separated from sheer advertising chaff. A committee of able pupils can do a major part of this, although the teacher is responsible for the material used.	Letter writing for such material can be a class project, each pupil writing to a different source. If there are not a sufficient number of sources for each pupil to investigate, the class may be divided into small groups, each responsible for writing to one source. A review of proper letter writing form may be needed.	Pupils should understand that only one letter should be sent to each source; that consideration of other people, whether individuals or companies, is highly important.
	7. Study maps and globes as sources of information. A variety of maps in sufficient quantity for class use may be difficult to acquire. Single copies may be shown through the opaque projector or transparencies may be made for use in an overhead projector. The class can then study the maps together.	a. Pupils should become acquainted with the various types of maps: relief, historical, population, photographic, pictorial, political, product, vegetation, landuse, and physical. They should be helped to see how each of these furnishes a particular kind of information. They should learn to read each type. b. Comparisons should be	The names of the various types of maps and the features of the maps may be added to the vocabulary list and to the flash card collection. Pupils can prepare oral descriptions of different maps or sections of maps.	

made of flat maps and globes. c. Longitude and latitude should be reviewed.		The approach as listed under I–E and II–A–*Guidance Aspects* should be continued.
8. Use films, filmstrips and recordings as sources of information.	a. Films selected for their appropriateness to the problem being studied are very helpful. After the film has been introduced it should be indicated that a discussion of it will follow the showing. Pupils should watch for material that gives information about their particular problems. b. The showing should be followed by a discussion of its major points. c. The data from a film seen by the entire class together with the discussion of it should be summarized by two or three pupils as a final step. d. A filmstrip may be shown to the entire class or be used by a small group or by an individ-	a. Emphasis should be on the recognition of main points and on how these apply to group problems. b. Recording notes from a film, filmstrip, or recording may need to be practiced. c. Discussion and listening skills are stressed as the need arises. See I–E and I–B–4 *English Aspects*.

Purpose	Possible Activities	Social Studies Aspects	English Aspects	Guidance Aspects
		ual. For individual use a viewer may be used. For a small group it may be shown against a bare wall space or on a screen in a corner of the room. e. A recording is used similarly by individuals, small groups, or the entire class.		
G. To encourage creative expression.	1. Pupils may make maps to illustrate the information they have collected: • hand-drawn map • flour-salt, clay or papier-mâché relief map prepared on a plywood board and colored with showcard paints • hand-drawn map with products drawn on it. Cutouts from magazines may also be used. • war map of a particular area • map drawn with crayon	a. Pupils should have accurate information about the areas represented: • location • size • altitude • topography • products • any other items represented b. The legend should be accurate and fit the map.	a. The map should have an accurate title. b. Labeled parts of the map should be correctly spelled. c. The oral description of the map should be clear and to the point.	a. The teacher must show interest in the illustrations even though he may feel that they are far from being artistic or perfect products. His interest helps a pupil gain a feeling of success and makes him willing to try such an activity again b. Such material should be exhibited in the room. c. It is frequently possible to involve a child who

			rejects book work in this type of activity. Success in this area often gives a pupil the status with his peers which later makes it possible to draw him into work of a more academic nature.
on cloth and pressed between sheets of paper with hot iron			
2. Models may be made as illustrations: • clay models • wooden models • papier-mâché models • paper models • dioramas	Pupils should have accurate information about the historical or geographic material which the model represents.	The oral description of the model should be clear and to the point.	
3. Puppets may be made to illustrate the material in a dramatic form: • hand puppets • paper-bag puppets • papier-mâché puppets (built on wire skeletons or over ballons)	Conversation developed for use with puppets should contain accurate data based on historical or geographic fact.	a. The conversation can be included as a part of the group's written report. This may also serve as a basis for lessons on the use of quotation marks. b. Pupils need to practice such a performance with their puppets in order that the play moves smoothly. They should be helped in developing the oral skills needed.	d. The preparation by the teacher of a model, a diorama or a puppet often says to children more clearly than words that such an activity is not childish but can be a great help in making a report interesting.
4. Creative activities may be in the realm of writing instead of hand activities: • a skit to introduce or close a group report	The data included in these should be accurate and the ideas should be developed clearly.	Many aspects of English may be taught through such an activity: • interesting introduction	

Purpose	Possible Activities	Social Studies Aspects	English Aspects	Guidance Aspects
	• a poem • a story • a song		• strong concluding sentence or paragraph • challenging title • good taste • use of vivid words • sequence of content • organization • correct grammatical form	
	5. Graphs, charts and cartoons are also excellent means of illustrating certain types of data.	a. Reading and understanding of various types of graphs is most valuable in the study of social studies. • profile or line graph • bar graph • circle graph • picture graph • time line b. The construction of a chart or graph illustrating simple statistical data is also important. As an example of how this is done, the teacher may develop data into a graph or chart on the transpar-	a. In the preparation of graphs and charts, the importance of a careful choice of words, so that the title will accurately describe the product, should be stressed. b. Oral skill in explaining graphs, charts and cartoons is a part of the English aspect of the activity. Pupils may need considerable help in learning how to do this.	

ency of an overhead projector while pupils watch. Special attention should be given to: • the title • column headings • data key c. Graphs and charts taken from newspapers or magazines can be used in teaching the use of such illustrations. These may be shown on a screen with an overhead or opaque projector.	
6. A small group of pupils may be responsible for preparing an exhibit for a bulletin board to illustrate its findings. The teacher may also challenge the pupils by a bulletin board arranged so that they may complete it. Example: List the names of 5 or 6 famous people of the place or period being studied. After each name place 7 or	The information should be accurate. a. Statements should be written in good form. b. Items in an exhibit should have clear labels that can be seen from a distance.

Purpose	Possible Activities	Social Studies Aspects	English Aspects	Guidance Aspects
	8 blank index cards. The question on the board might be: *"What were these people like?"* **Pupils** write on the cards as they find information. Each signs his name to his own contribution.			
H. To share the information found by the members of a group with the entire class and to test out its value toward solving the overall class problem.	1. Each group in turn presents its data orally to the class. Such presentations may take many forms: ● a panel discussion ● a round table discussion ● a skit ● a tape recorded presentation ● —— ● ——	a. All data collected need not be reported. Pupils should learn to select that which is most pertinent to the solution of the problem. b. The data should be accurate. c. The order of presenting the material as determined by the group members should depend upon the material and its logical sequence. d. Pupils should be able to indicate the source of information reported. e. The creative illustrations	a. Time should be spent in considering the various aspects of oral reporting. This includes: ● use of voice—modulation, distinctness, and pronunciation ● posture ● how to make an effective speech Use English or speech text for reference. b. An oral report should be presented in the pupil's own words. It should be *told* to the class and not read either from note cards or from a paper.	a. The degree of success or failure that pupils have in reporting orally is determined in no small measure by the teacher's actions. He must help pupils to understand that this is not the moment at which they fail or pass the course, but that this is only one part of the work, and that this is a learning situation in which everyone makes mistakes. b. The teacher must have infinite patience. He cannot expect a perfect

that have been prepared should be presented as a part of the group report.

c. The organization of data leads directly into simple outlining. This may be a group outline for planning the order of presenting the different aspects of the material and/or be a part of individual planning. Pupils will need help in making and using a simple guide outline from which they can speak.

d. The techniques of panel discussion or round table discussion may need to be taught.

e. How to explain or demonstrate illustrative materials during group reporting should be considered.

f. Words which the class might not know should be listed on the chalkboard by the group reporting or given to class members on duplicated sheets. Names of people and strange place names

product nor should he make his pupils feel that he expects this.

c. He must be ready to help at a crucial spot where breakdown is imminent. He is the supporter to the child and he must show interest, concern and helpfulness.

d. The teacher must serve as a model to the class. He cannot correct papers while reports are being given and he cannot indicate boredom at any time.

e. He cannot allow laughter, and wisecracks if a pupil cannot go on. Above all he uses neither of these himself. The teacher shows his faith in the pupil's ability, be it little or much, and helps him to go on.

f. If a pupil cannot manage to speak before the class, he should be allowed to choose 5 or 6 pupils to

Purpose	Possible Activities	Social Studies Aspects	English Aspects	Guidance Aspects
			should be included in this. A language teacher can give assistance in the pronunciation of foreign names.	whom he will report apart from the whole class. Such a child should be given special help in expressing himself in the everyday classroom situations.
	2. The class members listening to a report may be responsible for writing a *Listening Record*[3] while group reports are being given. Such a record may be divided into columns which have headings such as these: • Person reporting • Questions I want to ask • Points I can add • Points to be remembered	a. A *Listening Record* involves all pupils in the audience and keeps them alert to the contents of the report. b. It avoids interruptions of the report but is a way of retaining ideas of the members of the audience until discussion time. c. It serves as a basis for discussion following the group report.	Listening skills are a vital part of communication. These skills include: • listening for main ideas • listening for important details • listening for interesting details • listening in order to question • listening in order to add information	The *Listening Records* need not be graded. It is best to collect and read them rapidly and mark an OK at the top if a record is satisfactory. A helpful comment is worth more than a grade.
	3. A class discussion of the subject matter content should follow each group report • A summary by the group chairman of the main	The discussion gives an opportunity for asking questions and for adding helpful information. The teacher has a leading role in this activity. He must lead the discussion so that it involves:	Continued emphasis on discussion skills as described under 1–E and 1–B–4 *English Aspects*.	Continued work with pupils as under 1–E and II–A– *Guidance Aspects*.

points made by group members is a good springboard for the discussion. ● clarification of the ideas expressed ● addition by the teacher or pupils of data which have been missed ● implications of the information for the solution of the class problem ● inferences to be drawn from the information ● relationship of the data to information already presented by another group ● extensions of the data in the application to other problems	4. An evaluation of the group's work follows the discussion. In addition to self-evaluation by group members, there may be: ● An evaluation by the class audience ● An evaluation by the teacher A 3" X 5" index card written as a pupil reports serves for either audience and/or An evaluation may consider a number of things: ● ability of group members to work together ● the effort the group has put into the work ● creativeness of the group ● amount and value of information collected ● number of resources used ● reporting success ● improvement over previous efforts	Same as for *Social Studies Aspects.* a. A far greater emphasis should be given to the good things done, the successes, than to the errors and failures. Pupils learn faster from success than from failure. This does not mean to ignore errors, but to make sure that pupils are given credit for the things they have done well even

³*Ibid.,* p. 265.

Purpose	Possible Activities	Social Studies Aspects	English Aspects	Guidance Aspects
	teacher evaluation. Good points are indicated and possibly a suggestion or two for improvement is added.			though these may be very small. b. If oral evaluations are made by the audience the good points should be emphasized first. Negative criticisms should be made in a kindly manner.
1. To tie all the information of all groups together and draw conclusions relative to the final solution of the class problem	A final class discussion should consider all the data that have been presented by all groups: • The statement of the original class problem is reviewed • The chairman of each group repeats the main points made by his group • Important points are added by pupils and teacher • Through a discussion of all these points the class reaches a decision relative to its overall problem	The discussion deals with facts in the area of social studies. Again the teacher helps pupils to: • clarify • question • make inferences • organize • find relationships • draw conclusions	a. Continued emphasis is given to discussion skills as described under 1–E and 1–B–4 *English Aspects*. b. This final discussion may be followed by a relatively brief paper written by each pupil in which he reviews the decision reached by the class and the reasons for it.	

			This is a learning situation and one in which a teacher helps individuals according to their different needs. He should circulate around the room giving help wherever it is needed.
			a. It is well to have the rough draft written in class in order that the teacher may give assistance as needed. Exchanging papers in rough draft form and looking for errors and passages not clear enough to be understood helps pupils learn to proofread not only other pupils' papers but their own. The paper is later written in final form and handed in. b. Many things need to be reviewed: • introductory sentence or paragraph
		The content of this report is the data collected by an individual. It needs to be organized in correct sequence of events if the material is historical. It should also contain the pupil's reactions to the data.	
J. To test the conclusions reached.	In historical problems little or no action can be taken to test the validity of the conclusions reached by the class. In solving a class or community problem, further plans may be made for trying out the decisions reached.		
K. To assemble data into an organized written report.	Each pupil should write a report covering the data he has collected.		

Purpose	Possible Activities	Social Studies Aspects	English Aspects	Guidance Aspects
			• concluding sentence or paragraph • title • organization of data • clear expression of ideas • spelling • grammar c. Special emphasis should be given to the inclusion of a pupil's own reactions, feelings and ideas about the material in the report. d. A simple bibliography should be included in such a report. This may include: • the name of the book • the author • the copyright date e. The final corrected draft should be kept in the individual pupil's file folder. f. Lessons dealing with major difficulties follow such report writing.	

Conclusion

The above *Guide* demonstrates how learnings from one subject reinforce and enrich the other. See, for example, the "What do you think?" paragraph written to introduce the unit. (II–A–5). It samples a student's present knowledge of a social studies topic and at the same time serves as the basis for a lesson on proofreading. The teacher may note common errors in grammar, spelling, punctuation, and capitalization as a guide to further instruction in English. During the data-gathering stage of the unit, (II–F–3–8), poetry and fiction help students understand the place or period under study while the social studies content helps them gain from the literature. Letter writing is not just an exercise but a means of obtaining information or expressing appreciation to visiting speakers or to resource people who have been interviewed. Creative expression is encouraged at several points and various communication skills are used throughout the unit, with direct instruction being provided as needed.

Note, also, how rich are the opportunities for guidance. Throughout the orientation unit the teacher becomes acquainted with each individual student. Autobiographies and other student compositions (I–D–1–3) may indicate areas of concern that merit group guidance or individual conferences. Student social needs are kept in mind when the teacher forms small groups (II–D), and at many points students are led to consider how their actions affect other people (II–F–4–6, for example). Guidance comes easier to a block-time teacher because he has fewer students to deal with each day. Also, the double-period class gives him more time and a greater variety of activities in which to work with individual students.

Teachers will want to refer to the *Guide* from time to time throughout the school year, each time gaining further insights into the kind of teaching and learning embodied in the core idea.

Chapter 3

The Core Teacher

by Wayne Jennings

This chapter highlights some distinctive features of core by focusing on the core teacher—his role, how he accomplishes his tasks, and the type of person he must be to serve effectively in an unstructured core program. Dr. Jennings is past president of the National Association for Core Curriculum, a former core teacher, and a curriculum consultant for the St. Paul Public Schools.

There is controversy and confusion over just what a core teacher is and does. It is quite inadequate to define the core teacher as one who uses teacher-pupil planning and similar techniques, because all teachers are encouraged to work from the interests and needs of students and to use cooperative planning. Pinning the core label on the combined English-social studies class also is a considerable distortion of what the architects of the core curriculum intended. Yet, if these two ideas—the two-hour English-social studies block and modern methods of teaching—are subtracted from all the classes labeled as core, scarcely any would be left. Failing to see the core teacher's objectives, critics sometimes mistakenly assert that there is nothing distinctive about core.

The Core Teacher's Central Task

In an authentic core class, the teacher's role is that of a guide and facilitator in helping *youth map the program* they believe will develop themselves into effective citizens and mature people. This distinctly means that the teacher does not come into the classroom each day and tell the students what to do, as happens in most conventional classes. Instead, the teacher *and* the students: (1) think out what they need to accomplish, (2) together decide on activities or topics that they believe will achieve the aims they have established, and (3) evaluate to determine if goals are being accomplished and reformulate the program if necessary. These are not simple steps, and they are especially difficult for teachers who view their role as the authority who knows best what youngsters should learn.

Many teachers cannot accept the idea that students should have a large part in deciding what they are to study. They ask how it is possible for beginning students to know what to study when they do not yet know anything about the subject. Such a viewpoint is in conflict with modern learning concepts, especially those that stress student perceptions as the key to learning. Further, it can be argued that learning to do what the teacher says establishes an attitudinal climate that is better training for an authoritarian than for a democratic society.

Everyone needs to learn how to make good decisions. Children who have always been told what to do and whose concept of learning is to do what the teacher or book says will be awkward and clumsy at planning their own learning. But as students learn by actually making important decisions, they gain the skills needed to become the self-directed individuals so necessary in tomorrow's world of unknown problems. When teachers and students together decide what they need to do to make themselves better citizens, the classroom becomes lively and spirited. Young people work hard at self-appointed tasks and in the end become creative, hard-working citizens who think for themselves.

Because the core teacher's primary task is to develop effective citizens, it is essential that he have in mind the traits of a capable person in a democratic society. Although educators have spent years in defining goals and millions of words have been written on educational objectives, it is essential that each teacher be absolutely clear on what he is trying to teach.

Teachers must know what citizenship traits are being fostered in their classrooms and be able at any time to show how each classroom activity promotes learning that will be functional for life in our society. At the end of a unit or a year, the core student must demonstrate by *performance* that he is learning to participate, to respect others, to handle responsibility and to make wise decisions, to name but a few of the citizenship and human traits being encouraged in a core class.

Evaluation in the core class must be in terms of a demonstrated change in the direction of clearly defined objectives. A core student once asked of the teacher, "How come we never have any tests in here?" The teacher answered that they were being tested at that very moment; they were being tested every day on nearly every task. The teacher was observing how well they participated, how they treated the opinions of others, how well they expressed themselves, and the reasoning of their statements. He then asked the students what other traits they thought he was observing. Their answers were a thoughtful list of the characteristics of a decent, admired person and a good citizen. Then he asked the students who they thought should do the evaluating. The students wisely answered that they should learn to evaluate themselves and thereby know in what directions to improve.

In preparing for his year's work, the core teacher needs to (1) list the citizenship and personality traits that are to be fostered, (2) devise learning experiences that will do the job (e.g., an important experience would be shared decision-making on what is to be studied and how), and (3) decide how to evaluate to determine if the students are, in fact, developing into better citizens. To a core teacher, the attitudes, skills, and knowledge essential for effective citizenship are more important than the factual content of the topic or subject being studied.

For example, if a class were studying American Indians, the teacher would observe to see if students were working well in small groups, if they were making better reports, if they had a greater sense of self-worth and self-confidence, and so on. The students' ability to answer factual questions about the subject would be of distinctly lesser importance. This differs from the usual situation in which a student can score an "A" on his knowledge of Indians and never lift a finger or say a word throughout his lifetime to alleviate the lot of the Indian.

Unlike the core teacher, most teachers prepare for the school year by deciding what units of content they will teach. Education turns out to be mostly information gathering, despite the fact that people tend to forget most of the factual material they once knew. Ordinarily, much of what they do remember is obsolete. The typical adult is less effective as a citizen because the school never taught him how to initiate action, never developed a sense of social responsibility, and failed to keep alive the spark of curiosity and creativity that all are born with.

Many beginning teachers are annoyed if they have to teach anything but their subject matter. The teacher arrives in the classroom full of enthusiasm and finds assorted problems cropping up: a few children cannot read, some can read but do not want to, others are not enthusiastic about the subject, and so on. After failing in the attempt to enthuse the students, the teacher throws up his hands and asks, "Why doesn't the administration do something about these kids so I can work with those who want to learn?" These teachers do not want to bother with such student problems as paying attention, how to read, writing neatly, manners, getting assignments in on time—they want to teach! What they do not realize is that these problems *are* teaching. One has to start where students are. As Buckingham put it, many years ago:

> There are no misfit children. There are misfit courses of study, misfit textbooks, and misfit teachers. But in the very nature of the case there can be no misfit children. The child is what education is for. One might as well say that a man does not fit his clothes as to say that a child does not fit the school.[1]

If we think it is proper that all children be bright, poised, curious, creative and active, then that is what we should teach for. It is of crucial importance that the teacher define the traits suitable for development in his group of youngsters and then devise learning experiences that promote growth in the desired direction. In general, the core program seeks to prepare people who have "can-ness,"

[1] B. R. Buckingham, "Disciplinary Values in Individualized Instruction," *Educational Record*, Vol. 19 (January 1938), p. 74.

people who believe in themselves and are secure, seeking people, people who go on learning after graduation, people who care about other people and society, people who think critically, people who will take effective action to correct unsatisfactory conditions.

Accomplishing the Central Task of Core

Many citizenship traits are hard to define and teach, but if the teacher's aims are clear, ways will be found to accomplish them. Suppose we wish to increase *purposefulness* in our students. We would like students to realize that having a plan and working toward long-range goals often helps attain life's hopes and dreams. One way to develop purposefulness is to help students see that each activity in the class must have a purpose, that it must contribute toward the achievement of important class goals. When students ask, "Why are we doing this?" they demonstrate that they are learning purposefulness, and core teachers are delighted. Students come to see that things in life do not just happen by magic or because some arbitrary authority says so. They realize that they can influence the course of events. Core students will do more with their lives because they have developed the habit of thinking about and establishing values and goals to strive for.

Initiative is an important trait of the mature personality and the effective citizen. One core teacher's method of promoting initiative involved having students serve on a committee that had an important task to do for the class, such as arranging for a social hour or publishing a class newspaper. Operating with very few instructions from the teacher, they knew that failure to exercise initiative and come up with a good plan would be disappointing to the class. The evaluation, analysis, and discussion of the committee's plans provided many teachable moments for emphasizing initiative.

In searching for a learning experience to teach *personal responsibility,* one teacher encouraged several students to bring charges against their student council representative and to have him placed on trial for failure to properly carry out his responsibilities. The accused boy threatened several of the class members after school for this attempt to impeach him. During the trial, witnesses were called and their testimony exposed the threats as well as other vital information concerning the student's attendance and attention to student council meetings. The teacher was able to structure the situation in such a manner that students could see how the rights of both the defendant and the complainants were protected. It is likely that the boy will never forget that trial; certainly he was a better representative of his class during the remainder of the year. His desire to be well regarded by his classmates caused him to temper his tendency to bully his way. Moreover, every member of the class learned that each of us is liable for his actions and that he can be called to account for them by those affected. As a result of this incident, everyone, including the teacher, took his responsibilities to the class a little more seriously. In addition, they learned about initiative and justice, how to take action to correct a situation they did not like, and the importance of the careful preparation of evidence.

The point is not that class goals, committees, or trials are the best ways to teach purposefulness, initiative, and responsibility, but rather that these seemingly vague objectives can be taught if the teacher is willing to seek out techniques and shape lessons and everyday classroom events in this direction. The core teacher's role in developing attitudes and skills for citizenship is vastly more demanding and creative than the conventional task of teaching information.

On Knowing Young People

Good interaction and honest feelings are essential in the core classroom. Students must have confidence in their teacher and feel that he understands them, although he can never be a pal or one of them. The core teacher's role as guide implies the ability to give friendly advice and help. Writers in the field of counseling say that a teacher who knows the student well may be the one best able to provide the continuous kind of guidance he needs to deal with everyday problems. Moreover, in trying to determine how to accomplish a certain learning objective, the core teacher must gauge the effects on various students. For this he needs considerable knowledge about the young people he teaches.

In addition to the orientation activities suggested in Chapter 2, some schools schedule parent-teacher conferences. These provide valuable information for the teacher. Another step is for the teacher to hold individual conferences with students, going over classroom matters and, in some instances, personal problems. A variation is the group conference with three or four students. If the teacher lets the students talk—and they will if the situation is right—much understanding can occur on both sides.

Teachers will learn much about students by observing them as they perform various roles in the core classroom. The conventional teacher using textbook work much of the time learns little about his students. Simply being at the door of the classroom as the students enter gives the teacher an excellent opportunity to greet each person and to offer a personal comment to some. The teacher may learn much by watching young people around the school, in the school play rehearsal, in the gym class, in the lunchroom, and at school dances. One teacher breached miles of distance between himself and the boys in his class when he stayed after school to watch his core class play intramural football. There were no other spectators. The boys appreciated having at least one, and they thought the teacher was a "little bit of all right" for his interest.

It has been suggested that teachers visit the homes of their students. Few do for reasons of time. However, the choice does not have to lie between visiting all homes or no homes. A teacher could visit at least three homes a year. A visit is easily arranged. Some day when a student is working late after school the teacher can offer to take him home. The neighborhood and the child's house will be seen. Sometimes the teacher will be invited in. At other times the teacher may see the home if he stops by to help the child carry some heavy bit of apparatus for a class skit; or the teacher may stop to inquire about a student's long absence and to bring assignments.

The reverse kind of visit is good, too. Situations should be arranged so that students can see the teacher's residence. Some students do not quite realize that teachers are human beings who live in houses, use bathrooms, and mow lawns. Child-adult barriers are reduced when they discover these things. Much more is accomplished in the classroom where friendly attitudes of mutual respect and cooperation exist.

The Core Teacher's Self-Improvement Program

Since few textbooks or courses of study offer much help in teaching citizenship traits, each teacher must find the methods that work for him and for his particular group of youngsters. It is not necessary to start from scratch; there are plenty of ideas available. Simply talking over a problem with another teacher often yields a method. Some teachers are reluctant to expose the fact that they have classroom problems. The core teacher must be willing to discuss situations and avail himself of the stimulation others can give.

Additional ideas can come from books, such as those listed in the bibliography at the end of this book, from films, such as *Practicing Democracy in the Classroom* (Encyclopaedia Britannica Films) and *We Plan Together* (Teachers College Press), or from filmstrips, such as *A Core Curriculum Class in Action* (Wayne State University). Scanning educational periodicals and attending educational conferences also promote professional growth.

One good method of generating ideas is for several teachers to meet on a regular basis for an hour during a preparation period or after school. Discussion may start with a problem posed by one of the teachers, or the group may compare notes on a film, a book, or a periodical article.

Core teachers in one school meet each week and rotate the task of chairman so that they experience some of the feelings and problems that confront student committee chairmen. They set the agenda each week for the next meeting and soon discover how easy it is to forget to prepare for a meeting. Thus they learn not to berate forgetful students for the same offense, but rather to make helpful suggestions like keeping a things-to-do notebook or setting aside a regular time for certain tasks.

This same group tries out classroom techniques at their meetings, where it is safe to do so before launching a new method in class. They try brainstorming, role playing, evaluating one another, sentence stubs ("Our meetings are . . . "), use of an observer to report on the climate of the meeting, and buzz groups—all in order to gain familiarity with techniques they seldom experienced when in school or in training.

Once teachers become searchers for ideas they seem to become more creative. Ideas often arrive out of nowhere. One teacher, in the midst of a teacher-pupil conference, pondered how she might get a student to see himself in a less negative sense. Suddenly she knew what to say: "You know, Doug, I can see you as the editor of our next class newspaper. Why, I bet you could get that newspaper out in a week less than the last one by reminding the kids every day about their deadlines." As she talked, Doug sat a little taller and obviously felt a little better about himself. The teacher related this to her colleagues later and said she thought of the idea on the spur of the moment, decided it would work with this boy, and used it in building his self-concept. Doug's subsequent success as editor bolstered it even more.

Ideas for better teaching also arise as teachers take an active part in class activities and as they continuously reflect on their teaching. Indeed, homework for the core teacher is not so much outlining the next chapter for presentation, correcting papers, and making written tests as it is figuring out new situations or approaches to develop a certain attitude or skill, telephoning or writing a note to a student chairman, meeting with class officers after school, or attending a class social event. Because colleges have, for the most part, prepared subject-matter specialists, core teachers must learn on the job. When students select topics for study that the teacher does not know much about, there is no need for panic. MacConnell states:

> In the core program, the teacher finds himself the chief learner. Odd as that may seem at first, it will appear to be psychologically sound on closer examination. Often the teacher does not possess the best potential mind in the group. That, too, may be an odd, even a shocking thought to some teachers. Sober reflection, however, will convince most of us that it would be unusual if some pupil, or perhaps some dozen or more pupils, in our classes did not possess greater possibilities for mental growth and personal development than we. On the other hand, we possess, or should possess, the great advantages of a head start, of greater maturity and broad backgrounds that come from reading and other experiences. When these things are considered, it seems strange indeed if the teacher isn't the chief learner in any classroom since he who possesses most learns fastest. . . . No two of his classes ever cover the same material. With each pupil making a contribution to the learning of the group, the teacher soon accumulates much information that he otherwise might never have occasion to read or hear. Year after year of this helps him to see new meanings in his accumulated knowledge, to recognize relationships that have been obscure. It is the sort of cumulative process from which true wisdom emerges, each according to his talents and responsiveness.[2]

The core teacher also improves his effectiveness by being an active citizen. For example, he comes well prepared to faculty meetings; he is a participant

[2] C. M. MacConnel et al., *New Schools For a New Culture: The Story of the Evanston Township High School Core Program.* (New York: Harper & Brothers, 1953), pp. 140–141.

rather than a spectator. Active in teachers' organizations, he may write, speak to groups, give demonstrations, and hold office. He is involved in community events, too. Summer jobs in radically different kinds of work build understandings of people, labor and economics. Travel, study, politics, and the new acquaintances they promote help to make a person a more interesting and experienced guide and facilitator in the core class.

Teachers who see their primary task as "putting across" subject matter often consider further university course work in a teaching field to be the best route to more effective teaching. Core teachers, too, may profit from further study of literature, language, history, and the social sciences. But since core seeks to develop more effective people and citizens skilled in handling life's situations, better preparation for the core teacher might well be a variety of experiences out in the real world of people and events. For when the teacher has self-doubts and timidity about accepting a speaking engagement or researching information for a community agency, he can then understand somewhat better what he asks of his students in similar classroom assignments.

As he sits in a committee of teachers, some of whom could not care less about the task, he arrives at a clearer understanding of the problems his students face while working in classroom committees. Teachers often are intolerant of small talk in student committee work until they discover the amount that takes place in their own adult committees and recognize the value of humorous remarks that reduce tension. From such experiences teachers develop into more effective citizens. They begin to realize that adult democratic decision making in small and large groups is so agonizingly slow because adults have had little practice and almost no training in interaction or citizenship.

The Self-Confident Core Teacher

There are a number of situations when the core teacher needs above-average confidence in himself. In some schools there are only a few core teachers and sometimes just one. If other teachers are traditionally oriented, their reaction to the core program may be one of suspicion, defensiveness, and occasionally, outright hostility. Perhaps some see core as a threat to their established teaching patterns. They may say that the core program is a lot of foolishness, that it lacks rigor and depth, and that it is anti-intellectual. The core teacher must be prepared not only to explain the program but also to withstand what may be an emotional and irrational attack. In the face of criticism, a few core teachers have melted away and retreated to teaching subject matter as their primary objective. They did not have sufficient understanding of core or they lacked the perseverance and confidence to stand up for their beliefs.

The core teacher must be able to state clearly what he is accomplishing by his classroom methods—methods that on the surface may appear to lack rigor. Beyond this he needs a thorough grounding in the modern sociology, psychology, and philosophy that support the core curriculum. Any program that departs as substantially as core does from conventional teaching will be questioned. The core teacher must anticipate this and go out of his way to know the what and why of the core program. This book and the references cited in the bibliography should help in this process.

Sometimes it is the parents who have questions about the core program. Again, the teacher needs to be up on his homework to be knowledgeable about core and to possess the confidence to explain it to parents. The core teacher certainly cannot depend on the school administrator to do all the explaining. In the face of parents who consider themselves qualified to speak on classroom methods, it is good to bear in mind that it is usually the well-trained teacher who is really the expert. Teachers ought to have no hesitation in gently reminding parents that times have changed since they were in school and that a good deal of research supports the core concept. Parents are, of course, welcome to ask questions and make suggestions, but in the end it is the teacher who bears the responsibility for instruction.

Another problem in a school where there are few core classes is that some core students may wonder why their class is so different from the classes of fellow students. Often it is a very able student who first questions the value of core activities because of his previous success with traditional instruction. The child is not sure he will be so successful with the new demands of the core class, since they do not lie in the area of textbook assignments. Of course, it is essential that the students feel confidence in their teacher and in the activities of the class. If the teacher senses a problem in this area he must spend the necessary time explaining and working with students so that they understand and feel good about the class. Sometimes a student (not uncommonly another teacher's child) will persist in his opposition; it might be desirable to simply say, "Not every class, every year, and every teacher is the same. This year we will be working somewhat differently. I expect you to try as hard as you can to learn. Here are some things you can do to help our class. . . ." Some special project that both the student and the teacher recognize as challenging and worthwhile may help the student make the transition to core.

Some new core teachers are hesitant and apologetic in their own classrooms. Indecision is communicated to students and generally leads to a progressively worsening class atmosphere. The beginning core teacher cannot avoid some feelings of inadequacy, but he can overcome this to some extent by being extremely well prepared for class. A few students may challenge the teacher or test him to find where he draws the line on discipline. The confident core teacher states his expectations and invites the class to join him in determining rules and standards. He does not hesitate in enforcing the rules. Some teachers make the mistake of equating core teaching or democracy in the classroom with permissiveness. They are not the same! Teacher-pupil planning means *both* share in the planning (and not in an atmosphere of uproar, either!). The teacher is always an active partner so that the planning is done well. If things are going badly in class the teacher must feel free to talk over the difficulty with the class in order to remedy the situation. Beneath the actions of the core teacher is the confident attitude that he can and will find ways to cope with circumstances that arise.

Finally, the core teacher needs to realize that he should never be the hapless observer of a deteriorating situation, be it in the classroom, in the school, or in the community. There is more than confidence involved here. The core teacher must be a living, breathing example of an effective person who knows how to take action. He must take the offensive to strengthen and increase the core program where he believes this to be in the best interests of a sound educational program.

Conclusion

The core program that functions properly gives its students an exciting and very significant part of their education. The class is meant to be the heart or "core" of education for personal effectiveness and citizenship. Core students regard the genuine core class as a very important part of their school day. They spend more time in this one class than in any of the others, and some of the experiences they have in core will be remembered for life. In the core class, the teacher pays them a rare honor; he consults them, and their opinions affect how things will go. It is not at all unusual for students who have disliked school to find the core class one of the most stimulating experiences of their education. The hard-working core teacher is rewarded in many ways: the students are less apt to be bored; they seldom ask, "Do we have to do this?"; they go on to leadership roles in later schooling; they seem to like learning and digging for the facts; in big and small ways they show real appreciation for their teacher.

None of these things happen of their own accord or suddenly. They happen because the core teacher knows exactly what he is trying to do, works hard at finding better ways to accomplish the job, and has the confidence in himself to bring about a miniature democratic society in the classroom.

Unit II

Core and Team Teaching

Chapter 4

Team Teaching
in a Core Program

by Loren D. Tompkins

When asked what they need most in order to carry out an effective core program, teachers frequently list time during the school day when they can meet to share ideas. They seek the advice and counsel of their colleagues as they face the challenges of core teaching. Whether core teachers should be formally organized into teaching teams is another question. Mr. Tompkins examines this issue on the basis of his experience as teacher and Core Coordinator in Northern Hills Junior High School, North Topeka, Kansas.

The core curriculum, which came into its own in the 1930's, has survived the critical years of the 1950's, and is still quite widely accepted in the junior high school.[1] Today a new plan, team teaching, touted by some as the ultimate in educational practice, has arrived on the scene and is increasingly winning acceptance. Some educators see team teaching as a modern-day refinement and extension of the core idea, while others view the two concepts as diametrically opposed. Precisely what are the relationships between team teaching and core? Can team teaching and core be combined so that the strengths of both overcome the weaknesses of each? The answers to these questions depend upon the meaning assigned to each concept.

Team Teaching

Team teaching is a term of many faces. In the most general and most widely applied sense, it simply means giving two or more teachers joint responsibility for the education of a group of pupils larger than what is generally considered a normal size class. Inherent in this concept is the idea that there will be some type of differentiation in the functions of the various teachers, either as to subject-matter specialization or methodology.

---

[1] Karl D. Edwards, "A Study of the Incidence of Core Programs in the Fifty States," unpublished study, University of Kansas, 1966.

Unfortunately, the prestige attached to having a team-teaching program today leads to some deceptive use of the term. Often nothing more is meant than that the music or art teacher teaches fifteen minutes per week in the history class. Or the term is used to describe a program in which a history teacher and an English teacher coordinate their programs without ever actually occupying the same classroom at the same time.

At the other extreme, team teaching can be defined to encompass not only an organizational structure but also a highly complex philosophy of education. Such plans, resulting primarily from the work of J. Lloyd Trump, are unfortunately few in number and have been rather poorly evaluated. The acceptance of this type of philosophy entails modular scheduling, variable grouping of students, delineation of teaching responsibilities, use of paraprofessionals, new building arrangements, released independent study time for pupils, and the replacement of the centralized library with resource centers. Only schools accepting total commitment to the team approach find it possible to install the complete Trump plan.

We must look for a useful definition somewhere between these extremes. Perhaps team teaching is best defined by a set of descriptive criteria. Educationally sound plans of team teaching have the following common characteristics:

1. Group size fluctuates according to the learning task.

Different educational tasks call for different size groups. A lecture can be heard and understood as well by a hundred students as it can by twenty-five. Discussion, however, can be more effectively carried on by ten students in a situation in which the teacher is a catalyst rather than an authority figure.

2. Time arrangements fluctuate according to the learning task.

Many students and teachers are frustrated because of the rigidity of the traditional mosaic schedule. In one class a teacher may shortcut part of a science experiment or cut off a creative discussion because of time pressure, while in another a teacher may "pad" part of a period with busywork because an entire period is not necessary.

Team teaching proponents hope to deal more effectively with time allotments by adapting the modular or flexible schedule. Basically, this consists of breaking the school day into a large number of short periods, referred to as *time modules,* and assigning teachers different numbers of these modules according to the task at hand. Sometimes periods vary on a rotating basis, but automated scheduling makes possible varying time allotments daily. It should be noted, however, that even this type of schedule has two rigid features, since the entire schedule is confined by the outside limits of the school day and a definite number of subjects must be fitted into a given length of time. Modular scheduling is an ideal time arrangement to be used with team teaching, but flexibility in scheduling also may be achieved through some of the block-time patterns and back-to-back scheduling described in Part II of this book.

3. Emphasis is on cooperative planning by teachers.

There are numerous types of teacher teams, but all include members with differing roles based either upon academic specialization or upon teaching proficiency. Regardless of type of organization, the purpose is to create a "superteacher" by fusing the strengths of each team member into a joint effort. This fusion necessitates extremely careful and concrete planning among the teachers of the team. Besides coordinating the program, this can prove beneficial to the teaching effort by reducing duplication in the clerical tasks of teaching and by establishing a greatly expanded "pool of creativity" from which the teacher can draw. Without continuous joint planning it is probable that any team effort would result in chaos.

4. It is recognized that teachers vary in degree and nature of competencies, and that this variation is observable in the child's achievement.

Every teacher has specific strengths and weaknesses, regardless of his overall efficiency. The creation of a superteacher through teaming carries with it the idea that student learning will be superior if teacher weaknesses are eliminated. Studies which have been performed to date are surprisingly far apart in results and tend to be highly ambiguous. Yet it is in the area of student achievement that team teaching must ultimately stand or fall.

Core Curriculum

As defined in Chapter 1, core usually involves the assignment of a class-size group of students to a single teacher for a block of time in which instruction focuses on the personal-social needs of the pupil. As with the term team teaching, the core label has been applied to many different programs. Nevertheless, the following descriptive criteria appear to apply to all core programs:

1. Group size fluctuates according to the learning task.

Like team teaching, core utilizes varying size groups for various learning tasks. The core teacher structures committee work (i.e., small group) and individual work (i.e., independent study), as well as total class instruction (i.e., large group). Like the team member, the core teacher acts as a catalytic force and places great store in the theory of group dynamics and in Gestalt psychology. Unlike the team approach, however, in core the students ordinarily relate only to the core teacher rather than to several teachers, except for occasional auditorium-type programs or activities involving several core classes.

2. Time arrangements fluctuate according to the learning task.

As with team teaching, the core curriculum is not bound by the standard six- or seven-period day. Flexibility is provided by the block of time, varying in length from school to school, but usually consisting of one-third to one-half of the total school day. The individual core teacher is autonomous in distributing this time among the various learning tasks.

3. Core lies within the general education sector of the curriculum.

Core normally replaces language arts and social studies. In a number of core programs, especially in the seventh grade, science is included within the core, but this practice seems to be decreasing. The explosion of knowledge which has occurred in the field of science since World War II, as well as the growing departmentalization of science in the elementary school, suggest the need for a specialist in this field.[2] There are a number of programs combining the areas of science and mathematics, sometimes under the core label, but upon closer examination they often turn out to be either subject-area block programs or interdisciplinary team teaching.

For many years the idea of a "cultural core" involving literature, philosophy, music, and art was in vogue, but this was fraught with problems, including time demands, teacher adequacy, and curriculum restrictions. Recently there has been a growing acceptance of this type of program, but in the context of a team-taught course in humanities as described in Chapter 6.

4. Instruction in the core is based upon teacher-prepared resource units which are interdisciplinary in nature.

Even in an unstructured core program, much instruction is based upon students' needs as predefined and interpreted by the staff. An interdisciplinary resource unit may offer many valuable teaching suggestions.

5. Subject matter is taught in an integrated fashion.

As elaborated in Chapters 2 and 3, an attempt is made within the core to make learning a dynamic process in which the student is actively involved. Subject matter from various areas is tapped during the examination of problems.

6. Guidance is an integral feature of the core curriculum.

Perhaps the most characteristic, and also the most controversial, feature of the core is the placement of the guidance function within the block of time. Just what is meant by the term "guidance" varies from program to program. In some schools the entire guidance and counseling function is carried out by the core teachers, while in others the teacher merely performs a screening function for the guidance specialist. Teachers may lack preparation for this kind of service, and local staffing patterns may limit the effectiveness of this classroom-centered guidance. In the long run the important thing may be not the amount or kind of guidance duties carried on by the core teacher, but rather his feeling that guidance is an important characteristic of the program.

Some reasons for including guidance in the core are:

    (a) The block of time gives the teacher flexibility in scheduling so that he can include time for guidance duties.

    (b) The extended time period, when coupled with the extensive pupil-teacher interaction which is so characteristic of the core, creates an ideal climate for establishing the informal rapport which is vital to successful guidance.

[2] William F. Adams., "Science Teaching: Core *vs.* Departmental," unpublished master's thesis Washburn University, 1964.

(c) The core teacher, enjoying a close working relationship with the pupil, is often in an excellent position to make value judgments regarding test results and past records.[3]

What, then, is the relationship of core and team teaching? Team teaching is essentially a plan of staff organization designed to greatly improve the efficiency of education, whereas core is a curriculum organization built on a particular philosophy of education. Would it not be possible then to marry the core philosophy and curriculum to a team-teaching organizational scheme and develop a superplan of education featuring the strongest points of each? Opinion on this question is divided.[4]

Core Curriculum and Team Teaching—An Experiment

In 1959 these ideas were given a practical trial. Near Topeka, Kansas, a small rural high school district was in the throes of reorganization. The district at that time had only a four-year high school of about 500 students, but population pressures created the need for a new secondary school. The decision was made to construct a new building designed exclusively for junior high school students rather than to convert the existing senior high to a junior high school. This made it possible to design the building to suit the curriculum rather than the usual practice of designing the curriculum to fit the building. It was determined early in the planning stage that the school would feature a core curriculum, since both the core's emphasis upon the child as an active learner and the transitional nature of the program were felt to be highly desirable. Additionally, however, it was decided that the more desirable features of team teaching would be introduced in an attempt to counteract any possible weaknesses in the core program.

Physical Facilities

The building design called for six core rooms and a central library to be located in a cluster arrangement in a separate wing. Each room was hexagonally shaped and contained almost a thousand square feet of floor space, with closets and built-in cupboards for storage. Each room would comfortably accommodate sixty students seated in rows or provide seating and a separate work area for thirty students. Three of these rooms were placed side-by-side to provide a "core suite." Each room within a suite was designed with a common wall which was composed entirely of soundproof slab doors which, by means of an overhead track, could be opened to form an amphitheater with a capacity of two hundred.

Between the two core suites was a central library of 5,000 volumes. Included were conference rooms which would accommodate eight to twelve persons for small group work and an open work area designed for over a hundred pupils.

[3] Roy D. Willey and W. Melvin Strong, *Group Procedures in Guidance.* (New York: Harper & Brothers, 1957), pp. 423–437.

[4] Gordon F. Vars, "Can Team Teaching Save the Core Curriculum?" *Phi Delta Kappan,* Vol. 47 (January 1966), pp. 258–262.

The Curriculum

The subject matter was basically composed of content drawn from the areas of social studies, language arts, and science. The curriculum design resembled structured core and was based upon teacher-prepared interdisciplinary resource units. Subject matter from other areas was utilized at times.

The Staff

Undoubtedly the selection of the core staff received more attention than any other single item. The decision was made early in the plan to go outside the district to recruit teachers rather than to move teachers into the program from within the district. Recruiting started early so that a wide selection would be available. In all, fifty teachers were interviewed for the six core-team positions. Emphasis was placed upon obtaining individuals who could work easily with others, who were knowledgeable about and sympathetic to both the core curriculum and team teaching, and who were willing to experiment. Academically, each team was composed of a person with a background in English, one with a background in science, and a third with a background in core and social science. When the six teachers were contracted they attended a special summer workshop at the University of Kansas which dealt with both core and team teaching.

Scheduling

Because of the limited number of students attending the school, a total commitment to team teaching would have been impractical. It was necessary to provide flexibility in the team-teaching segment of the curriculum while supplying traditional structure for the remainder of the school. A three-period block of time was provided for the seventh-grade core, while a two-period block was provided for the eighth grade. The team members were given complete freedom to determine how the time within the block was to be spent.

Teaching Load

Each team member taught one three-period block class, one two-period block, and one single-period class in his area of specialization. All team members were also provided with one period within the school day for planning. Since the teachers themselves controlled the use of the block of time, one or two team members frequently were released for additional planning, research, and related teaching duties.

Large Group Instruction

It was felt by the staff that the initial success or failure of the experiment would be determined largely by the success of large group instruction, since this was the area which required the greatest amount of adjustment for both students and teachers. It was determined that large group instruction was to be used as follows:

1. Introductory unit activities.
2. General information activities.
3. Culminating unit activities.
4. Audio-visual presentations.
5. Guest speakers.

Teacher responsibility in large group presentations varied according to the nature of the activity. Normally all team members participated in the activities listed first and third above, while general information situations were assigned to the subject matter specialist in that area. The responsibility for the fourth and fifth activities, which were usually of a general administrative nature, were rotated among the team members. During periods of large group instruction the teachers not directly involved with the presentation were released for planning.

Class-Size Group Instruction

For administrative and guidance purposes a group of twenty-five pupils was assigned to a teacher for the entire term. This was referred to as his homeroom group.

Other groups varied in size, depending upon whether they were used to provide specialized information, follow-up discussion, or remedial instruction. These groups ranged from fewer than fifteen to as many as thirty-five, depending upon the activity being pursued.

Teachers were assigned to these groups according to their specialization and the task at hand, while students were assigned according to their needs. At times the membership and size of a group were constant for a period of several weeks, while at other times the groups changed several times each day.

Small-Group and Independent Study

Classes were further subdivided into very small groups composed of three or four members, with each such "committee" working on a different aspect of a large problem. These groups operated with a minimum of teacher supervision. Independent study experience for each student grew out of the committee work.

Team Responsibility

Each team was given responsibility for the instruction of a group of approximately seventy-five students. Only two conditions were placed on this freedom. First, each team was to stay within the framework of the teacher-constructed resource units as much as possible, and secondly, it was suggested that a ratio of roughly 1:1:2 should be maintained between large group instruction, class-size group instruction, and small-group and/or individual instruction.

Each team met for one period during the school day for planning and also met informally each morning before classes began. During these periods teacher assignments were made, various student groupings were developed, and schedules were worked out. To achieve the greatest flexibility possible, activities were planned at first on a minute basis. Later, it was decided that the logistics of such scheduling were overly complicated and it was abandoned for modular scheduling within the block. Once each week the entire core department met for one hour to discuss problems and determine progress.

Team Teaching and Core—An Evaluation

In addition to standardized testing to evaluate pupil progress in the various subject-matter areas, the staff and administration, with the aid of professional consultants, carried out an extensive subjective evaluation of the program. Several staff members and interested outsiders studied various aspects of the program as part of their work in college courses, and a research team from the University of Kansas did an extensive study of teacher-teacher and teacher-pupil relationships.[5] Seven major conclusions were reached:

1. Teachers felt they benefited from the close working relationship with other teachers. Several aspects of this team relationship were judged to be especially beneficial. Most frequently mentioned was the creation of a "pool of creativity" when three teachers attacked a problem, rather than leaving its solution to one individual. This was particularly noticeable in developing learning activities. Teachers also felt that they had more time during the school day for planning and constructing lessons. Surprisingly, this released time most often resulted from a division of labor in carrying out nonteaching duties, rather than from large-group instruction. Teachers often felt unprepared to direct follow-up activities unless they were actually present at the large-group presentations, especially when these sessions dealt with material outside their area of specialization.

2. Pupil interest waned during large-group sessions, especially those in which students were largely passive. This seemed to be influenced, not so much by the teacher or subject matter involved, but rather by extraneous factors such as time of day, length of session, group age, and group composition.

Teachers also felt that even the most effective large-group presentation resulted in extremely diverse levels of learning. This was not necessarily tied to student intelligence or overall achievement, but rather to maturity and the nature of the task. Generally, eighth-graders suffered less from this than did seventh-graders, but even on the higher levels a great deal of reteaching was necessary, thus reducing the effectiveness of the large group presentation. Generally it was felt by the teachers that many junior high school students had not reached a level of maturity required to function efficiently in a large group.

3. Flexible or modular scheduling generally was felt to be less desirable than open-block scheduling. In part this problem stemmed from time limitations

[5] "Predicting Success of a Teaching Team," unpublished study, University of Kansas Guidance Bureau, 1964.

created by the fact that the entire schedule was not built around modules. The fact remains, however, that the scope of the curriculum, the outside limits of the school day, and the necessity of correlating activities all require split-second precision when more than one teacher is involved in the learning process at the same time. Ordinarily the block of time is an effective answer to these problems since, with careful planning, it is both long enough and flexible enough to accommodate a myriad of activities. However, a true plan of team teaching cannot function within a block without some subdivision of time. The finer these subdivisions the more inflexible the schedule becomes. The amount of flexibility actually attained hinges upon the tolerance which must be allowed for time errors that result from poor coordination of learning activities. Thus, six modules in a block with a three-teacher team creates the possibility of eighteen errors, while one block of time with one teacher allows for only one error. This problem concerns only time flexibility and not the efficient use of time. In the latter case, the flexible schedule may hold an advantage since it demands a great amount of lesson preparation. This dubious advantage depends entirely upon the personality involved. Effective lesson planning and preparation are characteristics of good teaching, not of time allocation.

4. Team teaching interfered with establishment of the rapport necessary for effective classroom guidance. Perhaps the most serious problem confronting the combined program was in the area of pupil identification. Since the individual's teacher varied with the task at hand, it was impossible for the student to identify with any one teacher as "his" teacher.

The homeroom system, which had been adopted to remedy this problem, actually worked in reverse since the pupils, foraging for identification, tended to identify so closely with the homeroom teacher that establishment of rapport with the other teachers was hampered. It became necessary, both for the teaching and guidance function, to centralize guidance functions outside the program, thus sacrificing one of the strongest features of the core.

5. Pupil evaluation was a constant problem. Although many educators decry the practice, marking is a function of the school which is here to stay. Always difficult, the problem was compounded by the nature of the program. In keeping with the core philosophy of integration, it was determined to assign one grade for all the student's work in core. Originally the teachers expected that each team member would evaluate all work falling within his particular subject-matter specialty. It was soon discovered that most of the work each pupil completed could not be categorized easily. When it was possible to categorize it, the weighting of various aspects created problems galore. The complete, ongoing subjective and objective evaluation of pupil behavior, interest, and performance, normally so basic to a core program, was lost in the melee.

6. The logistics of team teaching destroyed the usefulness of the flexible resource unit. The resource unit, as conceived by the core teacher, is an open-ended instrument constructed around the needs of pupils and catering to individual differences. Learning activities derived from such a unit vary from

class to class in terms of both content and teaching time. Team teaching, on the other hand, requires a highly sophisticated system of coordination among the various teachers involved. Therefore, artificial limits must be placed upon the amount of time each teacher spends on any given activity, sometimes to the detriment of pupil curiosity and interest. Finally, it became impossible to coordinate activities well enough to allow joint culminating activities. At times teachers and their classes were forced to "mark time" while waiting for other team members to complete their work.

7. Student achievement under this plan was disappointing. Pupils did show a marked gain in achievement, as measured by standardized tests, but later experience with the same teachers operating within the traditional self-contained core classroom resulted in about the same level of achievement.

Conclusion

Based upon the above-described experience, some generalizations can be drawn regarding the relationship of core and team teaching. Unquestionably two ideas with so many similarities can be integrated, but the requirement that it be done in such a manner that the weaknesses of each is remedied causes pause for reflection. Merely integrating the plans for the sake of being different is both futile and expensive. Introducing a unique feature of either plan quite probably will not only cure a weakness of the other plan, but also detract from its basic strength. The resulting program tends to polarize around one plan or the other.

Team teaching opens doors to new concepts of teacher cooperation, pupil placement, and methodology which cannot be ignored. Educators may profit by closely observing the progress made in schools which have true team-teaching plans, just as they have from experiments with the core curriculum.

However, today's complex and dynamic society demands a kind of education that develops the total individual. Core, alone among the various approaches to education present today, goes beyond development of the intellect without ignoring or weakening this most primary function of education.

Chapter 5

Interdisciplinary
Team Teaching

by H. Edgar Pray

Teamwork and cooperative planning by teachers have been part of core theory and practice since the very early years. In contrast, some educators would replace the core curriculum with an interdisciplinary program taught by teams of specialists in several subject areas. The case for an interdisciplinary team approach to common learnings is made here by H. Edgar Pray, Assistant Superintendent for Instruction, Burnt Hills-Ballston Lake Central Schools, Burnt Hills, New York. He examines this alternative from a background of experience with both core and team teaching, more recently as principal of Van Antwerp Junior High School, Niskayuna Public Schools, Schenectady, New York.

A perennial search in the development of education for the junior high school years has been to find an organizational pattern which makes possible a blending of the child-centered and the subject-specialist philosophies. Too many junior high schools, in their effort to strengthen the content curriculum, have created highly departmentalized and depersonalized operations. On the other hand, some schools that have overemphasized the child-centered approach have created situations in which teacher effectiveness may be substantially curtailed.

Thoughtful junior high school educators over the years have proposed a number of solutions to this dilemma. Some have seen in the combining of subject areas under one teacher an opportunity to reduce the number of daily student contacts. For example, a teacher under a strictly departmentalized arrangement might be responsible for five classes averaging 27 pupils, a total of 135 students each day. Under a combined studies or block-time pattern the teacher's responsibility might be reduced to two groups, or 54 pupils, with his total time load remaining constant because of the additional commitments he has to this smaller number of students.

In fifteen years' experience with this approach the writer has found much to commend it. Certainly the teacher does have time and opportunity to "know" the pupil. Grass-roots guidance and core-based homeroom functions can be enhanced under such an administrative arrangement, and the correlation of content areas comes naturally.

Another approach, which certainly is not new but which seems to be gaining in popularity, is that of the interdisciplinary team organization. The rationale, format, and problems of the interdisciplinary team approach to common learnings are the concern of this chapter.

Traditionally the typical high school has a departmental, vertical type of organization. On the other hand, the conventional elementary school tends to be organized horizontally, with one teacher primarily responsible for the learnings in language arts, social studies, mathematics, and science. The educator's function at the junior high school level is to meld these two philosophies, with a balance of emphasis on the subject and the child. The interdisciplinary team may well be an answer to this problem. These patterns can be shown in tabular form.

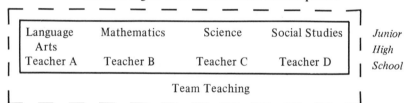

Vertical Emphasis

| Language Arts
Teacher A | Mathematics

Teacher B | Science

Teacher C | Social Studies

Teacher D | *High School* |

Horizontal Emphasis

| Language Arts | Mathematics | Science | Social Studies | *Elementary School* |
| | | Teacher A | | |

The Melding of Vertical and Horizontal Emphases

| Language Arts
Teacher A | Mathematics

Teacher B | Science

Teacher C | Social Studies

Teacher D | *Junior High School* |
| | | Team Teaching | | |

Rationale and Structure of the Interdisciplinary Team

The interdisciplinary team approach is based on at least four premises:
1. That teachers in junior high school need to be specialists in a single-subject discipline. With the ever-increasing demands for competency, it is not reasonable to expect a teacher to develop the background of content and method in more than one discipline to the level of effectiveness attainable when only one discipline is required.
2. That, while paying attention to the need for teacher competency in a single discipline, it is well to keep in mind the child-centered philosophy emphasized over the years in the elementary school. The elementary

teacher tends to know relatively few youngsters rather completely, and they know her well.

3. That the teacher team organizational pattern adds a new dimension, a stimulation resulting from the interaction of teachers who are planning together for the same youngsters.
4. That the team organization, because of its format, allows many opportunities to progress in the direction of large and small-group instruction and independent study.

How, then, can the interdisciplinary team be organized? A team can be composed of four teachers, one English, one mathematics, one social studies and one science, who all teach the same children. It should be noted that this is not the usual type of subject-matter team. Rather it is an attempt to offset the possible depersonalized aspects of the departmental pattern by bringing the teachers of the same pupils together to care for these children and their total educational program.

Team-planning sessions for teachers can take place during several periods a week at a time when a given team of pupils is attending physical education classes. In addition, during certain periods of the week entire teams of students can be assigned to study pools supervised by lay study hall aides. At these built-in times teachers are free to draw off pupils from the study pools for individual and small-group instruction.

At this point it may be timely to present both the teachers' schedule and a student schedule for a given team.

Program for the Teachers of Eighth-Grade Team 83

Periods	Monday		Tuesday	Wednesday	Thursday	Friday
1 9:10– 9:54	Free*		Free*	Free*	Free*	Free*
2 9:57– 10:41	Section 831	English	Same	Same	Same	Same
	Section 832	Mathematics	Same	Same	Same	Same
	Section 833	Science	Same	Same	Same	Same
	Section 834	Social Studies	Same	Same	Same	Same
3 10:44– 11:28	Section 832	English	Same	Same	Same	Same
	Section 833	Mathematics	Same	Same	Same	Same
	Section 834	Science	Same	Same	Same	Same
	Section 831	Social Studies	Same	Same	Same	Same
	Lunch and Homeroom		Same	Same	Same	Same
4 12:20– 1:07	Free		Free	Free	Team: large-group, alternate weeks	Free
5 1:10– 1:54	Draw-off		Planning	Draw-off	Planning	Planning

Periods	Monday		Tuesday	Wednesday	Thursday	Friday
6	Section 833	English	Same	Same	Same	Same
1:57–	Section 834	Mathematics	Same	Same	Same	Same
2:41	Section 831	Science	Same	Same	Same	Same
	Section 832	Social Studies	Same	Same	Same	Same
7	Section 834	English	Same	Same	Same	Same
2:44–	Section 831	Mathematics	Same	Same	Same	Same
3:27	Section 832	Science	Same	Same	Same	Same
	Section 833	Social Studies	Same	Same	Same	Same

*Except 1¼ periods per week for nonlanguage draw-off. Nonlanguage refers to the 20 percent of the pupils not taking a foreign language.

Program for a Pupil of Eighth Grade Team 83, Section 831

Period	Monday	Tuesday	Wednesday	Thursday	Friday
1 9:10– 9:54	Foreign Language	Same	Same	Same	Same
	Foreign-Language Lab	Music	Music	Foreign-Language Lab	Music
2 9:57– 10:41	English	Same	Same	Same	Same
3 10:44– 11:28	Social Studies	Same	Same	Same	Same
Lunch and Homeroom		Same	Same	Same	Same
4 12:20– 1:07	Arts	Arts	Arts	Alternate weeks: music large-group team large-group	
5 1:10– 1:54	Draw-off	Physical education	Draw-off	Physical education	Physical education
6 1:57– 2:41	Science	Same	Same	Same	Same
7 2:44– 3:27	Mathematics	Same	Same	Same	Same

Here are some plusses that can be derived from horizontal teaming:

1. Teachers tend to know each other better. Their efforts are correlated and a stimulation results from their interaction in planning together.

2. Teachers know students better, for they share information about youngsters.

3. Because it allows four teachers to work closely with approximately 108 pupils, the interdisciplinary team provides a framework for individualizing in-

struction and personalizing learning. For example, it is possible at times for one teacher to teach 105 pupils in a large group situation while the other three teachers each work with one student.

4. A guidance counselor can meet with a teaching team during planning sessions on a regular basis. This is a natural way to bring guidance counselors, teaching staff and children together in close relationship. Also, as the needs arise, the psychologist, speech teacher, principal, assistant principals, nurse, reading specialist, parents and others may meet with teaching teams during this built-in time.

5. During study-pool periods each team teacher may draw off the pupils he wants for individual and small group teaching. These are regularly assigned teaching periods when perhaps some of the most important teaching and learning take place. Often students take the initiative in this scheduling.

6. Because classes are scheduled back-to-back, the team teachers may plan long and short periods, schedule field trips, engage in large and small-group instruction, and not interfere with other classes. A given scheduling can be for a period or a day or a week or as long as it serves the needs of teachers and pupils.

Here are two schedules which show how the Team 83 program could be modified to accommodate either longer or shorter periods of time.

Double Periods for One Day (Team Subjects Only)

Period	Section 831	Section 832	Section 833	Section 834
1				
2	English	Mathematics	Social Studies	Science
3	English	Mathematics	Social Studies	Science
4				
5				
6	Social Studies	Science	English	Mathematics
7	Social Studies	Science	English	Mathematics

Half Periods for One Day (Team Subjects Only)

Period	Section 831	Section 832	Section 833	Section 834
1				
2	English	Mathematics	Science	Social Studies
	Mathematics	Science	Social Studies	English
3	Science	Social Studies	English	Mathematics
	Social Studies	English	Mathematics	Science
4				
5				
6	Available for team related purposes such as field trips,			
7	large group instruction, and other projects.			

7. Correlation among subject disciplines is enhanced. Language arts, mathematics, science and social studies tend to make up about two-thirds of the curriculum. The interdisciplinary team organization provides a setting in which cooperative planning can take place in the several subject areas. For example, a teacher responsible for science and a teacher handling social studies can plan and work together in the treatment of a topic on conservation. Not only are their efforts correlated, but a stimulation results from the interaction of teachers who are planning together for the same youngsters.

Correlation of experiences can also be strengthened in the other one-third of the curriculum, which includes such areas as art, music, and physical education. The opportunities to relate these subject areas with each other and with the academic areas are increased. For example, rhythm and dance in physical education can be rather nicely correlated with rhythm and song in music, and both can be related to social studies. Time for this cooperative planning can be built into the schedule.

8. School enrollment is divided into more manageable groupings. Sometimes a "house" or "school-within-a-school" plan is used for this purpose. In the typical house plan for a junior high school of 1,200, the school population might be divided into three 400-pupil units so that in effect there are three small schools or houses rather than one large school. In the interdisciplinary team organization, size reduction is accomplished through the four-section team, which makes possible units of approximately 108 pupils each.

9. Turning now to the vertical aspects of interdisciplinary learning, teachers may become specialists in one particular field at a given grade level. Teacher effectiveness is enhanced when teachers have time to study and plan in depth in a specialized discipline.

The task of those who teach at the middle or junior high level, then, is to keep in balance these two enormously important ingredients—the horizontal pattern with its accent on child-centeredness and the vertical pattern which places stress on subject field competency.

Our Experience with Interdisciplinary Teams

To further clarify the concept of interdisciplinary teaming, we shall examine the program of the Van Antwerp Junior High School of Niskayuna, New York. Niskayuna, suburban to Schenectady, has a population of about 17,000, with 4,700 pupils housed in five elementary schools, one junior high school and one high school. The junior high school, sometimes referred to as a middle school, has been organized as a grades 6-7-8 school for a period of eight years. We are in our third year of interdisciplinary teaming, the first year having been one of experimentation with three differing patterns. Presently the school has 1,140 pupils and ten interdisciplinary teaching teams. The following bulletins and reports give further details about the Van Antwerp program.

I. *Program of Studies*

This lists the number of periods per week for each subject at the three grade levels. Periods are 44 minutes in length.

Van Antwerp Junior High School—Program of Studies 1966-67

Subject	Grade 6	Grade 7	Grade 8
English	5	5	5
Reading	3*	—*	—*
Mathematics	5	5	5
Social studies	5	5	5
Science	5	5	5
French, German or Spanish	2	2½	2½
Foreign language lab	—	1	1
Art	3	2†	2†
Industrial or home arts	—	2†	2†
Music	2	2	2
Physical education	3	3	3
Draw-off periods	2	2½	2½
Total	35	35	35

*Plus remedial reading.
†Four periods per week for one semester.

II. *Teacher Load*

Earlier in this chapter the program of one teaching team was show. The following schedule indicates the total academic load of team teachers.

Program for Academic Team Teachers, 1966-67

Grade 6

Assignment	Periods Per Week	Explanation
Regular classes	20	
Reading	3	Developmental, sequential program for all pupils.
Team planning	3	Stress this year on subject correlation.
Draw-off	2	
Large-group		May use part or all of study pool period on occasion.
Departmental meetings (8:05 a.m.)	1	Curriculum development.
Other (8:05 a.m.)	1	Administrative, interdepartmental, etc.
Personal use	7	Free, planning, independent study, etc.

Grades 7 and 8

Assignment	Periods Per Week	Explanation
Regular classes	20	
Team Planning	3	Stress this year on subject correlation.
Draw-off	2	
Draw-off (non-language)	1¼	Handled by the 4 teachers; opportunity to work with non-language pupils.
Large group	½	Full period every other week for movies, lectures, etc.
Departmental meetings (8:05 a.m.)	1	Curriculum development.
Other (8:05 a.m.)	1	Administrative, interdepartmental, etc.
Personal use	8¼	Free, planning, independent study, etc.

III. Team Planning

The bulletin below was written in June, 1965, after the experimental year with interdisciplinary teaching. That year we emphasized the built-in cooperative team sessions. This bulletin had as its purpose the sharing of ideas among faculty members as well as a description for others of the "nuts and bolts" of cooperative planning.

When students leave the five elementary schools of our district they enter a single junior high school and become part of a departmental organization. It is important at this point that pupils be taught by teachers who have had a major concentration in one subject area. This transition from elementary to junior high school is difficult for some youngsters.

At Van Antwerp we try to provide a rather extensive program of orientation. Each spring, guidance counselors visit the fifth grades to describe the sixth-grade program. They confer with the teachers in order to learn as much as possible about each child. In addition, the fifth grades are invited on a tour through the junior high and parents attend an evening meeting as part of their orientation. In the fall, homeroom teachers and guidance counselors take time to help students adjust to their new environment.

Orientation is a continuous process, however. Because there is a need for each child to be known as an individual and to be known well by several adults, the staff at Van Antwerp has developed a team teaching program. Four academic teachers in English, social studies, science and mathematics all teach the same students. This academic team meets regularly three times a week to coordinate their efforts and their programs. Perhaps the most valuable personal benefit to teachers is the opportunity to exchange ideas on methods of approach, techniques which are successful, philosophies of teaching, and a feeling of assurance that they are working as a team. In order to spell out in concrete terms exactly what the academic teams do to improve the educational offering, the following items have been taken from team reports on each grade level.

Professional Activities Reported by Teams

Consideration of Individual Children
1. Behavior and emotional problems
2. Evaluation of progress
3. Meeting with parents to discuss an individual child
4. Changing schedules within the team to accommodate the needs of all children.

Consultation with Specialists
1. Guidance counselor
2. Psychologist
3. Speech teacher
4. Visiting teacher
5. Reading specialist
6. School nurse
7. Teacher of handicapped (blind)
8. Principal or assistant principal
9. Teachers of foreign languages, art, music, physical education

Correlation of Subject Areas
1. Each teacher describes coverage to date
2. Each teacher submits for discussion papers written by pupils in each subject area
3. Plan correlations around subject matter and skills. For example, conservation in social studies and science; written expression in all fields
4. Exchange materials

Discussion of School-Related Topics
1. Student council
2. Assemblies
3. Corridors
4. Homerooms
5. Cafeteria
6. Marking and reporting

Scheduling
A. *Regular Class Periods*
1. Subject-matter movies—all four sections
2. Speakers on special topics—for example:
    (a) Latin America
    (b) Health problems
    (c) Community problems
3. Laboratory periods for science
4. Library periods—social studies and English
5. Organization and evaluation of field trips

      6. Reading-study skills program
      7. Current events
      8. Large-group instruction
      9. Work with other teams to reschedule periods
    10. Clearance of major tests, large projects, homework assignments
  B. *Draw-Off Periods*
      1. Individual help for students
      2. Small group instruction in a particular area
      3. Assistance with a project or special reading
         (Note: One teacher on the team is responsible for maintaining a study place, one for taking a group to the library each of the five available periods.)

The faculty of the junior high school believes that through this team teaching organization and what this organizational pattern implies we can improve the educational program for each child. We hope that we are giving real attention to the need for subject-matter specialization while maintaining a sincere concern for the individual.

IV. *Draw-Off Period (from study pools)*

In May 1966, following the first full year of teaming, we asked teachers to report some of the ways in which they had used the draw-off periods. Here are a few of the items listed.

Make-up work (for absentees, students switching sections, or those new to Van Antwerp)
    Tests
    Homework
    Reading assignments
    Laboratory work
    Demonstrations
    Notebooks

Remedial work
    Basic skills: handwriting, reading, word attack, spelling, outlining, note-taking, reference skills, listening, problem-solving, interpreting source materials
    Help for slow readers or slow learners

Enrichment
    Special projects and independent study
    Seminar (once a week with able students)
    Movies of interest but not directly connected with the curriculum
    Historical gaming

Individual conferences
    Diagnosis and assistance with difficulties on tests

Help with composition, independent study
Counseling regarding personal and/or behavior problems

Group work
Group projects: rehearsing play, preparing bulletin board, choral reading, panel
Current events: discussed by representatives from each class, shared with each section the next day
Committee chairmen discuss their role in group work

Extension of regular class
Extra library period for research
Completing laboratory work begun during regular period
Laboratory clean-up period
Use of classroom reference materials

Other Implications of Interdisciplinary Teaming

Here are some additional insights derived from our experience.

1. At Van Antwerp we employ over twenty full-time and part-time lay teacher aides who, for rather nominal remuneration, perform numerous tasks for teachers. Among these are theme readers, mathematics correctors, typists, noon—period supervisors, language and science laboratory assistants, audio-visual aides and study-hall pool supervisors. This kind of assistance allows the teacher to spend his time and effort on the teaching task itself. Particularly important in the team organization is the job performed by study hall aides. Their supervision allows the team members to be free to work with children during draw-off periods.

2. Team teachers are assigned to four sections of children with the sections averaging about twenty-seven pupils each. Our experimental year proved that this organizational pattern is also possible with five-section teams although the results tend to be less satisfactory. In the five-section pattern a teacher devotes 25 rather than 20 of the 35-period week to formal classes, allowing less time to work with pupils in large and small group situations.

3. The interdisciplinary team with a four-section pattern is appropriate for the small as well as the large school. A school with 100 to 120 pupils per grade could be organized with one team per grade. To accommodate enrollment needs it is also possible to schedule a four-section team composed of two sections from one grade and two sections from another.

4. By scheduling classes opposite each other for two or more teams, pupils from several teams may be pooled when desired. For example, seventh-graders from four teams who have social studies the second period could meet in the auditorium for some appropriate large group presentation. If a double period were available, the presentation could be followed by discussion in small groups of varying size and composition.

5. Because pupils are organized in four-section teams, other team arrange-

ments are possible. At Van Antwerp Junior High School an entire team of students is scheduled at the same time in a related arts program which includes art, home arts, and industrial arts, Physical education classes, music classes, and foreign language classes also are organized on a team basis.

Some Pitfalls in Interdisciplinary Teaming

All organizational patterns have their pitfalls, and interdisciplinary teaming is no exception. One problem is that the four-teacher academic teams may receive so much attention that other members of the faculty might feel neglected. This is especially true when the team concept is first introduced. A simultaneous emphasis on the contributions and importance of other departments of the school can forestall the potential growth of professional jealousy.

Another area of concern is that of interpersonal relationships. When four people are closely related as a team and responsible for four sections of youngsters, the way in which they interact becomes extremely significant. Teams need to be staffed with great care and potential problems anticipated.

The method of grouping pupils should receive careful consideration. At Niskayuna we try to keep each team of students at a given grade level as similar as possible to the other teams at that level so there will be no high teams or low teams. Within the teams themselves there is some grouping according to achievement levels.

Conclusion

Because the interdisciplinary team provides the setting for a highly satisfactory blend of the child-centered and subject-centered philosophies, it attains some of the objectives of the core curriculum at the same time that each teacher remains a subject-area specialist. An additional bonus is derived from the fact that a tremendous potential is unleashed when a teacher emerges from the semi-isolation of the convential classroom to join his team colleagues in a cooperative effort to provide maximum educational opportunities for youngsters.

Chapter 6

Humanities Programs

by Parker LaBach and Mary Jane Rodabaugh

Interdisciplinary courses labeled Humanities, American Studies, and World Studies are gaining increasing acceptance, especially in senior high schools. They were found in 17.7 percent of the 7,237 accredited high schools surveyed in 1967 by Cawelti.[1] Humanities programs may approach core in philosophy if they focus on problems and emphasize the personal meaning of learning experiences. The authors of this chapter, a music teacher and an English teacher, were instrumental in the development of interdisciplinary programs for tenth-, eleventh-, and twelfth-graders in the University School at Kent State University, Kent, Ohio. Dr. LaBach is an associate professor of education at that university and Mrs. Rodabaugh is currently an instructor at Miami University, Oxford, Ohio.

As a general definition, it can be said that an instructional program in the humanities is concerned primarily with the study of man as a human being as seen through his literature, art, music, and those other elements of his cultural history which best show this essential human quality. Such a definition may be entirely too broad to be useful in establishing the place of the humanities in the curriculum or in formulating appropriate content and methods to be followed in teaching the humanities. There remain many unanswered questions, such as: Is there *any* area of study that is intrinsically foreign to a humanities program? Is the humanities a certain group of well-defined disciplines, or rather a *way* of looking at things? What should be the outcomes, in terms of meanings and understandings, of a study of the humanities?

The traditional humanist was a Renaissance scholar who interested himself in the study of the cultures of ancient Greece and Rome. In the wealth of these civilizations he found material which, combined with a contemporary genius for invention and discovery, provided insight into himself and his own times. He gained a heightened awareness; he became more "involved in mankind."

In succeeding centuries humanists have agreed that, indeed, "the proper study of mankind is man." Considered from today's point of vantage, the last half of the twentieth century, the basic humanistic idea remains the same. Man today seems particularly involved in a search for meaning and self-identity. The

[1]Gordon Cawelti, "Innovative Practices in High Schools: Who Does What—and Why—and How," *Nation's Schools,* Vol. 79 (April 1967), p. 61.

speed and complexity of today's world threaten to overwhelm contemporary man and to cause him to question the meaning of his very existence. However, the vast reservoir of man's past experience is still here for him to study; in fact, knowledge of it continues to grow. The quantity of material readily available for humanistic study is almost limitless. The problem for the teacher and the student then becomes one of sorting the record of man's experiences in such a way that the *individual human being can better understand himself, his relationship to his past, and his place in his own world;* in short, he can truly be "involved in mankind."

With the goal of a humanities program expressed in these terms, it becomes apparent that such a program is distinguished by its *approach to learning* and by the *kinds of meaning* sought from whatever content is included. The content itself, defined in terms of a particular course of study, is, of course, important; but it should not be too difficult, if valid aims of humanistic study are kept in view, to set up suitable criteria for the selection of materials and the organization of the instructional framework. It is important to remember that the problem is one of an embarrassment of riches, and that no two humanities programs need be alike.

The Meaning of Humanistic Content

If a humanities program is to truly help the student to know himself and to increase his sense of involvement in the human predicament, content studied must reflect this aim. An example here may serve to clarify some of the distinctions which need to be made. Most persons would agree that learning which is purely practical or technical, the "how-to" course, is not a part of the humanities; but what about the sciences—chemistry, physics, and so on? These courses are usually not taught in such a way that they have humanistic content. However, if the *history* of science, the philosophical and social consequences of scientific discoveries, the moral dilemmas raised by scientific developments, and other such topics are included, science does become one of the humanities. To carry the point further: the humanities are not concerned with such things as measurement, analyses of materials, or the strict application of the so-called scientific method, whether in the physical or social realm. In contrast, however, Einstein's opinions on war, Bertrand Russell's social views, and the impact of Freudian psychology on contemporary society are quite relevant. The physics of nuclear fission may not be in the humanistic realm, strictly speaking; but how can the threat of the nuclear bomb be omitted?

However, it is in the fields of literature and the fine arts that the meanings most relevant to the humanities are concentrated. It is through these media that man has kept the record of his civilizations and expressed most dramatically the character of his societies. Poetry, painting, architecture, and music are personal creations of individual men who, using a variety of techniques, have held the mirror in which we may best see ourselves. Of course, if we are to understand what an artist is saying to us we must become familiar with concepts of style and form; we must learn new ways of communication. Literature and the arts are not useful because they tell us facts or provide practical information. The truth in the arts is of a higher order: here we are not *reasoned with,* but rather *made to see, hear, feel, and understand* with a heightened awareness; we become emotionally committed. The unique satisfactions which come from literature and the arts do not result, as is sometimes supposed, from their merely imitating or describing life and nature. Works of the great creators are worlds within themselves, worlds in which life and nature are altered through such means as exaggeration, distillation, symbolism, and abstraction. Thus the student of the humanities must concern himself with *means of expression;* he must become familiar with aesthetic ideas used in literature and the various arts through the study of representative examples. In short, he must learn the languages of the arts in order to live with them and derive meaning from them.

Specific Content Areas

Literature

Poetry, drama, and the novel are the main sources of literary content in the humanities program. The student will usually find this content area more approachable at first than those of art and music, partly because he is already familiar with the language, and partly because of previous experience in English class with some representative works.

It is the use of literature within the humanities program which should differentiate this course from an English class. The student is encouraged to read to find himself, to view the work as a product of its time, and to relate the work to other creative expressions of the same period. Writing experiences must be planned to make the student progressively more independent in the selection of ideas which he develops. In the absence of textbooks, the teacher must assume the responsibility for providing background information and for relating the literary work to the period. Lectures, filmstrips, movies, and records must be used to stimulate the class. This method and the absence of a textbook, of course, force the students to develop note-taking techniques.

Specific literary works which are to be used in the humanities course will be determined by the organizing theme. It is usually the literature chosen which determines the focus of a twelfth grade humanities course. At other levels it may be that the topics selected for American history or world history will provide the nucleus around which literary works will be selected. The most obvious principle is chronological organization, but the literature teacher must always keep in mind that the representative works must provide a means of relating all creative expressions in a real rather than a forced manner. The quantity and quality of paperbacks available today give the teacher a free hand in the selection of literature.

Art

Painting, sculpture, architecture, and other visual and plastic arts are included in this area. Here the student is taught to *see* with greater comprehension, to derive the various kinds of meaning inherent in the art work. When the student can so relate to the work of art that he is aware of a dialogue taking place between himself and the work, the purpose of this area has been met.

The instructor is responsible for giving the student guidance and direction in using his eyes. This can be done with lectures, but always the student must have actual contact with the creative arts which are related to the theme under consideration. Slides, movies, filmstrips, and prints may be used, but many opportunities as well should be given the students to become familiar with the existing art in galleries near the community. The student should also be made aware of the application of art forms in the world around him, e.g., the influence of Greek forms in homes and public buildings in his community.

The artist, like the composer, the poet, and the playwright, can be a mirror, an iconoclast, a prophet, or an eclectic; he is an individual expressing his personal feelings. In any event, the artist's work projects humanistic values uniquely for all who can understand them. It is a purpose of a humanities program to sharpen visual perception, to provide the required eyes for seeing.

Music

The occurrence of music as an accompaniment to living is so common, its presence in the background of our activities so pervasive, that it might be expected that students could be easily led to understand it. One difficulty with this assumption is the very fact that music *is* so easily available; everyone *hears* music, and most people use it in a variety of social ways, but comparatively few people are accustomed to actively and consciously listening to it against a background of silence. Then, too, most students' experience in the performing of music has emphasized the activity of performance rather than the aesthetic values of the music itself. Needless to say, the typical and predominant musical experience of most students is with the popular music of the time.

The aim of music study in a humanities program should be analogous to that of art study: the student is led to *listen* more acutely and with a greater comprehension of the kinds of meaning with which music is concerned. Since music deals in abstract patterns of sound, considerable emphasis must be put on factors of form and style. *All* music has a purely musical meaning derived from its sound structure. Some music—program music and music involving words—has extramusical meaning as well. In either event, all music is a reflection of its time, a creative response of the composer to his cultural environment. Thus music should be considered alongside literature and art within the context of cultural history. Each in its own way is an equally valid expression of the life of man.

History and Other Disciplines

History, as the "artful recreation of the past, in obedience to factual evidence,"[2] is the context within which literature, art, music, or any other humanistic content is to be considered. History is necessary to provide coherence and establish relationships. Individual works of literature and the arts may be studied as examples from which we derive aesthetic and personal meanings rather than facts and information for "practical" problem-solving. But at the same time works of literature and the arts *are* facts, events in the course of cultural history, and any meaningful integration of them must rely on historical interpretation.

If a homely analogy may be used here, it may be imagined that the humanities is like a bowl of soup with many ingredients. Art, music, and literature might be compared to the meat and vegetables, the pieces of which may be relished individually or in various combinations. History, then, would be the stock or liquid, the medium in which the other ingredients move and have their meaning, and without which there could indeed be no soup at all. If the analogy may be carried even further, the need for other ingredients may be seen—various flavorings and spices which can serve to provide a particular character or perhaps clarify, unite, or intensify the flavor of the entire mixture. These last ingredients may be compared to such disciplines as philosophy, religion, and perhaps psychology; the concern of these disciplines with matters of individual existence, ultimate meaning, and patterns of life gives them a role which permeates the entire fabric of the humanities and which, whether studied directly or not, is never far from the surface.

If the analogy of soup with the humanities seems to the reader at this point to be far-fetched, let the reader be reminded that he may mix his own ingredients in any way he pleases, for the design of humanities programs, like the making of soup, is a highly individual process with an endless supply of material; but the result, in either case, may become in itself a work of art.

Organizational Patterns

The ideal curriculum centered in a humanities approach will be organized to provide a gradual introduction of the contributions that art, music, literature, history and philosophy have made to the understanding of man.

In the elementary school (K-6) the language-arts program may be the most logical area in which to introduce a humanities approach. Other areas perhaps equally suitable include social studies, art and music. Here the emphasis ought to be placed on releasing the creative potential in the individual student. By selecting specific themes or concepts for each grade level, each teacher can plan the reading, writing, art and music materials to relate to this theme or concept. Creative writing and creative dramatics provide the student with an opportunity to identify with reading materials through role playing. By careful integration of the music and art experience, the students' self-expression will be given additional enforcement. Appropriate themes, ideas, or concepts at various grade

[2]Philip H. Phenix, *Realms of Meaning* (New York: McGraw–Hill, 1967), p. 7.

levels might include: work and play (K), love (1), friendship (2), ourselves (3), others (4), liberty and justice (5), and space and time (6).[3] Students should become aware of both their own and other social and cultural traditions. Learning should begin with the experiences drawn from the child's own social and cultural environment. After the concept is familiar to the student, it should be applied to less familiar content, including that of foreign cultures. Obviously such themes or concepts cannot be considered as belonging to one grade level only; each must be considered or extended by experiences at all grade levels.

With the seventh grade the emphasis of a humanities program may be directed toward introducing the student to more formally structured experiences in art, music, and literature. If the teacher selects this grade level to summarize the concepts developed in K-6, the student might then be ready to extend such concepts to other cultures, especially those of non-Western man. An additional and unifying concept which suggests itself is that the student consider the human experience as part of certain social systems or cultures. Japan, for example, might well provide the focus of attention in a block-time program, with the emphasis on Haiku and Nōh plays in literature plus related art and music.

Since American history is found in the eighth-grade curriculum of most schools, the teacher might consider here the nature of personality and leadership as the organizing concept for a block-time program embracing social studies, language arts, music, and art. Biography and narrative poems on patriotic themes could be used to reinforce the concept. Music might be related through the study of the American folk song with an opportunity for student performance. In art, the portrait as a form and such analysis of style as is appropriate could be presented.

Beginning with the ninth grade, the humanities program should give greater emphasis to the concept of form. Man in response to his environment has given form to his creative needs. Drama in literature is one form which is most clearly responsive to the total impact of the environment on the creative mind. As a form, the drama can be related rather clearly with art and music. The block-time teacher can select representative plays which may serve as the means of exploring the time in which the works were created.

Through the ninth grade we have considered a humanities program as centered in one teacher, with other teachers and content assisting in the development of the central concept. To achieve the goal of bringing the student to realize his own identity and his relationship to the total culture, another form of presenting a humanities program may be used from grades 10 through 12. Here interdisciplinary classes taught by completely integrated teams will achieve the most satisfactory results. The following suggested programs are based on this premise.

[3]These suggested topics resulted from an exploration of a humanities curriculum for elementary school in an Institute in Children's Humanities. June-July 1966, Kent State University and James A. Garfield Schools.

World Studies

Selecting world history as the focus for the tenth-grade program, the history and English departments may develop an integrated program. With the aim of helping the students see themselves as human beings in a world of humans and of deepening their insights in respect to other culture groups, materials for study can be drawn from the traditional western European content or from non-Western cultures. It is not meant to suggest that literature play a supporting role to history. Instead, both departments should work toward an integration of the students' experiences so the total picture of a culture may be achieved. Assisting teachers from the areas of art and music should begin formal instruction in how to listen to music and how to see art. The basic forms in architecture, painting, music, and literature should be introduced through representative selections. It is obviously impossible to include in this course all the content which the departments involved would like to teach, but by pooling the resources of the subject areas and taking advantage of the special strengths in each department, a choice of areas of study can be made which will provide an introduction to important formal and stylistic concepts. With such a basis, subsequent programs can reinforce and add to these beginnings. All areas of concentration should provide content in history, literature, art, and music which are clearly related in a design the student can comprehend. It must be equally plain to the student that he shares this experience because it is found in his world.

A tenth-grade humanities program, then, will demand the use of several techniques. It should utilize team teaching with block-time or back-to-back scheduling of the English and history periods. The team must accept its professional obligation to select content appropriate to objectives and must direct the course to study-in-depth and learning-by-discovery rather than the memorization of factual material. In 1964 Charles R. Keller proposed that "post-holing" be used to solve the problem of coverage in history courses.[4] This method utilizes depth study of a few eras or topics selected from the total; chronological gaps are then filled in by "stringing wires" between the posts, keeping such factual contents to a bare minimum. These techniques are equally applicable to world studies, American studies and humanities programs in general.

American Studies

The American studies course at the eleventh-grade level represents a different approach to the understanding of our country's civilization, rather than a forced or artificial integration of subject-matter disciplines. It should attempt to unify and intensify the study of our cultural history by bringing together areas of study which are now needlessly compartmentalized or, in some instances,

[4]Charles R. Keller, "Needed: Revolution in the Social Studies," in Byron C. Massialas and Andreas M. Kazamias, *Crucial Issues in the Teaching of Social Studies* (Englewood Cliffs, N.J.: Prentice-Hall, 1964), pp. 38–45.

totally neglected. The aim of the course is the presentation of a total picture of our country using the varied resources and viewpoints of history and the social sciences, literature, music, art and others.

In no way does an American studies course represent a diluting of solid, traditional subject matter with frivolous or unrelated elements. The teaching team must plan and work together, each contributing uniquely toward well-coordinated units. Although the general framework may be chronological, a topical approach (post-hole) within the chronology will provide depth and flexibility. Various media through which better insights can be gained will be brought to bear on any specific topic or problem. Special interests of individual students can be given new outlets through independent study. The result can be an understanding of the interrelationships among the institutions which create our complex twentieth-century civilization, and the student's identification of himself as a product of, and a contributor to, this changing culture.

Until recently, secondary teachers have been limited by the textbook-centered course with its accent on coverage and chronology. The paperback revolution has freed the teacher from this restriction. In the teaching of literature the only restrictions now are those imposed by the teacher's imagination and the inherited supply of textbooks. It is now possible for the social studies teacher also to find materials around which to build an American studies course. A number of these resources are listed in the Appendix.

American studies courses for the eleventh grade are, of course, interdisciplinary, and are best taught by teams of English-social studies teachers with the assistance of art and music specialists. The team will have the responsibility of selecting the topics for the course, selecting the materials for the students, and working together to evaluate student progress. The scheduling of such classes should allow for large blocks of time, perhaps ninety minutes or more, which may be used flexibly by the team as the needs of the class dictate. The emphasis in such a course is not on the coverage of a body of factual information, but rather on directing student activities toward learning a few things well. The goal is the definition of American civilization as it is relevant to the student.

Humanities

Ideally, when the student enters a twelfth-grade humanities course he has had one or more of the courses discussed previously in this chapter and, therefore, has some understanding of how to listen to music, how to see art forms, and how to read literature. However, if students lack these experiences, the senior humanities course must provide them at the outset; in many situations, the twelfth-grade course is the only humanities offering. Suggestions for content and organization of such a course are difficult to make and must be considered by each school in relation to the strengths of the faculty, the level of student achievement, and the availability of time and equipment.

Since a senior humanities class has been the most commonly offered humanities-type course in the secondary curriculum, many forms of organization have been developed. These include great themes; great epochs or eras; chronological or modified-chronological patterns, some using the post-hole technique; survey courses of great books or great works; and aesthetic principles, i.e., form and design. Most have been organized around Western European culture, excluding English literature. Most of the courses are combinations of art, literature plus philosophy, and music. Some include history and the social studies.

Which organizing theme is used to provide a focus for the course is not as important as the attitude toward the content of the course. Many teachers seem to conclude that this course is the only one in which their students will be exposed to "culture," and thus rush the class into a gallop through the ages, resulting in mental indigestion for the students and exhaustion for the teachers. The purpose of this course is not to cram the student with *information* about great works, but rather to give them an opportunity to read, to listen to, and to see certain representative examples so that they may continue as consumers of such works with some basis for discrimination. This course is one in which the post-hole principle must be rigidly applied. Students do not need more facts; they need time to weigh and discuss the content in order to reach some evaluations on their own.

The senior humanities should be planned and directed by a team of specialists, all of whom should be present in the classroom with the students at all times. The planning should be so flexible that any member of the team can participate in the discussion without formal assignment of time. Lectures should be kept at a minimum; discussion among teachers and students should be encouraged; differing viewpoints are valuable for developing thought and discrimination.

Because the class must be exposed to many examples of art through slides and must listen to entire works of music for maximum learning, it has been found that, rather than designing a schedule for daily class meetings, it is more productive to meet in longer blocks of time less frequently. It is also advisable to have an instructional materials center to which the student can go for independent viewing of art slides or independent listening to music.

This course may best be organized around either the great epochs of Western man or style and form. Either focus for the course will provide the basic materials in literature, art, and music which can direct the student toward an involvement in it. Great epochs which may be included are the Renaissance, the Enlightenment, Romanticism, Reactions to Romanticism, and Contemporary Trends. The last two of these units, often unfortunately neglected, seem to require a particular emphasis and ample allotment of time. In the earlier units, representative works may be selected to direct the thinking of the class to elements of these epochs which have a relevance to contemporary society. Having selected certain works to be considered in depth, the teachers must provide the background information which will relate the works to the time in which they were created.

If the teaching team elects form and style as the focal point, the literature teacher may wish to use the drama (tragedy), the novel, and poetry as the forms, while the music teacher may develop concepts of form and style through study of the symphony, the opera, the song, and other organized structures in the various periods under consideration. The art teacher may select color, line, and form and apply these principles to representative works. The aesthetic approach has the advantage of cutting across the various periods of time to examine man's responses to his environment. It has the disadvantage of confusing some students who are unable to make relevant relationships. Which approach to select may be determined by the special fields of interest or competence of the teaching team.

Most senior humanities courses are electives designed primarily for the college-bound or superior student. If we consider that the purpose of such a course is to concern the student with mankind and to help him develop discrimination as a consumer of the products of our culture, it is clear that a humanities course should not be so limited but should be offered to all. With the multimedia teaching aids available today, almost any student can derive value from the humanities. Art and music are presented through the eye and the ear. Literature can also be presented this way through recordings, movies, and filmstrips. The students' progress can be evaluated by discussions of TV programs, movies, books and magazines which they read independently. A check list of such choices at the beginning of the course with subsequent discussions and evaluations among students and teachers can be a test of the success of the course. Students should be introduced to the cultural opportunities which exist in the community. Study trips to museums, lectures, and concerts can develop an appreciation of the community's resources. It may be for some students the only opportunity to become involved in learning how to live rather than in how to make a living.

Organizational patterns for humanities courses in the curriculum will vary. If the goals are worthwhile, then the earlier in a student's school experience such approaches to learning are introduced the more effective they will be. The emphasis of humanities courses in the elementary school should be on releasing the creativity in each student; by the seventh grade such concepts should have more formal structure; and by the tenth grade interdisciplinary courses can help direct the students' search for self-identity and an understanding of the world in which they must live.

The Selection of Humanities Materials

The humanities approach to learning may be adopted at almost any age or grade leve, may involve one or many particular disciplines, may employ one teacher or a team, and may be organized in one of several different ways. Therefore the selection of materials to be studied in any particular humanities course or program is an individual problem about which it is difficult to generalize. Certainly, a high degree of discrimination in selection is needed when the unique needs of each teaching situation are considered alongside the vast reservoir of material which is available.

However, it is necessary to derive some broad criteria for selection which are generally applicable and which aid the teacher in making good choices. Of course, there is no valid substitute for a broad background and rich experience in the humanities on the part of individual teachers. Then, too, purely personal factors, emotions, and even whims can color the teacher's judgment, and it is probably both undesirable as well as impossible to eliminate such subjective elements. A teacher can usually teach from his enthusiasms more effectively, all other things being equal. Moreover, some teachers like to experiment; such experimentation, if carried on intelligently, can usually provide insights into improving the program and can minimize the possibility of a static, standard course of study.

Nevertheless, while admitting the validity of these observations, the authors suggest the following specific criteria for material selection:

1. Individual works of literature, art, and music should possess intrinsic aesthetic value. Each should be worthy of the student's efforts to know it. Each should be potentially able to add some permanent dimension to the student's realm of aesthetic experiences.

2. Selected material should, generally, be representative of important styles, forms, techniques, trends, or cultural epochs. Important generalizations may be made from a study of the humanities, but these can only be made on the basis of knowledge of individual representative examples. In the arts the general is formulated from the particular.

3. The maturity and cultural backgrounds of the students must not be ignored. Materials should be selected so that there is the greatest probability that immediate meanings and understandings can be derived. However, it must be emphasized that teachers often err in this direction and "teach down" to students' most superficial preferences. Many worthwhile works can be appreciated at several levels; great works have the quality of seeming forever new, of being sources of ever-growing appreciation and understanding. Thus, appropriate materials will be those with which the student may have some immediate communication but, at the same time, he should be able to grow into and beyond them.

4. Materials to be studied should generally be relevant to the life of the student in today's world. The notion that humanities study is an inspection of a dead past should be avoided at all costs. This criterion probably implies, and rightly so, that a greater emphasis should be put on contemporary works than is often the case. In any event, the most worthwhile works are those having elements of universal truth or beauty with which we may communicate on contemporary terms.

Here it should perhaps again be emphasized that humanities study can be made important for all students, whether academically talented and verbally proficient or not. Some students can—and should—do more (and more difficult) reading than others. Some have a particular interest in art or music or can derive more meaning through these media than through reading. Moreover it should not be forgotten that there are many excellent films, filmstrips, and other audio-visual aids which can be of significant value to any student. In summary, then, there is such a wealth of material and such a variety of means of presenting it that no student need be denied an opportunity of sharing in humanities experiences. A small sampling of this material is listed in Appendix A.

Physical Facilities and Equipment

Better-than-adequate facilities and equipment are needed for humanities programs. What specific items are required will depend on the content of the program, but, in any event, quality should not be compromised in a learning situation demanding aesthetic understanding and appreciation.

If, for example, the visual arts are being studied, printed reproductions should be adequately large and reproduced with color fidelity. Thirty-five millimeter slides, showing works of painting, sculpture, and architecture, are becoming available in increasing quantity and quality and may be preferable to prints if shown on good projection equipment in a properly darkened room. An opaque projector is useful for showing small prints and illustrations from books and magazines. Adequate storage and cataloguing facilities must be provided.

For playing recorded music, a good turntable, amplifier, and speaker system must be provided. A wall-mounted stereo speaker system amply powered for the dimensions of the room is best. Parenthetically, it may be observed that the majority of school-owned phonographs, including nearly all that are portable, are nothing short of disgraceful. How can a student be taught to hear and understand what literally cannot be heard or is so distorted as to be irritating? If records are to be used, they must be properly stored, kept meticulously clean, and played with a diamond stylus in pristine condition. Such styli, by the way, are *not* permanent and should be replaced at least once per year.

Frequently played records wear out quickly. For this reason, it may be desirable to transfer the music to tapes, or to buy prerecorded tapes when available. This decision is particularly appropriate if a listening laboratory is maintained or if students play the recorded music themselves.

The room used for humanities study, or any modern-day program, for that matter, should be comfortable and pleasant to live in, should have flexible seating accommodations, a maximum of bulletin-board space, ample chalk-boards, a pull-down projection screen, table space, bookshelves, and opaque draperies for darkening the room. It may seem unnecessary to mention such items, most of which are found in many classrooms. It has been the authors' experience, however, that the demands put on a humanities classroom in terms of sheer quantity of material used and the variety of activities carried on exceed those put on most other classrooms, and that a humanities classroom is, indeed, a rather special place. Every effort should be made to make it a comfortable, functional, and stimulating place for teacher and student.

The best location for keeping materials and equipment will vary depending on the individual school's physical plant, the extent of the humanities program, and staff available to supervise students' out-of-class work. Ideally, the school library may be the best instructional materials center provided that facilities for listening, viewing, and individual study are available. Most schools have a long way to go in providing such facilities, which should be comfortable, easily used, and designed for the most efficient upkeep of the relatively expensive materials and equipment which are necessary.

Conclusion

The approach to learning undertaken through the humanities puts man himself in the center of things. The significant creations of man are studied and viewed as evidence of his humanness: his hopes and fears, his triumphs and defeats, his joy and despair. But man is a creature of the present as well as the past; hopefully, man may make his way into an unknown future where he will continue to create his evidences of being just as he has in the past. It is the student of today who must inhabit future time, who must prevail amid confusion and doubt, who must create his own style of life from whatever means are within his grasp. The humanities can provide him with the bases for a continuing dialogue with his world.

Unit III

Core and Other Innovations

Chapter 7

Independent Study

by James D. Wells

In a core class, students usually engage in independent study in order to contribute to the group's examination of some broad issue or problem. In recent years, other types of independent study programs have appeared; in some of them the student's work is quite unrelated to any of his courses. This chapter examines the many types of independent study being carried on in schools today, relates them to the core concept, and suggests effective ways to initiate and develop independent study programs. Dr. Wells, a former core teacher, is currently an assistant professor of education at the University of Miami, Coral Gables, Florida.

One of the primary goals of teachers is to make themselves less and less necessary in the lives of their students. As students become more proficient in the basic skills, as they become better informed and more aware of their own intellectual power, they should become more independent and personally adequate. Core teachers, utilizing small-group work and independent study and serving in roles such as educational leaders, guides, and consultants to their students, have always placed high priority on these goals.

These goals are basic to a democratic society. As Kimball Wiles put it:

> Self-directing citizens are essential if democracy is to continue to flourish. Democratic forms and procedures require that men and women reach their own decisions and assume the responsibility inherent in their choices. If the citizens do not exercise their right to participate in policy formation, freedom is lost by default. Unless a high percentage of the population cherishes and utilizes the privileges and responsibility of self-direction, a few members will make the choices and will impose their authority.[1]

The extent to which this goal is being met by our public schools has been questioned. Carl Rogers, for one, decries the trend away from freedom and the

[1] Kimball Wiles, *Teaching for Better Schools* (Englewood Cliffs, N.J.: Prentice-Hall, Inc., 1959), p. 28.

111

great pressures toward conformity, docility, and rigidity.[2] The current "youth rebellion" is, at least in part, a reaction to these pressures.

It has long been one of the goals of the public schools to develop fully participating and adequate citizens. As the explosion of knowledge accelerates and changes in society become more manifest, the pressures upon society to solve its increasingly complex problems are intensified. So too is the pressure on the schools to produce citizens capable of operating effectively in their society. In order for citizens to be able to cope with their problems, they must embrace education as a continuing process—one that does not end with the completion of their formal schooling—and they must acquire the skills of continued learning.

If the schools are to develop citizens that are self-directed, participating, informed, and adequate, rather than conforming, docilely unimaginative, and uncommitted, they must provide students with ample opportunities to learn on their own. Conventional homework and individualized assignments by the teacher are not adequate. Needed is genuine independent study, defined as follows by Alexander and associates:

> *Independent study* is considered by us to be learning activity largely motivated by the learner's own aims to learn and largely rewarded in terms of its intrinsic values. Such activity as carried on under the auspices of secondary schools is somewhat independent of the class or other group organization dominant in past and present secondary school instructional practices, and it utilizes the services of teachers and other professional personnel primarily as resources for the learner.[3]

Thus independent study focuses primarily upon providing opportunities for students to learn to study on their own, with teachers and others serving as resource people. This definition also implies that students must find and achieve the intrinsic values in learning, discover new ideas and techniques, gain self-confidence, and learn how to make use of the vast stores of knowledge available to them.

The Development of Independent Study Programs

Independent study is referred to in many ways in educational publications: honors study, honors seminars, self-directed study, individual research, and individual study. Many experiments with independent study in the United States have been conducted at the college level.

Independent study has a prominent place in many team teaching programs, notably those stimulated by J. Lloyd Trump and the Commission on Staff Utilization of the National Association of Secondary-School Principals. Numerous independent study programs have been reported in the *NASSP Bulletin.*

[2]Carl R. Rogers, "Learning To Be Free," *Readings in Curriculum,* Glen Has and Kimball Wiles (eds.), (Boston: Allyn and Bacon, 1965), p. 210.
[3]William M. Alexander et al. *Independent Study in Secondary Schools,* (New York: Holt, Reinhart & Winston, 1967), p. 12.

Some indication of their popularity is evident in a recent listing of innovations in junior and senior high schools that are participating in the Association's administrative internship program. Thirty-one of the 78 schools reported independent study programs.[4]

A number of experiments in independent study carried on in the University of Illinois High School have been reported by Jackson, and others.[5] The first project centered around a course, "Advanced Problems in Science," which was open to gifted students in science so that they might obtain advanced study in their chosen fields, independent of formal instruction. Evaluations by students were positive, and there were no adverse comments about the program's effect upon college experiences. One conclusion was that a course such as this would be a desirable and inexpensive way to allow the few gifted students in a school to have a special experience in science. It was felt that the success of such a course would depend upon careful selection and early guidance of students, and upon the willingness of the supervisor to trust the students admitted to the program.

In another project, "A Method of Teaching Chemistry in the Laboratory," it was found that by the end of the course students could be given a large share of the responsibility for planning and carrying out laboratory activities.

A third project, entitled "Increased Responsibility for Seniors," studied means of easing the transition from high school to college by excusing seniors from study halls and making them responsible for managing their own time outside of regularly scheduled classes. In a follow-up study, the authors concluded that these students did not differ significantly from the class of 1958, which did not have the benefit of self-management in their senior year. Comparisons were in terms of grade point average and the number of hours the students reported that they spent studying during the freshman college year. Also reported were: no negative opinions about the project, a significant reduction in teacher time devoted to study-hall supervision, and a judgment on the part of the faculty that the project was successful. In a fourth-year French course, students spent two periods per week with the teacher and three periods per week in independent study, using records, tapes, and other aids. The French teacher felt that the students learned as much as they would have in the conventional five periods per week of classroom instruction.

In a biology course, much effort was put into developing materials to be used in the laboratory to help students learn to work on their own. It was reported that a significant number of techniques were learned, and sufficient experience was gained to establish the feasibility of students doing independent study in science.

In a number of publications, B. Frank Brown has reported favorable student

[4]"Synopsis of Innovations at NASSP Internship Schools, 1966–67" (Washington, D.C.: National Association of Secondary-School Principals, 1967).
[5]See the January issues, 1959, 1960, and 1961, of the *Bulletin of the National Association of Secondary-School Principals.*

reactions to independent study in the nongraded program of Melbourne High School.[6] In one of several articles on the program in this school, Whitmire described the personnel involved, facilities available and utilized, admission requirements and procedures, course requirements, and problems involved in the program. She concluded:

> When the responsibility for learning rests with the student rather than the teachers, the student's experience is more dynamic and beneficial. Working independently encourages self-discipline and self-reliance, characteristics desirable for advanced study, and good equipment for living in a competitive world.[7]

In a follow-up of graduates of Wayland, Massachusetts, High School, Griffin reported that those who went to college reflected favorably upon a program utilizing independent study as well as large and small group instruction. He felt that these students showed greater readiness to study independently.[8] Marquette stated that three ingredients were vital in making independent study successful at Valhalla High School in New York State, where enrollment in the program increased from two to twenty-three students in less than three years. These ingredients were student projects, student planning, and close staff guidance.[9]

Among Congreve's findings in a pilot project at the University of Chicago Laboratory School were: (1) The most capable students according to ability and achievement sought out the most independent-type programs; (2) Only half of the freshman students in a high-ability group felt comfortable and wished to continue with a situation where they have the opportunity to plan their programs, select the mode of study, and take the consequences for their selections; and (3) It was possible to organize and operate a school program for 175 students wherein they operated with a great deal of freedom without having the school "disintegrate for lack of order."[10]

Fromm described independent study at Lakeview High School, Decatur, Illinois, where three levels of independent study were utilized. Among other things he felt that all students are not sufficiently self-directed to operate in this new environment, although sampled student reaction to the program was positive in nature.[11]

[6]B. Frank Brown, *The Nongraded High School* (Englewood Cliffs, N.J.: Prentice Hall, 1963) and Education by Appointment: New Approaches to Independent Study (West Nyack, N.Y.: Parker Publishing Company, 1968).

[7]Janet Whitmire, "The Independent Study Program at Melbourne High," *Phi Delta Kappan*, Vol. 47 (September 1965), p. 45.

[8]William M. Griffin, "Wayland, Massachusetts, High School Program for Individual Differences," *Bulletin of the National Association of Secondary-School Principals*, Vol. 47 (March 1963), pp. 118–127.

[9]Don Marquette, "Independent Study: Effective Program or Waste of Time?" *School Management*, Vol. 8 (September 1964), pp. 124–125, 128–130.

[10]Willard J. Congreve, "The University of Chicago Project," in David W. Beggs and Edward G. Buffie (eds.), *Independent Study* (Bloomington: Indiana U. P., 1965).

[11]William Fromm, "Independent Study with Team Teaching," in David W. Beggs and Edward G. Buffie (eds.), *op. cit.*

Independent study programs in selected North-Central Association High Schools were studied by Reavis. Three major organizational patterns were identified:

1. A seminar group with a teacher serving as the director.
2. A group of students assigned to a teacher acting as a coordinator with no regularly scheduled times to meet.
3. Students working with individual teachers using student-scheduled conferences.

Reavis also found school satisfaction with independent study in twenty-one of twenty-four schools. Providing time for teachers to work with students was the most crucial problem noted. Seniors participated most, and superior academic attainment was a requisite for admittance into independent study. Credits in Carnegie units for independent study were given in four out of five of the schools surveyed. Ninety-two percent of the teachers included in this study reported favorably on the knowledge gained in independent study; the students reported a lower knowledge gain than did the teachers.[12]

The first comprehensive survey and definition of independent study in secondary schools was that of Alexander and Hines.[13] This study reported findings obtained from questionnaires and interviews with school administrators, independent study coordinators, teachers, and students involved in independent study. The publication by Alexander and associates, cited earlier, draws upon this research and explains what independent study is, how it affects secondary education, and how it may be introduced into a school's program.

Types of Independent Study Programs

Ten distinct types of independent study programs were observed and delineated by Wells.[14] This study included twenty-four secondary schools located east of the Mississippi River. Types were defined primarily in terms of their time-organizational structure, as follows:

Program 1

A regularly scheduled class in the school's instructional program which normally requires that students work independently (e.g., journalism, advanced courses in art, industrial arts, music).

---

[12]Peyton Reavis, "Independent Study Programs in North-Central Association High Schools," unpublished Ed. D. dissertation, College of Education, University of Arizona, 1965.
[13]William M. Alexander and Vynce A. Hines, *Independent Study in Secondary Schools*, USOE Cooperative Research Project No. 2969, University of Florida, 1966.
[14]James D. Wells, "Independent Study Students in Secondary Schools, and Their Expectations and Satisfactions in Independent Study," unpublished Ed. D. dissertation, University of Florida, 1966.

Programs of this type are seen in most secondary schools. Independent study of this type is characterized by:

1. Being a regularly scheduled class in the school.
2. Student election of the course.
3. Criteria for admittance to the course, including past success in basic courses and having acquired the necessary skill and/or ability to pursue the work on a more mature, sophisticated, and advanced level of competence.
4. The high degree of creativity and imagination evident in the products of the student's work.
5. A high degree of teacher-pupil interaction in all phases of the work, from the initial planning stages of what, how, and why the work is to be done, to the culmination of the project in the form of various kinds of products.
6. A high degree of student involvement in all stages of the work, with the teacher serving as guide and consultant.
7. An observed high degree of enthusiasm and satisfaction on the part of most pupils and teachers.
8. The use of an extremely wide variety of instructional media, materials and resources.

Differences noted include:

1. Grading policies.
2. Degree of freedom which the teacher allows the student in selection of the material to be studied or the work to be done.

Program 2

Vocational or work experience programs in which students work independently, in or out of school, so that they will develop salable skills.

The student engaged in this type of program is basically oriented toward the world of work, toward gaining both skills and experience which will help to make him employable upon completion of his high school education. Factors held in common by students in this type program are:

1. The voluntary nature of their entrance into the program—all students in this type of program elect to enter it.
2. The knowledge that the skills and experience in the program will help to make them employable after they leave school.

The student in this program appears to gain a more realistic and mature attitude toward both work and earning a living in the adult world.

Differences among various programs within this category are:

1. Grading policies and amount of credit given.
2. Time arrangements and duration of time at work.
3. Types of skills and work being done.
4. Criteria for admission to the program.

5. Level of skill being learned.
6. Remuneration, some students receiving pay while others work entirely for the reward of obtaining needed skills and experience.

Program 3

A regularly scheduled class in the school's instructional program which provides all students with some class time for independent study in order to accomplish a long-term class assignment that is required of all members of the class but which may be individually planned in terms of the specific topic or problem studied.

There is a rather fine line of distinction between this type of program and the usual student "term paper" or long-term research project. Genuine independent study is distinguished by the degree of teacher-pupil planning which transpires in the selection of the individual student assignment, by the degree of teacher-pupil interaction which occurs as a direct result of the individual assignment, and by the amount of independent study time which is given to students. This type of independent study is a basic procedure in many core classes.

Varying among teachers and schools are:
1. Grading policies.
2. Degree of freedom given in the selection of the area to be studied.

Program 4

Some released time given from a regular class so that students may work independently on individually planned studies in addition to class assignments.

In programs of this type, the student is given varying amounts of time during which he is released from regularly scheduled classes to enable him to pursue a topic, project, or area of special interest. The amount of time given or the number of classes from which the student is excused varies among individual teachers, school departments and programs, and individual schools. The duration of the released time from class also varies, as does the kind of required product that results from the student's independent study. For example, students may give oral as well as written reports. Grading policies are another variable.

In this type of independent study, the work the student does during his released time is individually planned and agreed upon by both the student and teacher. Also, the student is responsible for all work done in the class; that is, he is required to do all assignments and to take all tests given during the period he is released from class.

Program 5

Some released time given from a regular class so that some students may work independently on individually planned studies *in lieu of* class assignments.

This type of program is similar to Program 4 except that the student is *not* held responsible for any class assignments or tests which are given during the period he is released from class for independent study.

Program 6

Independent study as part of a program of instruction organized around large- and small-group instruction.

Students study common subject matter and are taught by a team of teachers. The major purpose of the independent study is to allow the student to gain both added breadth and depth in the topic or unit under study in the large and small groups.
Variable in these programs are:
1. Grading policies.
2. The amount of time given the student for independent study.
3. The amount of freedom given the student to select individual areas of study.
4. The amount of freedom of movement within the school building.
5. The requirements established for the end product of the work.

Program 7

Seminar groups which are smaller than ordinary classes and in which students work independently, at least part of the time, on common or individual topics, units, or problems.

Seminars that are not part of large-group or small-group instruction have several factors in common. Usually, the students are selected with high ability, high achievement, and high motivation as basic criteria. However, that is not always the case. In one program, designed to reduce school dropouts, students were selected on the basis of low achievement and low motivation. Another characteristic held in common by these programs is the size of the group. In the Wells study, seminar group size ranged from a low of 3 students to a high of 25, with an average of 11.
Variable aspects of this type of program are grading policies and the amount of time spent in class working as a group and out of class working independently. Many programs give time blocks from several days to several weeks for out-of-class work. Another variable is the degree of freedom given the student. In the selection of areas of study, some students have a wide degree of choice, while others are required to study in an area directly related to units or topics being dealt with in the seminar group at the time. In some programs the student is allowed almost complete freedom of movement within the school building, while in others, specific designated areas are assigned where students may work and study. Some programs are highly formalized in the manner in which the final product of the independent work is presented, while others are quite informal. In operation, seminar groups often resemble miniature core classes.

Program 8

An individually planned program of curricular study with regularly-scheduled time to study independently, in or out of school, with a minimum of teacher direction and supervision.

Independent study programs of this kind appear to be as flexible, as free, and as innovative as any of those observed. There appears to be a relatively high degree of individualization of instruction and encouragement of the student to assume individual responsibility in conducting his work.

Programs of this type are characterized by:

1. A high degree of teacher-pupil interaction and planning in all phases of the work, from the initial planning stages of what, why, and how the work is to be done through all stages in the process of doing the work to the final culmination in the form of various kinds of products.
2. A high degree of pupil involvement in all stages of the work.
3. A high degree of enthusiasm and satisfaction on the part of most pupils and teachers.
4. The teacher serving in a consultant or guidance role, rather than being the prime mover in the process of learning.
5. The use of an extremely wide variety of instructional media, materials, and resources.
6. The broad and extensive use of community resources, e.g., persons, libraries, laboratories (both in public and private institutions), and social and governmental agencies and institutions.
7. The wide range of subjects and curricular areas available in which students could choose to work.
8. The high degree of creativity and imagination in many of the students' final products.
9. The repeated observation that these programs are adding both depth and breadth to the school curriculum.

Programs of this nature vary in flexibility of time, grading policies, and methods of presenting the final product of independent work.

Program 9

A curricular program in which the student assumes nearly complete responsibility for his use of regularly offered independent study time.

Programs of this type emphasize, as their primary goals, the development of student responsibility for learning how to learn. They are characterized by the following:

1. Some independent study time is provided the student each week, with the student exercising options with respect to how he will use this time.

2. A wide range of subject areas, from which the student may choose those in which he prefers to study.
3. A high degree of freedom of movement within the school, with the student having a number of work and study areas from which to choose.

Varying among the programs of this nature are:

1. The degree to which the student may use his independent study time for work not directly related to formal classes in which he is presently enrolled.
2. The amount of school credit and the grading or evaluation of work done during independent study time.

Program 10

Individual extracurricular enrichment study with students working independently before or after school or on weekends.

Students working in this type program seem to be highly motivated. They appear to be keenly interested in the area in which they are working and, in most cases, are pursuing this type of work *without* being given the incentive of a formal school grade or school credit. Personal satisfaction and keen interest appear to be the important motivational factors characteristic of the students in this program.

Many pupils in this type program are pursuing their work, not only within the school, but also in many areas and facilities in the community. Students engage in a wide variety of work ranging from science and government to drama and public speaking.

Programs in this classification vary as follows:

1. Length of time spent on any one project.
2. Areas and types of work done by students.
3. The setting or locale where work is done, with a wide range found both in and out of school.

Student Reactions to Independent Study

The Wells study included the reactions to independent study of 388 secondary school students. They ranged in age from 12 to 19 years, with a median age of 17.1. Almost 50 percent were 17 years old. The balance between boys and girls was almost equal. The grade level ranged from 7 to 12, with 60 percent in grade 12. Students were engaged in independent study in almost all subject areas, but almost half were in English and social studies. The overwhelming majority of students (89.8 percent) were planning to attend college after they completed high school; about 70 percent were aspiring to enter professional or managerial occupations.

Approximately 84 percent of the students had entered into independent study voluntarily. A majority (58 percent) were engaged in a library-research type project. Over half the students (53.9 percent) were in their first semester of independent study. Almost 55 percent of the students said that they spent more time studying in independent study than they did for a regular course.

Student expectations and satisfactions were obtained by "opinionnaire." Generally, female students expected more from independent study than did male students. When student expectations were studied by subject area, there were distinct differences. The highest expectations for independent study were held by students in the nonacademic subjects, while students in the academic subjects held the lowest expectations.

Student expectations also varied according to the type of independent study program in which they were working. The following types are listed by rank order, from highest expectation to lowest.

Student Expectations of Independent Study

Rank	Type of Independent Study Program
1	Vocational work experience
2	A class which normally requires considerable independent study
3	Some released time *in addition to* class assignments
4	Some released time *in lieu* of class assignments
5	Nearly complete student responsibility for use of independent study time
6	Individually planned programs
7	Seminar groups
8	Independent study as part of a large-group–small-group instructional organization
9	Extracurricular enrichment
10	A regular class with long term assignment required of all but individually planned and carried out by the student

Students working in independent study were generally well satisfied with this arrangement. However, there were very marked differences when satisfaction was studied by subject area, with home economics ranking highest. Of the six top-rated subject areas, all were nonacademic with the exception of number 5, science. The fact that students were least satisfied with independent study in social studies has special significance for core teachers. Group interaction is essential for many learnings of this type.

Significant differences in student satisfaction also were found when they were analyzed according to type of independent study program. When ranked from the highest to the lowest in student satisfaction, they were as follows:

Student Satisfaction with Independent Study

Rank	Type of Independent Study Program
1	Vocational work experience
2	A class which normally requires considerable independent study
3	Individually planned programs
4	Seminar groups

5   A regular class with long term assignment required of all but individually planned and carried out by the student

6   Some released time *in lieu* of class assignments

7   Extracurricular enrichment

8   Independent study as part of a large-group–small-group instructional program

9   Nearly complete student responsibility for use of independent study time

10   Some released time *in addition* to class assignments

Educators planning to introduce independent study might well note the discrepancies between student expectations and satisfactions with certain types, such as the plan of providing released time for independent work in addition to regular class assignments. Note also the high student satisfaction with individually planned programs and with seminars. The close teacher-student relationships inherent in these programs, as in the core curriculum, undoubtedly contribute a great deal to student satisfaction. In the long run, the structure of a program is less important than its philosophy. Little is gained when independent study is viewed merely as another way to cover subject matter.

Independent Study in Core Programs

Several types of independent study may be found in block-time and core classes. The following selected examples illustrate the varied nature of independent study currently being carried on throughout the country.

P. K. Yonge Laboratory School, University of Florida, Gainesville, Florida

Independent study is an important part of the core program in this school. It provides opportunities for students to work in an area of special interest as well as a means of dealing with different ability levels. The program includes grades 10, 11, and 12 and involves 270 students enrolled in core classes. This number represents one-half of the total number of students in the high school. Students utilize all of the facilities of the high school as well as many community resources. Their independent study work may culminate in both oral and written reports, construction projects, and bulletin-board displays.

O'Neill Junior High School, Downer's Grove, Illinois

Individualized or independent study in this school is designed to meet the individual needs, interests, and abilities of the students. Independent work relates primarily to the social studies aspect of the block-time program and includes 300 students in grade 7. This figure is one-half the total student body of the school. Many facilities are used by students, including the school, village, and private libraries, local businesses, large corporations, and governmental agencies.

Student activities revolve around individual research, with the teacher guiding their work and helping them locate instructional materials. Students give oral or written reports which include charts, maps, drawings, and display using artifacts. One student project was an attractive and informative written report on the new states of Alaska and Hawaii, supplemented by original drawings. Another student's report on Mexico included a chart of resources, a time line to depict its history, recordings to explain its music, and artifacts to illustrate its crafts.

Seneca Junior High School, Penn Hills School District, Pittsburgh, Pennsylvania

A unique structure, organized around a core workshop, characterizes independent study in this school. Students volunteer for this workshop and the number of students participating at any one time has ranged as high as 96 seventh-and eighth-grade students. The program provides opportunities for students to do individualized research, to develop oral and written communication skills, to enrich the study of an important era of American history, and to increase appreciation for our American heritage. Students utilize the school and public libraries, art facilities, resource speakers, and a wide range of audio-visual equipment. Students evaluate the results of the core workshop as well as showing completed work by oral presentations, written reports, demonstrations, dramatizations, and visual display material. The time utilized for the study varies from one to five weeks.

Evanston Township High School, Evanston, Illinois

The Combined Studies Department at this school incorporates independent study in a block-time instructional organization. The purposes of independent work include enabling students to pursue specific interests at considerable depth, developing greater curiosity, improving motivation, expanding understandings, teaching the process of inquiry, and allowing students to examine concepts, test opinions, and answer questions about particular subjects. The process of independent study is an integral part of the Combined Studies program and includes grades 9 through 12. Students elect to take Combined Studies classes; therefore, their independent study, too, is voluntary. Facilities utilized include the school and public libraries, audio-visual materials, and resources from other school departments. Learning activities include lectures or discussions revolving around a paper presented by a student, demonstrations and exhibits, as well as group reports and panels. School credit and grades are given for independent study work. The time element varies among teachers.

Initiating and Developing Independent Study Programs

The suggestions which follow are intended to provide guidelines for teachers and administrators who are interested in providing increased opportunities for their students to work independently. The focus is on specific questions which should be answered before initiating a broadly based and extensive program of independent study.

A serious attempt to initiate independent study should begin with an examination of the purposes and objectives for such a program. The study by Alexander and Hines disclosed the following values of independent study as ranked by 300 school staff members in 36 secondary schools:

1. Provides for needs and interests of the individual.
2. Develops independence, responsibility, self-direction.
3. Allows study of topics beyond the regular curriculum.
4. Increases achievement in the special area.
5. Improves student performance beyond high school: in college, vocational, or technical training.
6. Permits maximum use of instructional resources.
7. Provides opportunity for study under optimum conditions.
8. Improves articulation between high school and college.
9. Raises level of performance in other areas.[15]

After purposes and objectives have been delineated, the type (s) of program which might best fit local circumstances should be designed and organized. As the structure of the independent study program takes shape, consideration should be given to the following questions:

1. What kind of facilities will be necessary in order to conduct the program satisfactorily? Facilities which are commonly used by students engaged in independent study include:
    (a) The school library or resource center
    (b) Individual study carrels and workrooms
    (c) School shops and art rooms
    (d) Community facilities including business and government laboratories, public and private libraries, and government offices
2. What kind of equipment and materials will be required? Students often use:
    (a) School textbooks, library reference materials, vertical file materials, as well as teachers' books and materials
    (b) Equipment and materials normally found in the school's industrial arts shops, art rooms, electronics classrooms, mechanical-drawing and drafting rooms, and science laboratories
    (c) Educational media such as tapes (both video and audio), recorders, projectors of all types, and personally manufactured visuals photographed on acetates
3. How should teachers' and students' schedules be arranged to facilitate independent study? The scheduling of independent study may be very flexible or very precise.
4. How should independent study be evaluated?

[15] William M. Alexander and Vynce A. Hines, *op. cit.*, p. 51.

The time factor is extremely variable among programs of independent study in current operation. Depending upon the type of program which has been designed, scheduling may be a simple operation or quite burdensome and tedious. For example, a teacher who is operating in a block-time or core program may simply allow individuals, small groups, or the entire class to use all or part of the block of time for independent study. In contrast, some schools schedule students with as much as 30 percent of their time unassigned, a portion of which may be used for independent study. The teacher should be aware at the outset, however, that unless scheduling and the time factor are given careful attention, guiding students engaged in independent study can impose a burden upon their already heavy and taxing schedules.

School personnel should engage in their own "independent research study" to gather both objective and subjective data with which to evaluate the program. Several different programs might be initiated, with periodic evaluations and comparisons using student achievement tests, attitude scales, observation of work habits, study skills, and final products. The long-range effects of the program may be determined from follow-up studies of graduates of the school who are either in college or are employed in the community.

A series of system-wide conferences or workshops might be conducted in order to evaluate programs as well as to exchange ideas. Both interschool and intraschool visitations and observations might prove helpful. The use of community resources should be coordinated in order to minimize overburdening certain businesses, agencies, or individuals.

Many schools at present have given a teacher some released time to serve as coordinator or director of independent study in the school. Among the functions of this coordinator are: (1) providing for evaluation, (2) communicating ideas among teachers and schools, (3) providing a home base for teachers and students engaged in independent study, (4) coordinating programs, policies and procedures within the school, and (5) providing continuity for the program from year to year.

Conclusion

Research to date indicates that both teachers and students see many values in independent study. Core teachers, who have long used several forms of independent study, should welcome the expansion of this idea into other courses and programs. Whether it is part of the core or operated as a separate program, independent study promotes both individual development and such common learnings as self-direction and the skills essential for continued learning.

Chapter 8

Core and the Nongraded Curriculum

by Gordon F. Vars

A small but growing number of secondary schools have established programs variously described as nongraded, ungraded, continuous progress, and the like. This chapter identifies three types of nongraded programs and examines their compatibility with the core curriculum approach to common learnings.

One aim of the core curriculum is to dissolve barriers between subject matter areas. In contrast, the nongraded curriculum removes arbitrary barriers between grade levels. The present system of dividing students into grades based primarily upon age arose in the mid-1800's as a means of systematizing students' progress through school. In this familiar arrangement, mastery of the subject matter and skills assigned to one grade level entitles the student to "pass" to the next. Promotion is usually on an annual basis, with the month of June representing a period of crisis for students and teachers alike.

Annual promotion based on grade-level standards works particular hardship on those who are either above average or below average in ability. The less capable student too often fails and must repeat the grade; the especially capable student often finds his only escape from boredom to be skipping a grade, with its attendant gaps in knowledge and problems of social adjustment. While the graded system serves most average students reasonably well, intensified concern for individual differences in the late 1950's revived the search for a sequential organization that makes greater allowances for human variability.

Types of Nongraded Programs

The term nongraded, when applied either to a curriculum or to a school, tells only what it is *not*, not what it is. This ambiguous term fits many different programs in which grade-level designations have been removed or deemphasized and students are allowed to progress through their school years more or less at their own rate. To date there appear to be three main types of nongraded programs.

What might be called a *single-sequence nongraded plan* is based on the premise that all students both can and should learn the same things, but not necessarily in the same length of time. Content and skills in each subject-matter area are broken down into performance levels, steps, concepts, or units and arranged in a carefully designed sequence. Each student works his way through this curriculum at his own rate of speed, without regard to his chronological age, the number of years he has been in school, the particular time of the year he masters one level and is ready for the next, or his progress in any other subject area.

Each student may work independently, often utilizing some form of programed instruction devices or materials, or he may be placed in a class with others working on similar levels. Such a class might contain a very able twelve-year-old, an average thirteen-year-old, and a slow fourteen-year-old, all working at the same performance level in a particular subject. Since the class contains students working at several levels, grouping within the class and individualized instruction are essential. Mastery of all the content or skills assigned to a particular class entitles the student to transfer to a different class working on higher levels. In theory this transfer may take place at any time during the school year, but most schools reassign students at regular intervals, usually to coincide with report-card periods.

In essence, this type of nongraded curriculum replaces a single grade-level standard with several smaller performance level standards. Instead of three large hurdles to jump between the end of elementary school and the beginning of high school, for example, the student may have seventeen smaller ones. A student may require more time than his peers to master the learnings at a particular level, and hence be "left behind" by them, but there is no failure in the usual sense of the word. That is, no student must repeat an entire year's work. Grade skipping, too, is eliminated. The able student may require only two years to move through a sequence that takes the average student three years and the slow student four or more. Each student begins in the fall where he left off in the spring, sometimes with the same teacher, sometimes with another.

Performance-level nongraded programs have received rather widespread acceptance at the elementary school level, especially as applied to reading instruction. Children from self-contained classrooms representing several age or maturity levels are regrouped for a portion of each day according to their reading ability. Some elementary schools also set aside a second portion of the day in which students are sorted and instructed according to their performance in mathematics.

A secondary school that has achieved prominence for its nongraded performance-level program is the Middletown High School in Rhode Island. This is a six-year school in which subject matter has been broken down into many specific concepts and skills to be mastered in sequence by the students. For example, the six-year English curriculum consists of 212 levels and social studies, 441.

Instead of a single sequence or track, with students moving along it at different rates, the nongraded program proposed by B. Frank Brown consists of several parallel sequences or "phases." This plan closely resembles the form of ability grouping known as *tracking*. The major difference is that students are assigned to tracks without regard to grade level or year in school. This approach to nongrading may be called a *multisequence nongraded plan*. Even when all students are studying the same social studies topic or the same literary selection, the subject matter in each track differs in complexity or depth; hence, it is essentially a different curriculum. In Melbourne High School near Cape Kennedy, in Florida, students are assigned to phases or tracks on the basis of their scores on standardized achievement tests, without regard to age or year in school. They shift from phase to phase whenever they and their teachers judge this to be desirable.

As in the case of the single-sequence nongraded plan, students may study in class groups, by themselves, or both. Secondary students in the Brigham Young University Laboratory School, for example, spend approximately 50 percent of their time studying individually.

In a third major type of nongraded program, learning sequences are only loosely structured in terms of broad units or topics that are presumed to have significance for students of diverse age or maturity levels. Students whose ages differ by as much as three or four years may work together on such a unit, with small groups or committees formed according to interest. Such an approach may be called the *multiage unit plan*. When not engaged in studying the unit, students may be subdivided on a different basis, such as performance level, for work on skills, or they may work individually.

The Torrance, California, schools have had multigraded elementary school classes for a number or years. At Nova High School in Fort Lauderdale, Florida, units of approximately one month's duration form the organizing elements of the nongraded program. Multiage unit programs at Emporia, Kansas, and Kent, Ohio, are described later in this chapter.

Under the multiage unit plan there is a danger that a student may either repeat a unit or topic in succeeding years or miss one entirely. A student who changes phases in a multisequence program faces similar difficulties. Therefore the curriculum must be planned on a two-, three-, or four-year cycle, depending upon the length of time most students spend in a particular building. For example, East Central High School in Tulsa, Oklahoma, is on a three-year cycle in a correlated English and history program. During the 1966–67 school year, all students studied world literature and world history, followed the next year by British culture and the next by American culture.

Many nongraded programs are staffed with teaching teams. The team format provides a necessary degree of flexibility in grouping and regrouping students, as illustrated by a number of programs described in this book. Moreover, "teachers of nongraded classes are more likely to realize that their separate talents are insufficient to meet the many needs of their pupils, and they will inevitably look to their colleagues as sources of help and reinforcement."[1]

Current Status

Despite its strong theoretical appeal, the nongraded idea is still far from

---

[1] *Middle School: A Report of Two Conferences in Mt. Kisco on the Definition of Its Purpose, Its Spirit, and Its Shape* (New York: Educational Facilities Laboratories, 1962), p. 22.

widespread acceptance, especially at the secondary level. Cawelti found nongraded programs in less than 5 percent of the 7,237 accredited high schools he surveyed in 1966.[2] Beggs and Buffie make the following explanation:

> The spread of nongraded schools has been both alarmingly slow and surprisingly rapid. Contrasted with the increased introduction of new programs in science, mathematics, and foreign language, the non-graded movement has been slow in development. But there are no federal funds to sponsor institutes, prepare guides, and concentrate on development for the nongraded school, as there have been for the content revisions. Also, the introduction of the nongraded concept implies widespread faculty participation in this innovation. In changes of course content, only the particular teachers of the subject field are called upon to alter their programs. In spite of these factors, the nongraded organization has increased in use in recent years at an unusual rate, considering the adoption of this concept implies the rejection of the traditional way teachers were taught to teach.[3]

Nongraded core programs are rare. Diligent search of educational publications, correspondence with experts in the nongraded curriculum, and a request for information circulated among members of the National Association for Core Curriculum turned up only two established programs of this kind. These are the programs at Roosevelt High School, Emporia, Kansas, and the one at Roosevelt School, Ypsilanti, Michigan, described in Part II of this book.

Implications for the Core Curriculum

Nongrading represents a novel approach to sequence, the vertical dimension in curriculum design. Core is an interdisciplinary, problem-centered approach to the horizontal dimension, sometimes referred to as the *scope* of the curriculum. Both single-sequence and multisequence nongraded plans are at variance with the core concept because they are aimed primarily at mastery of subject matter or skills. When separate sequences are prescribed for each of the academic disciplines, even a block-time program is not feasible. Each sequence would be likely to have a different number of steps or performance levels, and students would seldom progress at the same rate in each. Combining subjects under these circumstances would appear to be out of the question.

Suppose, instead, that broad problem areas are arranged in a prescribed nongraded sequence. By definition, core problems are those for which there are no ready answers; they are major personal and social issues likely to plague mankind for many years to come. How can any student "master" the concepts, values, and skills inherent in a study of "Problems of Intergroup Relations," or "War and

---

[2] Gordon Cawelti, "Innovative Practices in High Schools: Who Does What—and Why—and How," *Nation's Schools*, Vol. 79 (April 1967), p. 72.

[3] David W. Beggs, III, and Edward G. Buffie (eds.), *Nongraded Schools in Action: Bold New Venture* (Bloomington: Indiana U. P., 1967), p. xiv.

Peace," or "Finding My Place in the World of Work"? True, in many core programs certain problem areas are assigned to specific grade levels, but there is no assumption that students will master one before they tackle another.

Sequence in a core program is based more on psychological, than on logical principles. Recognizing that grade placement is usually arbitrary at best, a core teacher usually is free to determine sequence through teacher-student planning, capitalizing upon existing interests of the students, current world happenings, or problems uncovered in carrying out previous units. This kind of flexibility would be impossible in any rigidly sequenced program, graded or nongraded.

Core learnings are more like the insights gained by a number of explorers, each plunging into a relatively unknown wilderness, guided only by a vague map supplied him by an "old timer" (the teacher). Each brings back a slightly different picture of the new territory, varying according to his route, his motives and purposes, his background and ability. In core the main emphasis is upon continued refinement and enlargement of the learner's perceptions, not just the accretion, bit by bit, of a predetermined sequence of facts, concepts, or skills. One of the reasons why mathematics has seldom been absorbed successfully into core is the incompatibility between a highly sequential discipline, like mathematics, and the problem-centered approach.

Further complications arise from the idea that a student under either a single-sequence or a multisequence nongraded plan may move through the program at his own rate of speed. Accelerating individual students through a core program may hamper the development of teacher-student rapport and destroy the group spirit core teachers work so hard to achieve. Both group guidance and individual counseling by the teacher is difficult in a class where even a few students are coming and going.

Some of these drawbacks might be minimized in a tightly knit school-within-a-school or interdisciplinary team program in which teachers and students are well acquainted. Interdisciplinary teams are used in the nongraded middle school program in Liverpool, New York,[4] as well as the Bloomington, Indiana, SCAP program and the Component Curriculum in Ypsilanti, Michigan, both which are described in Part II of this book. Further experience with this approach is needed to determine its effects on group morale.

But the core curriculum is not just a series of problem-centered units. Many skills are involved—reading, writing, speaking, listening, critical thinking, use of the library. These skills might well be developed through carefully sequenced, nongraded learning experiences provided for students drawn from several core classes. A reasonable amount of regrouping across grade lines for this kind of instruction need not impair the *esprit de corps* being developed in the core class nor interfere with the problem-solving process. The nongraded approach is a natural extension of the individualized instruction in skills commonly provided by core

---

[4] Robert J. McCarthy, "A Nongraded Middle School," *National Elementary Principal,* Vol. 47 (January 1968), pp. 15–21.

teachers. Programed instructional materials, too, have their place in this aspect of the core curriculum.

The multiage unit approach to nongrading offers fewer difficulties when applied to core. A broad problem area seldom is limited to a particular grade or age level, so its study may well include students of several age, maturity, or grade levels.

The Nongraded Core Program at Emporia, Kansas

Before staff changes forced modification of the program, multiage units and individualized instruction characterized the core program in Roosevelt High School at Kansas State Teachers College.[5] The program consisted primarily of social studies and language arts, taught in a two-hour block of time to students who would ordinarily be classified as seventh- and eighth-graders.

After an orientation period of two to three weeks, in which the three core teachers became acquainted with new students, class groups were formed without regard to the student's year in school. Students were assigned to one of three levels according to teacher observation of the following areas of development:

(a) Social and/or emotional maturity.
(b) Ability to organize ideas or material logically, to make associations and to draw conclusions.
(c) Initiative and self-discipline.
(d) Competence in using the basic skills of oral and written composition.
(e) Extreme shyness or withdrawal tendencies.

Teacher-pupil planning was an almost constant process in the core classes. Teacher and pupils cooperatively developed units or individual problems for learning in accordance with the maturity levels within each group. During his junior high school years each student explored problems in many areas of social science: geography, history, anthropology, sociology, economics, and current affairs. In literature he examined ideas and themes in keeping with his level of maturity; Man and Nature, Human Friendships, Sportsmanship, and Responsibility were a few popular topics.

After choosing a unit, surveying references, and determining what information they needed to learn, students and teacher prepared a study guide for the unit. It included (1) spelling words that would be needed or that had been misspelled on compositions and other writing during previous units, (2) questions covering the unit being studied, (3) unfamiliar vocabulary words that students would meet during their study, (4) plenty of suggestions for individual or small group projects for those who completed the study early, (5) short stories and books that pertained to the unit, and (6) references on various reading levels. The entire class might be considering the same problem, but references, readings and projects varied according to individual needs, abilities and interests. During the core period the teacher worked with individuals, small

[5] Information supplied by Jeanette Bigge and Betty Campbell, associate professors of education at Kansas State.

groups, or the entire class as needed. Small-group work and panels or other group presentations replaced work on individual study guides during certain units.

Through the use of small, flexible groups, individual conferences and group instruction, skill development in language arts was individualized. When the teacher evaluated short compositions, the student was present and helped to discover and correct errors. When several students showed similar weaknesses, the teacher grouped them for work on needed skills. Other students might be working on social studies, literature, spelling or reading while the teacher gave attention to individuals or small groups. Teachers met each week to discuss the needs and progress of individual pupils. Teacher-pupil conferences were a part of each week's learning activities. A pupil moved from group to group at any time that he and the teacher agreed that his progress and growth warranted it. His chronological age or grade level was not a factor, and he did not have to wait until the end of the grading period, semester, or year.

Carefully planned and guided reading programs were an important phase of individualizing instruction. The teacher allowed much free choice in book selection, but offered guidance in accordance with her knowledge of the student's reading level, problems, and interests. Teacher and students cooperatively planned interesting ways in which books could be shared. Simple forms provided a record of books read by each student.

Student evaluation revealed almost complete satisfaction with the nongraded core program. An eighth-grade girl said: "The fact is that I don't see any other way to learn. I do not think I would know half as much as I do if I had to stay with group instruction or follow the interests of others and the teacher." Said another student: "There is too much repetition in a more formal program. We do not have to repeat just because all of us are not of the same level of ability in learning. Everyone is more relaxed because each learns according to his ability and can learn more if not pressured. We learn what the other fellow knows and we share our knowledge."

Bigge and Campbell conclude:

> Sixteen years of continued experimentation with the core program have convinced us that the flexibility and block-time scheduling of core provide the framework for a program of individualized instruction which may give careful attention to the changing needs and interests of each adolescent.[6]

Multigrading at Kent State University School, Kent, Ohio

In this experimental program, two teachers combined approximately 50 seventh- and eight-graders into one large class for the study of the history, geography, government, and current social problems of their state. Committees

[6] See also Jeanette Bigge and J. T. Sandefur, "Social Integration Through a Core Program," *Social Education*, Vol. 27 (March 1963), pp. 134–136; Charles Niess, "A Non-Graded Program for the Small High School," *Bulletin of the National Association of Secondary-School Principals*, Vol. 50 (February 1966), pp. 19–27.

were formed primarily on the basis of interest in a particular topic or question. The actual age and grade distributions of the resulting small groups were as follows. Notice that the correspondence between age and grade level is somewhat less than perfect.

Committee Composition in a Multi-Graded Unit

Committee Topic	Group Membership by Age and Grade				
	Age			*Grade*	
	12	13	14	7	8
Geography	3	2	2	5	2
History					
A. Indians	0	3	4	3	4
B. Local History	0	1	3	0	4
C. State History	1	6	0	5	2
Government	1	1	1	2	1
People	1	1	1	1	2
Business and Industry	1	3	0	3	1
Schools and Colleges	0	1	2	0	3
The Arts and Architecture	1	3	2	2	4
Recreation	0	3	1	3	1

Early in the unit, each student selected three people with whom he would like to tour a historical museum. The sociogram of these choices revealed eight choices across grade level lines. When the sociometric test was repeated three weeks later, prior to a second field trip, there were only five cross-grade choices. Presumably the intervening weeks of study in cross-graded committees accounted, at least in part, for the change.

At the end of the five-weeks' unit, students were asked how they liked having the two grades work together. The table below shows that opinion was rather evenly divided, with boys somewhat more favorable than girls and the seventh-graders somewhat more favorable than the eighth-graders.

Attitudes of Seventh and Eighth-Graders Toward a Mixed-Grade Class

Favorable		*Noncommittal*		*Unfavorable*	
Seventh-Graders		Seventh-Graders		Seventh-Graders	
Boys	7	Boys	1	Boys	3
Girls	4	Girls	2	Girls	4
Total Seventh	11	Total Seventh	3	Total Seventh	7
Eighth-Graders		Eighth-Graders		Eighth-Graders	
Boys	6	Boys	4	Boys	3
Girls	3	Girls	2	Girls	5
Total Eighth	9	Total Eighth	6	Total Eighth	8
Total Favorable	20	Total Noncommittal	9	Total Unfavorable	15

Some student comments reveal both the values and the drawbacks of this approach.

Favorable

A seventh-grade boy: "I think it was great because I got to know the eighth grade better."

A seventh-grade girl: "I think it's fun. You learn a lot from the older kids."

An eighth-grade boy: "I think it was all right. They added some important ideas to our group."

An eighth-grade girl: "I like to have kids in the seventh (grade) working with us. It gives us a bigger variety of kids to work with and it is more fun."

Unfavorable

A seventh-grade boy: "I didn't like it because I felt that seventh graders were inferior to the eighth graders in knowledge."

A seventh-grade girl: "In a way I like it, but then I don't, because I (was) afraid they might say something sometime about the way you do things."

An eighth-grade boy: "With two grades working together there are two sub-groups in the group and this causes problems when there is a mixed committee. Also, in this case the eighth grade made a bad example of behavior for the younger children."

An eighth-grade girl: "The kids are nice, but we end up learning on their level. I haven't learned anything significantly new this summer. But, it was a switch and I still enjoyed it."

Further experimentation is needed to determine whether incompatibilities between age groups decrease over longer periods of time. The teachers in this experiment experienced difficulty evaluating student performance, since the usual class comparison was inappropriate. More sophisticated, individualized evaluation procedures are needed with cross-graded classes.

Age group conflicts may be a less serious problem in senior high school. B. Frank Brown says: "It makes not the slightest difference to the senior doing remedial work whether he is sitting next to a sophomore or a junior student so long as he feels that the work he is doing is worthwhile and that, at last, he is learning something useful."[7] However, peer group relations are so important to junior high students that it is unlikely they could be this blasé about their fellow classmates. Further experimentation is needed to determine precisely how the spread of maturity levels found in a nongraded group affects both learning and group morale.

Conclusion

Experience with nongraded approaches in core is too limited at present to draw firm conclusions. Theoretically it would appear that a strictly sequential

[7] B. Frank Brown, *The Nongraded High School* (Englewood Cliffs, N.J.: Prentice-Hall, 1963), p. 127.

approach would be appropriate only for the skills component of the core curriculum. The multiage unit plan might be useful if the spread of the students' maturity levels is not so wide as to hamper the development of group morale. It would appear that a fair trial of the nongraded curriculum at the secondary level cannot be made until elementary school programs have been nongraded sufficiently to minimize students' identification with a particular grade-level group.

Chapter 9

Core and the Middle School

by Kilmer D. Rivera and Gordon F. Vars

The 1960's have witnessed accelerated discussion and experimentation with the middle school. This intermediate institution usually embraces grades 5 through 8 or 6 through 8, whereas most junior high schools include grades 7 through 9. Some educators view the middle school as a distinct new institution, while others see it as merely a modification of the junior high. In any case, what effect may a shift in grade-level organization have on the desirability of core for youngsters during their "in-between" years? This question is examined from a theoretical viewpoint and then illustrated by an account of the development of a middle school core program in the West Irondequoit Central Schools, Rochester, New York. Mr. Rivera, a teacher and former Core Department Chairman in this district, also has served as consultant to the Odessa-Montour Falls Central School District near Watkins Glen, New York. For several years Dr. Vars assisted the West Irondequoit core staff in program development.

The widespread acceptance of block-time and core at the junior high school level stems primarily from two factors. First, such a program provides a desirable transition from the self-contained classroom typical of the elementary school to the completely departmentalized program common to senior high. Hence core classes are found most frequently at the grade level a student enters first in junior high, usually grade 7. The transition function also is reflected in the way many programs taper off, extending for three for four periods in grade 7, dropping to two or three periods in grade eight and to two or none at all in grade nine.

Block-time and core programs also find favor at the junior high school level because they enhance the guidance role of the teacher. As they approach and pass through puberty, young people especially need the help of adults who know them well as persons, who are specifically charged with their guidance, and who provide the problem-centered instruction within which guidance may be most effective.

A number of present-day middle schools are merely junior high schools under another name; all the usual arguments for block-time and core apply. If the middle school includes grades five and six, however, the need for block-time or core is intensified. For many years it has been accepted that a self-contained classroom, with one teacher responsible for instruction in most subjects, is best for elementary school children. When children are with the same teacher most of the day, they have a home base and a coordinating center for their school activities. Alice Miel, in assessing the value of the self-contained classroom, cites arguments that closely resemble the values of block-time and core discussed in Chapter 1. Acknowledging that these potential advantages are not always realized, she concludes her case for the self-contained classroom as follows:

> If a type of organization has more promise for accomplishing certain goals (better mental health, more integrated, more complete learning), then our best course is to work toward the realization of the potential that is there. . . . The intelligent course is to continue a type of organization which invites and facilitates interrelatedness and attention to learning that falls between subjects and that makes it easier for a teacher to provide for all the ways in which a child may learn differently from his classmates.[1]

These characteristics are especially desirable for fifth- and sixth-graders in a middle school, which is apt to be a larger and more complex institution than the typical elementary school. Junior high school educators frequently testify that seventh-graders are "lost" for several weeks when they first enter a junior high school. How much more difficult must be the adjustment of fifth- and sixth-graders! Thus complete departmentalization, as practiced in many junior high schools, is especially inappropriate in a middle school. No doubt some of these considerations account for the fact that, of the twenty school systems identified in a National Education Association study as having middle schools, a vast majority were only partially departmentalized, especially in grades five and six.[2]

Block-time and core programs may be easier to staff in middle schools, since they usually fall within elementary teacher certification regulations. Junior high school administrators offer prefer to staff their core programs with elementary teachers. Whereas secondary teachers tend to consider themselves subject-matter specialists, elementary teachers are more likely to be concerned with the child's all-around development. Theirs is a broader preparation that usually includes specific techniques for teaching skills and for developing broad units of study. In the absence of teacher preparation geared specifically for core teachers, elementary programs that include modest depth in one or two teaching fields, as required for certification in some states, would appear to be most ideal. Of course, no program of preservice teacher preparation eliminates the need for continuous in-service development of teachers or for effective leadership on the part of school adminstrators.

In short, the core curriculum has special merit for a middle school because it

[1] Alice Miel, "The Self-Contained Classroom: An Assessment," *Teachers College Record*, Vol. 59 (February 1958), pp. 286–287.

[2] "Middle Schools," *Educational Research Service Circular*, No. 3 (Washington, D.C.: National Education Association, May 1965), p. 3.

preserves some of the best features of the elementary self-contained classroom as well as the values evident from more than thirty years of experience with the core concept at the junior and senior high school level. Furthermore, a major obstacle to the development of core programs at the secondary level—the shortage of qualified teachers—may be minimized when the middle school is constituted of grades in which elementary certification is acceptable.[3] Let us turn now to a specific example of core program development in three middle schools in New York State.

Core in West Irondequoit

The tree-lined streets and neat homes of West Irondequoit could easily serve as the movie set of a typical American middle-class suburb. Residents, many of them professionals and highly trained workers, enjoy an income level that is exceeded by only two or three other communities in the Rochester area.

The district has eleven elementary schools serving kindergarten through fourth grade, three middle schools serving fifth through eighth grade, and a high school, which customarily sends in excess of 80 percent of its graduates to institutions of higher learning, principally colleges and universities. Some school facilities are over forty years old and some were erected within the last decade. West Irondequoit enrolls about six thousand youngsters from a wide range of ethnic and religious backgrounds, plus over 120 children from Rochester's inner city, who are bused to the district voluntarily. Until recently, teachers' starting salaries were the highest in the area.

Early in the 1960's the district embarked upon a program of change under the leadership of Mr. Earle W. Helmer, Superintendent of Schools, and Miss Helen Rice, Coordinator of Curriculum Planning. This included the reorganization of the district's middle schools along the lines suggested by George D. Stoddard of New York University in his book, *The Dual Progress Plan.*[4] Stoddard divides instructional areas into what he calls *cultural imperatives* and *cultural electives.* The cultural imperatives are the common learnings; that is, those which are deemed essential for the development of responsible and effectively functioning adults within the present framework of American society. The cultural electives, on the other hand, are those considered desirable but not essential for all citizens to master.

Three instructional areas are considered to be cultural imperatives: health and physical education, the language arts, and the social studies. Instruction in the language arts and the social studies is provided by one teacher in what Stoddard calls a *core* class. Cultural electives like mathematics, foreign languages, art, or music are taught by specialists, utilizing, wherever possible, a nongraded

[3] Gordon F. Vars, "The Middle School: Implications for the Core Curriculum," in Thomas E. Curtis (ed.), *The Middle School* (Albany: Center for Curriculum Research and Services, State University of New York at Albany, 1968) pp. 216–231.

[4] George D. Stoddard, *The Dual Progress Plan* (New York: Harper & Brothers, 1961).

approach. Thus the Dual Progress Plan represents a semidepartmentalized organization of the school day. It seeks to retain the best features of the self-contained classroom (through the core class) while simultaneously offering the advantages of classroom instruction by specialists. In West Irondequoit the Dual Progress Plan is in operation only in the fifth and sixth grades. It currently involves about 300 children in each of the three middle schools. The seventh- and eighth-grade programs are departmentalized.

Initially, the "core" was simply a block-time curriculum and it was tried on an experimental basis in only one of the middle schools. During this experimental year, the emphasis was on information and feedback: informing the parents about the nature of the total program and assessing feedback from parents, students, and teachers concerning the practical aspects of its operation. Orientation sessions were held with parent groups and informational flyers were sent to their homes. Questionnaires were filled out by parents, students, and teachers. Reactions, particularly those of students and teachers, were overwhelmingly favorable, and the next year the Dual Progress Plan was extended to the other two middle schools.

Once reorganization under the Dual Progress Plan had been accomplished in all the middle schools and a normal routine had been established by students and teachers, the nature of the core program itself was brought under closer examination. Should it continue to operate as a simple block-time curriculum? Teams of consultants from the University of Rochester met with teachers during the second year in an effort to determine the type of curriculum that would best meet the educational needs of the students. A majority of the core teachers indicated a preference for *unified studies*. It appeared to offer the best possibilities for a smooth transition from the self-contained curriculum with which they had been familiar. This plan was adopted and has since come to be called the *combined subjects curriculum.*

In the combined subjects class, the social studies serve as the instructional vehicle or medium for learning experiences in language arts. Thus, student efforts in communication through reading, writing, speaking, and listening concern primarily the social studies topics under study. As often as possible, the social studies learning experience is simultaneously a language arts experience.

Social studies content for the two grades is essentially a cultural-geography approach to man's history, from his earliest beginnings through the exploration of America. Life patterns in various cultures and civilizations are compared to illustrate the many ways that man has devised to meet his basic needs. Content is divided into the following units:

Grade Five

I. How Do We Find the Missing Parts to the Puzzle of the Past?
II. How Did Our Earliest Ancestors Survive in a Harsh World?
III. What Do the People of Today Owe to the Civilizations of the Near East?

IV. How Did the Nile River Give Birth to a Mighty Civilization?
V. Why was China a Land of Fable to Other Men for So Long?
VI. How Can We Repay Our Debt to the Glory That Was Greece?
VII. How Did a Tiber Village Become Mistress of the Mediterranean World?

Grade Six

I. A New System of Living Arises in Europe
II. New Forces Create Changes During the Middle Ages
III. The Beginnings of Modern Nations in Europe
IV. Men Are Stirred by New Ideas
V. The New World
   a. Explorers and Geography
   b. Pre-Columbian Indian Civilizations
VI. The New World of Latin America
VII. The New World of Canada

The Program in Operation

The schedule below shows that a student spends approximately one half of the school day in the combined subjects class. During this same part of the day, two weekly periods of forty-two minutes each are allotted to physical education.

Foreign-language instruction (French or Spanish) is scheduled within the cultural imperative half of the day merely as a matter of convenience. A sixth-grader may have study hall instead of foreign-language instruction if his

A Sixth-Grade Student's Schedule at West Irondequoit

Period*	Monday	Tuesday	Wednesday	Thursday	Friday
1	Combined subjects	Same	Same	Same	Same
2	Combined subjects Foreign-language†	Same	Same	Same	Same
3	Combined subjects	Same	Same	Same	Same
4	Combined subjects	Physical education	Combined subjects	Physical education	Combined subjects
5	Mathematics	Same	Same	Same	Same
6	Art	Study Hall	Vocal music	Art	Vocal music
7	Reading	Same	Same	Same	Same
8	Science	Same	Same	Same	Same

*Each period is 42 minutes long. Passing time is three minutes.
†Foreign-language instruction for twenty minutes daily.

fifth-grade experience reveals low achievement potential and marked disinterest in foreign language.

During the other half of the day, the student moves about from teacher to teacher for instruction in mathematics, science, developmental reading, art (two periods a week), and music (two periods a week). One period a week is provided for a study hall. Some students have combined subjects in the morning; others, in the afternoon. A combined subjects teacher ordinarily has both a morning and an afternoon group.

It will be noted that developmental reading, while inherently an area of major importance in the language arts complex, is not included in the combined-subjects half of the daily schedule. This area of the language arts is deemed of sufficient importance to warrant the use of especially trained reading instructors, and it is therefore scheduled in the departmentalized half of the day. Furthermore, since students are grouped heterogeneously in core classes and homogeneously for the departmentalized half of the day, reading classes can be scheduled to take advantage of this grouping practice.

The heterogeneous grouping in combined subjects, incidentally, represents a departure from the homogeneous grouping recommended by Stoddard. This feature of the former self-contained organization in the district was retained as a matter of local preference. It could be argued that the combination of both heterogeneous and homogeneous grouping gives students a much wider circle of bona fide social contacts than would be the case with homogeneous grouping throughout the school day. Moreover, changes in a student's schedule that are required by adjustments in the ability grouping during the departmentalized portion of the day cause only minor disruptions in a student's social contacts.

Several social studies textbooks are used to provide for the wide range of student reading abilities in the combined subjects class. Where possible, this same multitext approach is used in the selection of reading materials for literature. In some units a student may choose from as many as four different textbooks. Classroom sets are provided on the basis of a 1–2–1 proportion for the slow average, and superior readers, respectively. Disagreements or contradictions in information from different texts help to show the students that, while books are useful tools, they are not infallible.

The library is vital to the success of the combined subjects curriculum. Students use the library to research social studies topics for individual or group projects and reports, and they visit the library often to make selections for personal reading.

Sometimes books in heavy demand are placed on overnight reserve. This prevents a monopoly of such material by a single class, e.g., the first group to begin a particular unit of study. It also enables the librarian to purchase a variety of books on a given topic rather than multiple copies of the same book, thus creating a broader reference base for research activities. The overnight loan policy also is applied to student use of filmstrips and filmstrip viewers. Records, tapes, and film loops, however, are restricted to use within the library. Special classes are arranged as the need arises for a lesson in some specific library skill.

In order to keep abreast of new developments in education and to discuss problems common to the department as a whole, meetings of all the combined subjects teachers are held once a month. This district-wide department meeting is alternated with meetings of the combined subjects faculties in the individual middle schools.

Development of Curriculum Guides

At the time the decision was made to adopt the unified studies or combined subjects approach, curriculum materials available consisted of lists of approved textbooks and short two- or three-page topical outlines for fifth- and sixth-grade social studies and language arts. It was apparent that more extensive curriculum guides were needed, particularly for teachers who were new to the district and who had little or no teaching experience. It was felt that these guides should, indeed, *guide* the teacher toward desirable techniques of classroom operation through the inclusion of as much step-by-step and how-to-do-it information as the collective efforts of the curriculum writing teams could provide.

In the summer of 1963 the first writing team started work. During the next three summers writing teams, with the help of consultants, revised and expanded this material. In each instance it was phased into classroom work during the school year immediately following and revised the next summer.

One publication that resulted from this endeavor is *An Introduction to the Combined Subjects Curriculum,* which is designed to give the teacher a general orientation on the program. It describes the Dual Progress Plan, indicates the place of combined subjects in the K–12 curriculum spectrum, and explains the use of other curriculum publications. It details the topics, sequence, and suggested time allotments for the social studies units which are the medium for language arts learning. Finally, it states the educational objectives of the curriculum in relation to both skills and personality development, defining these in behavioral terms.

The *Manual for Teachers* focuses more directly on classroom instruction in the combined-subjects class. It deals with structural linguistics, speaking and listening skills, composition skills, and some generally useful instructional methods. The section on structural linguistics, new and relatively brief, merely establishes an experimental instructional sequence in the "new English" for grades 5 and 6. The district is currently testing some English textbooks that have a strong linguistics orientation in both grammar and composition. If adopted, these may eliminate the need for a more detailed expansion of this section. The section on speaking and listening skills contains a sequence for grades 5 and 6 that is part of the district's K–12 program.

The composition section of this manual focuses on the structure of the paragraph. Fifth-grade students are taught to manipulate the single paragraph for a variety of purposes. In sixth grade the writing is directed toward multiparagraph compositions. Topics related to most of the social studies units in each grade are suggested for each category in the list of writing objectives.

The instructional methods and activities described in the manual are useful in any instructional unit. "How to Conduct a Field Trip," "Getting a Poetry Program Started," "Using Current Events Materials," and "Preparing a Class Newspaper" are illustrative titles.

The Unit Teaching Guide

Unit Teaching Guides provide teachers with practical information on the instructional organization and development of combined subjects units. Each guide contains a time line showing important events that occurred in the period under study. A suggested vocabulary list includes both social studies and language arts terms, limiting the introduction of new terms to about six per week. Of course, the teacher may adjust the vocabulary studied to the abilities and interests of the students in his class.

Paralleling a detailed social studies content outline for each unit is a column that lists pertinent page numbers in a variety of textbooks. Brief code words, such as "skit" or "panel" refer the teacher to appropriate learning activities that are described more fully either elsewhere in the same unit guide or in the *Manual for Teachers*. A portion of a social studies content outline may be found in Appendix B.

Also listed are the reading, writing, listening, speaking, and study-reference skills that are to be reinforced or introduced during the unit. All the language arts skills are not necessarily emphasized in each unit, but the entire sequence receives attention in one unit or another during the two-year period. A column parallel with the list of skills cites pertinent learning activities that are described elsewhere in the same guide or in a different curriculum publication. (See Appendix C.)

Map and globe skills are listed in selected unit guides. As in the case of the language arts skills, they are arranged in sequence from the simple to the more complex.

Literature serves three functions in combined studies. It reinforces social studies learnings, serves as a vehicle for instruction in language arts skills, and is enjoyed for its own sake. West Irondequoit teachers found that reading anthologies of the type generally encountered in elementary classrooms were not suitable for combined studies. They generally contained little material directly related to the social studies, few had the same literary content at different reading levels, and the literary quality of the stories varied greatly. Instead, the staff chose specific works that could act as extensions of the social studies content and that represented, in the original or in adapted form, literary creations of a widely recognized excellence.

Selections related to the fifth-grade social studies content include: readings from the *Old Testament,* an adaptation of a fourth-century Chinese tale entitled *The Superlative Horse,* readings from Greek mythology, *Aesop's Fables,* and, in adapted form, the *Iliad* and the *Odyssey.* Sixth-grade selections include paperbacks entitled *King Arthur and His Knights* and *The Seven Voyages of Sinbad,* and two versions of Mark Twain's *The Prince and the Pauper.* For each story, the unit teaching guide contains suggested discussion questions for the teacher and a student reading guide, which lists details of plot, setting, and characters for him to examine as he reads. Parallels drawn between historical narratives and contemporary situations are used as springboards for discussion of modern-day moral and ethical problems.

The section describing "Initiatory, Developmental, and Culminating Activities" specific to that unit are printed on blue paper for easy reference. These activities are designed to help the teacher create interest in a unit, sustain this interest during the development of the unit, and end the unit, hopefully, with the intellectual appetite only whetted. Both group and individual student activities are listed. As mentioned above, these activities are indexed next to applicable topics in both the social studies content outline and the language arts skills list for each unit. (See Appendix B.)

Listed separately on yellow paper are art and music activities which correlate with the social studies content of the unit. These are activities deemed especially suitable for combined studies rather than for music or art classes. However, courses of study for music and art classes also correlate with the combined-subjects curriculum. Thus, a combined-subjects class in grade 5 might consider the music of prehistoric man in connection with the concept of communication. In the music class this concept of music as a form of communication may be more carefully explored. The students may make different types of musical instruments as they might have been created by prehistoric man. During the study of a unit on medieval life, a sixth-grade student committee might present an oral report and exhibit on the Gothic style of architecture. In the art class, students might study stained glass as an art form and then create some of their own designs.

Each unit guide also contains a comprehensive list of resource materials and their sources. Included is a reference bibliography for the teacher, a student bibliography of both fiction and nonfiction books, lists of a variety of audio-visual materials (films, filmstrips, tapes, recordings, slides), and in a few cases, portions of historical documents. Near the back of each guide is a complete textbook listing, including estimated reading difficulty levels (easy, medium, difficult).

An unusual feature of the West Irondequoit unit teaching guide is the section on classroom questions. It is designed to acquaint the teacher with a broad variety of questions, particularly those that might be used to instruct the student in critical thinking or to measure his abilities in this area. Utilizing the analysis of thinking found in the taxonomy of educational objectives edited by Benjamin Bloom,[5] sample questions were prepared by district core teachers and organized into two major categories:—recall and critical thinking. The recall questions give the core teacher a general idea of the scope and detail presumably dealt with by his colleagues in other core classrooms. The critical thinking questions encourage him to lift the level of his questioning so as to stimulate such thought processes as translation, interpretation, application, analysis, synthesis, and evaluation.

Guidance and Evaluation

An important contribution to the combined studies program is made by the guidance department of the West Irondequoit middle schools. At the present time there are two guidance counselors in each of the middle schools. One of these works primarily with students in the fifth and sixth grades. Personal counseling, parent-teacher conferences, student schedule changes, group standardized testing, and the maintenance of personal information and test data on each student are all areas of regular concern for this guidance specialist.

Some of the standardized tests that are given under the direction of the guidance counselor include the *Iowa Tests of Basic Skills,* the *Lorge-Thorndike Intelligence Test,* and the *Sequential Tests of Educational Progress* (STEP) in science and mathematics. Test results are made available to teachers and are discussed with students during individual conferences with the guidance counselor. Results also are available to the parents upon request.

The guidance counselor is especially important to the combined-subjects teacher as a source of feedback from the students concerning the effectiveness of the classroom program. He also may help teachers to better understand student behavior and performance in the classroom. A former counselor (now at the district high school) chose to conduct a quasi-instructional program through the medium of monthly half-hour guidance sessions with each combined studies group. The teacher was not present during these guidance sessions, and the topics discussed ranged from smoking to lunchroom behavior, as well as the students' feelings about school or classroom routine. The counselor always preserved the anonymity of sources when presenting feedback to the teachers, whether it was complimentary or not.

A student's progress is indicated on report cards sent home six times a year. Separate marks are given in *English, Spelling in Written Work, Writing* (handwriting), and *Social Studies.* Marks are recorded in letter symbols which match the numerical scale used in the seventh and eighth grades. A committee of teachers and administrators has been formed to explore better ways of reporting and evaluating student progress and achievement.

[5] Benjamin S. Bloom, et al., *Taxonomy of Educational Objectives, Handbook I: Cognitive Domain* (New York: David McKay Company, 1956).

Conclusion

In summary, what can be said about the strengths or weaknesses of the combined studies program as it operates in the middle schools of West Irondequoit?

The weakness seem to be relatively few and of a minor nature. The guidance department, for example, does seem to have a hectic time of it, for a short period, when planning student schedules and trying to make all the pieces fit. Then, too, the multiple-text approach could create a whopping bill if each child were to have a copy of each text. The purchase of partial sets of textbooks creates occasional problems when a specific topic is not covered in all the available texts and there are not enough other materials suitable for a common reading assignment. This type of problem is quickly solved once teachers within a grade arrive at a system of sharing textbooks.

The advantages, on the other hand, are big ones. Teachers can now concentrate their efforts in two instructional areas, instead of the many subjects taught by the typical elementary teacher. Class preparations are fewer in number and can be more intensive. There is now more time to plan original approaches to instruction, more creative lessons, and ways to more strongly motivate students. Unlike the usual secondary teacher, core teachers have only two groups of students, so they can know each child as a person and adjust instruction to his individual needs. In short, the teachers and the students like things the way they are in preference to the way they were before the combined studies program was introduced.

Will the combined subjects approach be extended into grades seven and eight? Will the program evolve into a full-fledged core program? Curriculum development thus far in West Irondequoit has proceeded from the bottom up, with much emphasis on teacher involvement. This relatively slow but steady process works well in districts with little teacher turnover. Curriculum development procedures in which administrative and supervisory personnel exert more direct influence are described in Chapters 11 and 12.

Chapter 10

Core and the Culturally Disadvantaged Student

by Morrel J. Clute

Core curriculum concepts have proved successful with all kinds of students—gifted, average, or slow; boys or girls; rural, small-town, or big city. Here Morrel Clute examines the special values of core for culturally disadvantaged youth and describes programs designed to prepare teachers for work with this type of student. Dr. Clute is a professor of education at Wayne State University and coauthor of Teaching and Learning in the Junior High School (Wadsworth, 1961).

"Sometimes when you're on a trip you meet a real tall man that makes you stretch a little and you think maybe you can make it."

With these words a fifteen-year-old potential dropout described his positive feelings for his experiences in "Operation Go." This student was referring to a special summer program, a federally funded project under the direction of the Division of Extended School Programs in Detroit, Michigan. Initiated in 1965, "Operation Go" has been expanded from the initial two projects to programs in twenty-two junior high schools within the city. Although it is too early for data from the follow-up studies now under way, there is considerable evidence that a significant number of potential dropouts have been salvaged from the educational and social scrap heap.

"Operation Go" is probably typical of hundreds of projects throughout the United States that are designed to help American youth whose "growing up" has lacked the kind of growth-nurturing experiences needed for finding personal meanings in traditional school programs. Nearly all such programs for the educationally disadvantaged are built around these central tenets of the core curriculum:

1. The learner must be involved, must begin where his own interest permits him to begin.
2. Past experience is the only basis for making meaning from his perceiving; becoming more knowledgeable is enhanced through broadened experience.

3. Learning is dependent upon all the things the learner is, particularly how he feels about himself, his feelings of worth, what he believes he can do, what he believes he cannot do, and his perception of the risk involved in venturing into the unknown.

4. All learners are unique, each different from the other, bringing different experiences to each new understanding and therefore different meaning.

5. Such differences are to be accepted and cherished because they represent the true state of the human society; this acceptance makes possible the cooperation necessary for a functioning community.

6. The fundamental goal of education is to help each child become a self-respecting, functioning citizen of the human society; respect for others can exist only when there is respect for self.

These tenets are not restricted to the core curriculum, of course, but they are too often violated in conventional school programs. The crucial problem is to fill that vast void that exists as a result of specialization, departmentalization, and the frantic search for the magic in the subject fields. In the past we have frequently lost our perspective about curriculum and have perceived curriculum as something to teach—not something to teach *with*. We have provided little opportunity for students to integrate information and to make personal meanings from the data which is fed to them. Arthur Combs says:

> The problem of learning always involves two aspects: providing new information or experience and helping the individual discover the meaning of information for himself. We, as educators, have allowed the provision of information to become our preoccupation. This has resulted in our failures being largely human problems, breakdowns of personal meaning—almost never failures of information. There is a vast difference between knowing and behaving—knowing comes through the possession of information, behavior from the discovery of personal meanings.[1]

The Renaissance of Core Curriculum Concepts

Educators who have for years advocated teacher-pupil planning and problem-solving as practical approaches to helping students discover personal meaning are about to witness a tremendous rebirth of these concepts. This will come about, not because of any pressure group or salesmanship, but simply because the conditions of today make it necessary.

There are many reasons why there is increasing use of core curriculum concepts in school programs and practices. The massive commitment of the federal government to education has focused national attention on those students who traditionally have not found school worthwhile. Until federal inter-

[1] Arthur Combs, from an address delivered at the 1967 convention of the Association for Supervision and Curriculum Development, Dallas, Texas.

vention, the school's concern for students who did not fit the predetermined curriculum has been minimal. All schools have students who are labeled as nonachievers, underachievers, slow learners, retarded, or remedial students. Regardless of the labels, the existence of these boys and girls is evidence that the inflexible, subject-centered curriculum is inappropriate to the learning needs of children who lack growth-nurturing experience. National concern for disadvantaged youth has made it popular and appropriate for schools to depart from the traditional practices, those dictated by the concept of curriculum as content to be taught without regard to the experience background of the learner. With federal funds, schools are designing special projects in an effort to find effective ways to help young people overcome their educational handicaps. Typical names for these projects reflect their purposes: "Operation Help," "Project Save," "Upward Bound."

These programs are usually characterized by extended time blocks. Students may be assigned to a special separate school with a special staff for the whole school day, as is the case in Hazel Park, Michigan, with "Project Save," or they may spend two-to-four-period blocks with the same teacher, as represented by the "Personalized Curriculum Program" (PCP) in Flint, Michigan.

Intensive effort is made in each of these programs to humanize the relationships among the students and between teachers and students. Students in programs which are successful consistently report that teachers listen to them, plan with them, and encourage them in their individual or group interests. One student, pleading that his class be permitted to continue together for another semester, stated that his teacher was a good teacher because he let them take responsibility. In the student's words, "He doesn't always do it for us."

The second reason why the national climate is supportive of core is the reaction to the national curriculum reform movement, which has emphasized the subject disciplines. The hysteria which swept the nation following the Russian sputnik brought federal funds into the education arena. Massive amounts have been spent on an intensive study of the subject fields in the hope of finding more pertinent concepts and more effective methods to help students discover these concepts. John Goodlad estimates that since 1957 more than nine million dollars has been spent on curriculum reform in the field of mathematics. Comparable amounts have been spent in similar efforts to improve the curriculum in science, foreign language, English, and social studies.

The results of such intensive study of the subject fields could have been expected: a vastly increased number of concepts have been identified, they have been sequentially ordered, and more and more of these concepts have been moved downward toward the first grade. In the meantime, the walls between subjects grow higher and make it more difficult for a student to find meaning in his world through the discovery of relationships between and among the subject fields. As subject fields becomes more isolated from one another and specialized subject instruction reinforces the concept that a curriculum is to be taught, there has been less time and effort spent on what is fundamental. *The fundamentals,* those things which enable an individual to survive in a complex human society, have to do with *a person's sense of responsibility, his respect for himself, his respect and concern for the rights and welfare of others, and his capacity for service—both to himself and to his community.* Fortunately, in recent years greater concern is being expressed about the responsibility of the school for nurturing these values, attitudes, and feelings, which are vital for young people living so close together in modern society.

We are horrified by mounting acts of violence, hostility, and aggression throughout the nation. The summer riots in our large urban centers are monstrous demonstrations of defiance of law and order. The rioters seem to have one characteristic in common—they are young, very young. Race, religion, or other factors commonly associated with such civil disturbances seem only a part of this mob scene. Primarily it is youth in rebellion against feelings of degradation, poverty, and maltreatment; it is youth testing its power. One could well ask how many of these young people found reasons for self-respect in their growing-up years. Did the practices and behavior of school people simply maintain the usual prejudice against those who had limited experience with which to deal meaningfully with the academic orientation of the school? Or did the practices help young people see alternatives, consequences, or promise?

Teacher Preparation

If learning is changed behavior, as we so often say, the school must be more concerned with what students feel, think, or believe and less about "what are the facts." This calls for teachers who believe in young people, who understand their needs, who know how to plan with them and facilitate their learning. The fallacy of the conventional teaching concept must be exposed. As a twelve-year-old girl from an inner-city junior high school said: "Ya can't teach 'em if they don't want to do it." The idea that a teacher is one who presents content is appropriate only for a static society, not for a changing, dynamic one. The concept of teacher that is needed is that he is one who facilitates, who opens the door to new experiences, invites, excites, accepts. He must be one who uses himself effectively, who knows something about what he is, and who recognizes above all else that each child must find a satisfying way to learn.

Can colleges and teacher education institutions help people become this kind of teacher? The many ramifications of this problem were explored years ago in a definitive monograph by the ASCD Commission on Core Curriculum.[2] Here are some things that are being done currently at Wayne State University.

First, we have lost faith in the traditional concept of student teaching as a means of developing this potential in teachers. Too often a student teacher merely learns all the mistakes of the past. This does not prepare him for the

[2] *The Preparation of Core Teachers* (Washington, D.C.: Association for Supervision and Curriculum Development, 1955.)

teaching responsibilities of today. Educating each child in America calls for more than minor repairs on the status quo.

We have, therefore sought every opportunity to provide experiences for prospective teachers that will help them to know "kids" as they really are—experiences that demand planning and living with them. We are finding great return from the experiences people have while working in schools or summer camps. Such summer projects include "Operation Go" in Detroit and Highland Park's "Traveling Classroom," where the curriculum content grows out of teachers and students working together. For several summers, student teachers have been part of the Highland Park teachers, team which has taken disadvantaged secondary students on a 6,000-mile classroom jaunt around the nation, all of it cooperatively planned.

One of the most rewarding experiences for our students is spending the summer as a teacher with the Job Corps. After three months of working with high school dropouts who are seeking a second chance through this program, most of our students return confident that they can help such students and, most important of all, they are unafraid.

An experiment with closed-circuit television is equally promising. An experimental course was developed in the summer of 1965 at Wayne State University, and a similar program was conducted in 1966 at the University of Connecticut, with the assistance of Wayne State educators. As offered during the summer of 1966 at Wayne State, the course Education 6014 involved two classrooms: a racially integrated junior high age group of inner-city children, and a class of teachers and administrators taking the course for credit. The main content of the five-week program evolved from continuous observation by closed-circuit television of the daily activities in the junior high classroom.

Class I (The Television Class)

The students, chosen through the counselors at three Detroit junior high schools, were boys and girls from underprivileged school areas. As news of the class spread, friends brought other friends until the enrollment had to be cut off at forty participants, thirty-five Negro and five white. Sessions were held from 9:00 to 11:30 a.m., four days a week, in a room designed for television production.

The television class was conducted along the lines of a core curriculum; that is, it dealt with "broad units of work, or activities, planned by the teacher and the students in terms of needs as perceived by the group."[3] It was an unstructured core, since no basic curriculum plan was set up in advance. The problem-solving approach to learning was employed, involving goal-setting, problem selection, group activity, individual effort, group interaction, continuing evaluation, and cooperative assessment of accomplishment.

[3] Roland C. Faunce and Morrel J. Clute, *Teaching and Learning in the Junior High School* (Belmont, Calif.: Wadsworth, 1961), p. 87.

Problem-solving, or reflection-level teaching, is considered by many educators to be the highest level of teaching-learning, since it requires creative thinking. It is different from memory-level learning which stresses rote memorization of factual material. It is different also from understanding-level learning which produces generalized insights directed toward a goal. According to Morris Bigge, reflection-level or problem-solving learning requires "more active participation, more criticism of conventional thinking, and more imagination and creativeness" on the part of the students. He goes on to say that "the classroom atmosphere is one of teacher-student mutual inquiry within which genuine problems are developed and solved."[4]

Can such a teaching-learning approach succeed with culturally disadvantaged children? Do they have the background, the verbal and written skills, the intellectual capacity to profit from such a teaching method? These questions were of paramount concern to the teachers observing the integrated classroom.

To implement the problem-solving approach, the teacher and students together developed the units of study from topics of mutual interest. The students divided into groups to investigate and prepare presentations in areas such as: Teenage Problems (Prostitution, Pimping, Drunkeness, Unwed Mothers), Interracial Marriages, Teenagers and Parents, and Viet Nam.

Class II (The Teacher Observers)

The forty-seven teacher-observers were graduate and undergraduate students taking the course for eight hours of credit. Teaching and/or administrative experience of the participants ranged from none at all to more than ten years. The primary objectives for the course were to change the stereotype that many teachers have about the learning potential of Negro children and to demonstrate that an inner-city, integrated class can be taught in a problem-solving manner.

After two hours each day of viewing the TV class, the teacher-participants analyzed, interpreted, and evaluated the methods, activities, and outcomes they had observed. Each class member wrote a weekly evaluation of the TV class and his reactions to the course in general.

Despite the difficulties involved in doing an "after-the-fact" study, an evaluation of the impact of Education 6014 on the teacher-observers was conducted to seek answers to these questions:

1. Did the teachers feel they gained a greater or at least different understanding of the learning potential of culturally disadvantaged youth?
2. Did the course successfully demonstrate that an inner-city class can be taught using problem-solving techniques?
3. Did the teacher participants perceive closed-circuit TV observation as a valuable technique for preservice and in-service teacher education?

An open-ended questionnaire, sent to the forty-six members of the class

[4]Morris L. Bigge, *Learning Theories for Teachers* (New York: Harper & Row, 1964), p. 325.

who completed the course requirements, was returned by 74 percent of them. To determine the values derived from the course, previously stated course objectives were used as categories under which the responses were classified. Additional categories were set up as they emerged from the data. Comparing responses according to the participants' teaching experience, level of education, and experience in integrated schools, the following conclusions were drawn:

1. Almost three-quarters of the participants felt they gained a better knowledge of teacher-pupil planning as a teaching technique. Of the teachers who had never taught in integrated schools, 91 percent saw great value in this teaching method. Not unexpectedly, this demonstration of teacher-pupil planning was of most benefit to participants working on their Bachelor of Arts degrees, and somewhat surprisingly, almost equally of benefit to those working on their doctorates.

2. Almost half of the participants felt they gained a better understanding of cultural differences. Here again, those with no experience in integrated schools gained the most. This was as hoped and expected.

3. Demonstrating the desirability of a relaxed classroom atmosphere and warm teacher-pupil relations was not a stated objective of the course, but half of the participants felt this was one of the greatest values gained. This value seemed most apparent to those participants with one year of teaching experience and least apparent to those who had never taught. A small amount of experience makes one at least aware of the problem, even if not skillful enough to do anything about it.

4. Another outcome which emerged from the data concerned the exchange of ideas between experienced and new teachers, both white and Negro, that was made possible during Education 6014. One-quarter of the participants mentioned this as a value gained. As was to be expected, this exchange of ideas was most important to those with little teaching experience.

5. The course convinced at least 15 percent of the class that standardized intelligence and achievement test results are not applicable to the culturally different. The teacher-observers were not told the ability ratings of the television students until the end of the course. Much to their astonishment, they discovered that the children had not been especially chosen as the brightest available for the class. Indeed, with one or two exceptions, they were rated average or below average by the school personnel who selected them.

6. Over three-quarters of the respondents declared that they were motivated to proceed differently in their teaching, with 43 percent of the responses specifically mentioning increased use of teacher-pupil planning. Another third of the responses related to better teacher-pupil interpersonal relationships. It was apparent from the remaining responses that the teacher-observers in Education 6014 were motivated to try a wide variety of new approaches in their teaching methods.

7. Although the number of comments concerning the value of closed-circuit television for teacher education was not as great as for the other questions, the tone of the responses indicated a strongly favorable feeling. Eighty-four percent of the responses were in favor of using this technique. It was significant that all of the six class members who had never taught praised TV observation for giving them a better understanding of teaching methods. A quotation from one of the questionnaires summarizes the values of this approach: "Closed-circuit TV observation is valuable for beginning teachers and for mature teachers who want to try new methods but don't know how to go about it, who are in a rut, or out of touch." Negative comments, which numbered only four of the twenty-five responses, mainly expressed concern that children tend to act unnaturally when on camera.

In conclusion, the available evidence indicates that Education 6014 achieved its objectives to a considerable degree. Most teachers gained a better understanding of the learning potential of culturally different youngsters as they witnessed a demonstration that inner-city children can be taught by problem-solving methods. In the opinion of the participants, closed-circuit television observation was shown to have considerable value for teacher education. An unanticipated plus was the strong conviction many teachers developed of the need for warm, understanding teacher-pupil relations.

This description of the closed-circuit television project is not intended to be a prescription for how to prepare core teachers, but it is representative of efforts that must be continued if we are to meet the most pressing problems facing education today.

The Broader Perspective

Our concern must not be limited to the culturally disadvantaged. Loud and clear across the land, high school and college students complain that education is not relevant to life needs or life problems—either in its content or its methods. The static, locked-in curriculum will always be irrelevant, but it will continue as long as we believe that information is knowledge and that knowledge can be transferred to the student with or without his consent. This belief almost guarantees that curriculum will not be relevant to the resolution of such problems as racism, deterioration of democratic ideals, finding identity for self, and developing social values.

Student feelings are vividly revealed in this statement from a high school underground newspaper, in an article describing student efforts to improve communication between students and the administration:

> I hope the man (principal) has finally seen that we're not just a bunch of snotty-nosed bastards concerned only with our shallow little lives and that we really hope to change this world, that so far we have

not had any say in its administration, and furthermore that we will not pimp out in our responsibility as have our parents.

Add this one by a California sophomore, Mark Kleiman, from a paper titled, "High School Reform":

> What I remember most about my school is that there is a ten-foot fence around it. In parts, there are three rows of barbed wire strung along the top. What concerns me most about the fence is not that it keeps me in—but that it keeps the rest of the world out, admitting only those portions of "reality" which the administration deems safe for us to view. Those responsible for our education have done their utmost to create an artificial community on the high school campus; a community which will demonstrate to us that it is better to "adjust" to an unsuitable society than to change the society into something in which we can live with dignity. If we are to lead meaningful lives, and do more than pass on our problems to the next generation, we shall have to break out of that artificial community. It is to that end that this is being written.

Kleiman's prescription for how to make education relevant is brief and to the point:

> The educative process should be a learning experience for both teacher and student. The teacher and his students should sit down and freely discuss the topics of the course and the method of study. The idea is workable. At least it worked for all the great philosophers.

Paul Goodman agrees:

> It seems stupid to decide a priori what the young ought to know and then try to motivate them, instead of letting the initiative come from them and putting information and relevant equipment at their service. It is false to assert that this kind of freedom will not serve society's needs—at least those needs that should humanly be served.[5]

Student unrest, revolt, and demands to be involved in the decisions affecting their own education and destiny represent a more potent force than any that has heretofore influenced teaching reform. Students are demanding in teachers' behavior the kinds of skills, attitudes, and understandings that the advocates of core curriculum have been recommending for years.

Conclusion

Whether he works with disadvantaged, privileged, or "just ordinary" students, in a core class, a conventional subject-matter course, or a special program, today's teacher must keep in mind these simple facts:

[5] Paul Goodman, "Freedom and Learning: the Need for Choice," *Saturday Review*, May 18, 1968, p. 73.

1. Every child who comes to school is different in some way and to some degree from every other child.
2. The only thing a child brings to school with which to make meanings out of all of his perceptions is his own unique experience.
3. Since he is unique and his experiences are unique, the meanings he makes will likewise be unique.
4. Every child needs self-enhancement and desires to learn, to know, to do.

Teachers who *act* on the basis of these facts accept students for what they are—the sum total of their experiences. They begin the educational process where the students' awareness and interests enable them to start. And they utilize all their professional skills to help students identify their interests and to plan with them for individual achievement. Whether these teachers are called core teachers is irrelevant, for what is needed in the world today is teachers who can facilitate learning and nurture humanness.

Unit IV

Developing a Core Program

Chapter 11

The Role of Central Office Personnel in Core Program Development

by Robert C. Hanes

Effective leadership is essential in any educational endeavor. It is especially crucial in the initiation and development of a program that differs significantly from conventional practice, such as the core curriculum. This chapter examines the leadership role of the school system's central office personnel, especially those responsible for curriculum coordination and supervision. Successful core programs have been developed in a number of the school systems under the direction of this chapter's author. Dr. Hanes is presently Assistant Superintendent for Secondary Education, Charlotte-Mecklenburg Schools, Charlotte, North Carolina.

There exist today various views concerning the role of central office personnel in organizing and administering curriculum programs. One popular view is that central office personnel should serve as expert resource people to support curriculum decisions made at the individual school level. The central office staff would serve as stimulators of new ideas, purveyors of information concerning innovative approaches to teaching, and proponents of various curriculum approaches. The actual decision as to whether to proceed with a curriculum innovation is left with the principal and his faculty. Once they decide to pursue the development of a program, the principal calls upon the central office staff for expert advice or logistical and technical support and for frequent consultive help. Thus a variety of curricular programs may be operating within the same school system in different schools. It is the job of the central office person to keep in touch with these varied programs and to share with other schools his observations concerning the more successful of them. Through this process, it is believed, central office staff may help other schools in the system adapt successful curriculum programs to their needs.

Another popular view is that the central office staff has the primary leadership responsibility for the initiation within the school system of action leading to curriculum change and development. Here it is assumed that curriculum decisions are made at the central office level and are implemented on a system-wide basis. Principals and classroom teachers may be involved heavily in the decision making process. The final decisions, however, are at the central office level, since the decisions reflect the curriculum direction toward which the entire school system will move. Even in this kind of central office arrangement a curriculum decision may not be implemented simultaneously in all schools within the system. It may be appropriate, in some cases, to reach a curriculum decision affecting all schools but to initiate curriculum action only in one or two schools. This gives the central office staff and others within the system an opportunity to work closely with a relatively small group of people. This arrangement also provides a concrete illustration of the curriculum design for principals and teachers of other schools to view carefully before they implement this design within their own schools. On the other hand, a curriculum decision which has been carefully planned and which has every likelihood of success built into it may be implemented at one time on a system-wide basis. The size of the system and readiness of the teachers to implement the curriculum change are but two important factors which must be considered by central office personnel before deciding whether a curriculum proposal should be implemented in a few schools initially or in all the schools at the same time.

How Central Office Staff May Operate

The views reflected in the remainder of this chapter are based upon the assumption that curriculum planning and direction is on a system-wide basis and that the central office staff members exercise crucial leadership in the planning and direction of curriculum change.

There are many values inherent in a curriculum organization which allows a school system to move in the same direction. It is obvious that this arrangement provides the broadest possible basis for support. The weight of authority, prestige, and school-wide resources may be brought to bear by the central office staff in implementing a system-wide curriculum plan. Such a broad move on a system-wide basis also emphasizes the likelihood of considerable philosophical unity as a basis for the curriculum change. A system-wide curriculum development also allows for the reduction of professional jealousy between various schools and their faculties. All schools are involved in the same curriculum activity and are moving toward the same goal.

Curriculum development on a system-wide basis carried out by positive leadership at the central office level brings to bear the larger resources of the school system on the curriculum area. This is especially obvious in the development of curriculum materials. Central office staff generally have a broader background of preparation as well as broader experiences, which tend to assure more professional materials. Central office personnel also have at their disposal the greater opportunity for securing outside consultative help as it is needed.

They are in a position to arrange more effective in-service programs than are principals and teachers in individual schools. Since public relations and public interpretation are often crucial to the success of a curriculum change, the larger resources of the central office may be in the best position to exercise these responsibilities. The news media tend to look toward the central office as a source of information. In addition, the central office is better prepared for the publication of its own interpretative materials and usually has a regular channel for the periodic distribution of such materials. Central office personnel are also more likely to be available for public-speaking engagements involving the interpretation of curriculum changes.

It must be assumed that central office personnel involved in curriculum development do not operate in a vacuum. Crucial to the success of system-wide curriculum development is the active involvement of principals and classroom teachers. Curriculum plans developed solely at the central office and then "sold" to principals and teachers have little real likelihood of success. Teachers and principals must be involved in the actual developing process of curriculum change. The initiative for the change, the source of many ideas, and the general leadership for the change may and probably should come from central office personnel, but central office staff are only partners with principals and teachers in the actual process of curriculum change. Any curriculum activity of central office personnel which ignores this important feature is not likely to be successful.

The development of a core program involves both curricular and administrative decisions at the central office level. It is, therefore, imperative that central office staff with both administrative and curriculum responsibilities be involved in the development of any core curriculum plans. If the central office is so organized that the instructional responsibilities are held by directors of specific subject areas, it is crucial that all subject areas directly involved within the core concept be included from the very beginning in the planning. These subject matter specialists should be involved to the degree that they both understand the purpose of the core program and appreciate ways in which other subjects may support it. It is certainly essential that subject matter specialists at the central office level be sufficiently involved so that they do not see the organization of the core program as a threat to their specific subject areas but rather as a device for strengthening and enlarging the impact of their subject areas upon pupils. Because the very structure of the core program involves certain administrative decisions, central office personnel with administrative authority must be involved in all planning. Such administrative support facilitates the actual implementation of any core program and is, indeed, essential if the program is to be begun smoothly.

Just as the possibilities are great in the core program begun on a system-wide basis, so are the risks. Failure on the part of central staff to perform their functions successfully will undermine the program in every school in the system. Once such a program is questioned, it is extremely difficult to restore the community's confidence. The values of a system-wide approach, however, are so great that this risk is certainly worthwhile.

Beginning a System-Wide Core Program

Any number of ways exist for initiating a core program on a system-wide basis. The alert central office leader will capitalize upon whatever appropriate arrangement presents itself. One of the best ways of stimulating interest in a core program is to search out a relatively small group of teachers whose grasp of the nature of the learning process has progressed to the point that the problem solving approach which crosses subject-matter lines is included in their own classrooms, regardless of the curriculum structure of the school system. These teachers, once identified, should be drawn together in informal discussion groups in order to build upon and strengthen their support of this type of teaching technique. Frequent arrangements for these teachers to visit core programs in nearby areas will further stimulate their interest. If any principals in the school system have expressed an interest in this type of curriculum arrangement, they should be included also in the early discussion groups. Frequently, a few principals may be found whose general understanding of the learning process is such that they may enthusiastically endorse the concept of core teaching if these concepts are presented to them in a positive and enthusiastic way.

Once an informal group of teachers and principals have worked together for awhile discussing curriculum matters in a general way, it may be desirable to suggest that the size of the committee be enlarged to include at least one teacher from most of the schools in the system which may eventually be involved in core programs. After this group has worked together for awhile, it is most important that a presentation be made to the principals of all of the schools in which core programs may be introduced. With proper preparation, the principals' group may decide to launch a plan for the implementation of a core program within their schools. This is more common at the junior high school level than at the senior high school level simply because of the greater general curriculum freedom that exists in most areas at this level.

The wise curriculum leader in the central office will have done a great deal of preparatory work with the principals before this topic is presented in any sort of formal way for study, review, and possible action. Participation in state, regional, and national core curriculum conferences may help measurably in building this kind of background. Periodic discussions with the principals concerning such topics as child growth and development, the nature of the learning process, and the structure of knowledge may be invaluable in the preparatory activities.

If the principals' group agrees to undertake activities leading to the implementation of a core curriculum, two other groups should be involved as quickly as possible. The first of these is the board of education. The members of the board should be advised that a curriculum reorganization is under way. If several members of the board are particularly interested in the curriculum area, it may be advantageous to include these board members as *ex officio* participants in curriculum planning sessions. Even if this is not possible, the members of the board should be made to feel that they are a part of the curriculum study.

Very early in the process, the principals and central office staff should move to include a much larger classroom teacher group in the study of the core curriculum and its possible implications. Each school faculty considering this curriculum approach should have representation on all system-wide curriculum committees. In addition, study groups should be created within the building faculties themselves. There seems to be a close relationship between the degree of involvement of classroom teachers in the planning process and the initial success of a core program. This kind of relationship probably exists in any type of curriculum reorganization. It does, however, seem to be especially obvious in the implementation of core programs.

Once a sufficiently large number of the professional staff is involved in the study of the core curriculum to the point that the beginning of a program seems imminent, central office leadership should initiate plans for these lines of action:

1. A plan for the organization of the schools in which a core program is to be implemented should be developed. This involves decisions concerning (a) the subject areas from which the program may draw subject matter, (b) the general approach to core curriculum itself—that is, whether the program should be completely unstructured, should have a high degree of structure, or something in between, (c) the relationship of the core class to other phases of the school curriculum, and (d) the cost to the school system for implementing these curriculum adjustments.

2. A plan should be developed for the preparation of curriculum materials. Experience seems to indicate that at least one curriculum guide or bulletin is most important if a new core program is to be introduced. More elaborate curriculum guides, as described in Chapter 9, may be prepared as the program develops.

3. A decision must be made concerning whether or not all the schools in the system start at the same time or whether the program will be begun in a few schools and will spread in an orderly way to other schools.

The plans for school organization require a great many administrative decisions which relate to the instructional program. Local school administrators as well as the school superintendent should be involved in making the decisions. The clearer the curriculum structure is worked out and the more specific the plan for the timetable for beginning a core program, the greater the likelihood of success. This is especially true in a large school system where direct communication is not always possible.

The development of curriculum materials for a new core program may serve at least two purposes. First, the provision of guidelines must be set so that all teachers move into the new program in approximately the same direction and have some security in knowing what the goals of the program are, what subject areas are involved, how course guides may be developed, how core classes may be organized, and so on. A second and sometimes more important value of the curriculum materials is that their preparation may provide extensive in-service training for many teachers prior to the implementation of the program. Although a great many teachers might resist specific in-service training activities which may prepare them for core teaching, these same teachers are very much interested in the development of curriculum materials and will often happily involve themselves in professional committee work leading to the preparation of curriculum bulletins. A core curriculum bulletin cannot be very well prepared without including a great deal of material concerning the teaching techniques involved in a core class. Working through the many topics that may seem appropriate for a core curriculum guide will help the teachers involved to get ready for their own teaching.

One popular device is to organize a graduate course in core curriculum in cooperation with a nearby school or university. A field project of the course may very well be the development of a curriculum guide for the school system. If such an important by-product is to be gained by the school system, it is not inappropriate that tuition charges for teachers be paid by the school system. Thus the teacher receives a sort of scholarship from the school system as well as certificate credit, while the school system receives the benefit of a prepared curriculum guide and a nucleus of teachers who have had specific preparation for core teaching.

There is no one best approach for developing a system-wide core program. These suggestions, however, all grow out of practical experience in major school systems. The most crucial factors seem to be (1) the involvement of large numbers of professional people, (2) the presence of active, effective leadership at the central office level, and (3) the preparation of a clear plan of action which may be easily interpreted.

Maintenance of Support and Direction

Once a core program is begun in several schools of a school system, its continued success depends to a considerable degree upon the sensitivity of the central office staff and principals to the need for supplying frequent interpretation of the program. In depth, the interpretation must be done by the individual school principal and his faculty. Such things as open house presentations, newsletters, Parent-Teacher Association programs, and student interpretation through frequent summaries of classwork are but a few of the activities that the individual school may carry on. At the central office level, care must be taken to see that the news media are provided frequently with interesting stories of core class activities and interviews with teachers and students. In addition, the central office ought to suggest periodically special programs for Parent-Teacher Association Council meetings, school board meetings, and civic club meetings dealing with the core program.

Frequently, the central office staff will support the implementation of the core program with a great deal of in-service activity and public interpretation. These efforts usually meet with a good deal of success and the program is effectively launched. It is often forgotten, however, that in just three years a whole new group of parents and students may be within the schools in which the core program is operating. These parents need to have the program interpreted for them just as carefully as did the parents who were in the program initially. The curriculum in a given school or a given grade level does not really become meaningful to many parents until their youngsters are actually involved. Although they may have heard generally about a program when their youngster was in an earlier grade, they do not follow in nearly so much detail the purposes of the program and its method of operating as they do when their own youngster is involved. Thus the interpretation of the core program to the entire community is an ever-continuing process which ought to be a regular part of the central office responsibility.

Another area of responsibility which the central office staff should feel concerning a core program is that of the selection of teachers. In most school systems a good deal of the initial interviewing of prospective teachers is done by central office personnel. During this process, central office personnel ought to be alert constantly to search out teachers whose interest and background have prepared them to be effective core teachers. In this process the central office staff must interpret accurately the program as it is operated and have some clear estimate of the kinds of skills which are needed by effective core teachers. The greatest single difficulty faced by core programs today is the lack of trained teachers who are capable of implementing the concept effectively. With this in mind, the single most important activity in which the central office staff may engage on a day-to-day basis is the recruitment and selection of qualified teachers. It is also helpful to prepare discriptive literature concerning the core program to be circulated with the brochures concerning the school system in general. Central office staff also ought to make regular contacts with teacher training institutions whose programs are designed to prepare core teachers.

One effective way that the central office staff may help in the recruitment of well-prepared core teachers is in cooperating with teacher training institutions for student-teaching placements. If the teacher training institution has a preservice program which offers broad preparation to the students, a student-teaching experience in a core class is a most effective way of identifying potentially successful core teachers. Representatives of the school system have an opportunity to observe the student teacher at work over a relatively long period of time in a variety of circumstances. At the same time, the student teacher has a great deal of practical preparation for teaching in the core class. Specifically, the student teacher has an opportunity to develop a basic grasp of the philosophy of the local school system. Many new teachers spend a good part of their first year coming to understand this. Thus the recruitment, selection, and placement of new teachers is enhanced by the district's active promotion of student teaching in core classes.

A third area in which the continuing support of the central office is important is that of evaluation of core programs. The central office staff usually has at its disposal testing materials and the personnel to administer various kinds of tests. Also available, generally, are trained staff members who have preparation for designing evaluation activities. This kind of data is essential both in the interpretation of what the core program is doing for the students and in pointing the direction for changing and strengthening the program. Too little has been done by school systems in the field of evaluation of core programs.

A fourth area which the central office may be supportive of the system's core program is in taking leadership for the selection, purchase, or preparation of appropriate curriculum materials. Central office staff have at their demand a much wider range of sources of material which may be appropriate for core classes. At the same time, central office staff are usually skilled at reviewing classroom materials of all sorts and may therefore look at a piece of material with practiced eyes. Since the purchase of material also has budgetary considerations, the central office staff are in the best position to know the district's financial resources and to discover ways in which essential pieces of material may be purchased and placed in the classroom. This kind of broad support from the central office staff also tends to make possible a basic collection of materials for all core classrooms regardless of the financial condition of the individual school or the students who attend that school.

The determination of the direction which a core program is moving in a school system is generally brought about by the interrelation of a number of factors. Chief among these are the interpretation and reinterpretation of the program, the selection and recruitment of teachers, the selection of instructional materials and the preparation of curriculum materials. Effective involvement of the central office staff in all of these activities gives them an opportunity to influence the direction in which a program will move.

In-Service Programs

The orientation of teachers during the inauguration of a core program is simply the beginning of in-service activities. The continued success of the program will require active in-service activities and programs, usually developed and directed at the central office level. The following represent some successful in-service activities:

1. Organize each school faculty so that there is a grade-level representative on a system-wide core committee. Plan intensive in-service activities for each grade level committee. Have each of these committee members repeat the in-service activities with the faculty members from the school which they represent. Much of the planning and many of the activities carried out by the system-wide committees should be initiated by the participants themselves. In this way, the in-service program is likely to deal with the expressed needs of the teachers.

2. Help the principals plan their schedules so that a number of core teachers have planning time together, i.e., a grade level, or a half a grade, or a third of the core teachers, etc. Prepare discussion guides which may be used by the principals in meeting with these teachers.

3. Invite outstanding consultants to the school system periodically for a system-wide meeting. These are usually of a more inspirational nature, but this does serve a valuable purpose. Often this is effectively related to a semisocial activity such as a banquet or a breakfast. Educational television is an excellent medium for this type of in-service activity.

4. Publish a core newsletter or bulletin for the system, in which many teaching ideas are shared. Use teachers to help publish the bulletin.

5. Encourage membership in state, regional, and national core curriculum organizations and arrange for staff members to participate regularly in their meetings. For information, write to The National Association for Core Curriculum, Inc., 404F Education Building, Kent State University, Kent, Ohio 44240.

6. Invite a state, regional, or national group to hold a conference in your system. Many of the activities involved in planning such a meeting have considerable in-service significance.

7. Conduct regular discussion sessions with the principals' group. This keeps the principals informed and involved. It also provides a valuable source of feedback to central office personnel.

Conclusion

A core curriculum may have its greatest impact if it is developed and implemented on a system-wide basis. The central office personnel have a key role to play in this process. This role, which involves both supervisory and administrative personnel, is, first of all, one of leadership. Adequate central office leadership will set the tone and direction of curriculum development. Such leadership will make possible community and school board acceptance. It will be able to arrange for financial support for materials and teachers. The central staff can effectively stimulate and direct the preparation of curriculum materials, the recruitment of teachers and the conducting of in-service programs. Finally, effective evaluation may best be carried out on a system-wide basis.

Chapter 12

The Role of the Principal
in Core Program Development

by Ralph E. Chalender

In a very real sense, responsibility for the total program of a school rests with the building principal. As a consequence, he plays a key role in the success of a core program. This chapter delineates some specific ways that a principal may provide leadership in curriculum development, guidance, evaluation, and public relations in a school that operates a core program. For many years Dr. Chalender was principal of Milburn Junior High School, Shawnee Mission, Kansas. He is now superintendent, School District 49, Overland Park, Kansas.

Curriculum change in American schools has been a slow process. Concerning change or modification in curriculum, Caswell's statement, made almost two decades ago, still rings true:

Change in the curriculum of American schools is not a fad nor is it an indication of a footloose, unstable educational system. Rather it is an essential feature of the social process essential to realization of the democratic goals to which our country is committed; it is an inevitable application of our prevalent conceptions of the nature of learning; it is a result of living in a culture which does not stand still and of which change is the most assured characteristic.[1]

In order to properly introduce a concept such as core curriculum to the school community, the principal must remind the public that change has been a major aspect in the growth of America. Changes in our culture have come rapidly since 1860. It is the task of education to teach citizens the nature of the changes that are taking place and to help them acquire skills which will enable them to make effective adjustments to new situations. Through its emphasis on contemporary problems, the core curriculum makes a major contribution to this endeavor.

[1] H. L. Caswell, and others, *The Changing Curriculum* (New York: Bureau of Publications, Columbia University, 1950), p. 20.

The Principal and Curriculum Development

The most important and challenging responsibility of the school principal is that of curriculum development. In the absence of a system-wide program of curriculum development, as described in Chapter 11, he should establish and supervise staff committees that develop general aims and objectives for the core program. He may wish to involve selected parents and students in this process. In any case, aims and objectives should be shared with parents and pupils in a variety of ways. Some schools find it effective to print them on report cards. Others present this information to parents at open meetings. Many core teachers write letters to parents explaining the general aims and objectives of each unit of work.

The partial listing below illustrates the kinds of aims and objectives which a principal could present to parents. Of course, objectives should be reevaluated and revised at frequent intervals.

Illustrative Core Program Objectives

I. The student should gain command of the common integrating knowledges and skills by developing the ability to:
    1. Speak easily, with freedom from gross errors.
    2. Organize and present ideas clearly and consecutively in oral language.
    3. Listen attentively to oral expression from others.
    4. Organize and express thoughts in written form.
    5. Read critically.
    6. Use source materials correctly.
    7. Develop one's spelling vocabulary.

II. The student should understand and practice desirable social relationships by developing:
    1. Trustworthiness, reliability, obedience, kindness, courtesy, and loyalty.
    2. Respect for authority.
    3. Leadership.
    4. Initiative.
    5. Worthwhile leisure-time activities.
    6. Respect for the rights and contributions of others.
    7. Cooperation.
    8. An appreciation for the interdependence of all people.
    9. An interest in civic functions.
   10. Moral and spiritual values.
   11. An appreciation for beauty.
   12. An appreciation for family life.
   13. Participation as a family member.
   14. Self-acceptance.

To be most useful to core teachers, curriculum guides should take the form of resource units. For purposes of this discussion the resource unit is defined as: "a systematic and comprehensive survey, analysis, and organization of the possible resources (e.g., personnel, problems, issues, activities, bibliographies) and suggestions as to their use, which a teacher might utilize in planning, developing, and evaluating a proposed learning unit in the classroom."[2]

Since the principal is responsible for the curriculum of the school, he must constantly supervise, guide, direct, and evaluate the development of resource units by committees of teachers, curriculum specialists, and other staff members. This is a never-ending process; units should be continuously reevaluated. The principal serves as a resource person, attempting to locate the latest and best curricular material. This should be an interest and a responsibility of the school principal even in schools which are large enough to employ curriculum specialists or in districts where curriculum guides are prepared on a system-wide basis.

A suggested organizational form which principals might use in developing resource units is as follows:

I. Statement of significance
II. Objectives
III. Outline of content
IV. Activities
    A. Introductory
    B. Learning
    C. Culminating
    D. Continuing
V. Sources of information
    A. Bibliographies
    B. Films
    C. Excursions
    D. Speakers
    E. Others
VI. Evaluation

The resource unit, with its outlines of suggested content, serves as a flexible guide in the development of a teaching-learning unit adapted to the needs of a particular class. Teacher-pupil planning is most important in developing the teaching-learning unit. This planning is a process in which the teacher and pupils plan learning experiences that will have meaning and interest for all concerned. It provides opportunities for pupils to use initiative, to assume responsibility, to develop skills in problem solving, to achieve a critical attitude toward their own work, and to learn through experience the art of working with others. In planning a teaching-learning unit and developing it with his class, the core teacher may follow these steps:

1. Preplanning by the teacher

[2] Harold B. and Elsie J. Alberty, *Reorganizing the High-School Curriculum,* 3rd ed. (New York: Macmillan, 1962), p. 422.

2. Presenting the introductory activities
3. Pupil-teacher planning
   (a) Setting up objectives
   (b) Organizing for work
        (i)   Groups or committees
        (ii)   Independent work
        (iii) Class chairman
        (iv)   Whole-class work
4. Carrying out the learning activities
5. Presenting culminating activities
6. Evaluating pupil progress and the success of the unit

Since learning experiences are chosen through teacher-pupil planning, the content of a unit is never twice the same. Nevertheless the principal may find it desirable to have staff members outline some of the subject matter which is included in the core program. Although not all core enthusiasts would agree, this writer is of the firm conviction that structured content is essential. A number of programs have been criticized because parents did not understand what subject matter was likely to be included in core units. Outlines such as those presented in Appendix D may help parents visualize how various subject areas can be drawn upon in a core curriculum. They should understand, of course, that in core there is no guarantee that specific content will be covered.

Some parents (and teachers, too!) do not accept the open-ended, problem-centered type of education that core represents. They may oppose a program if they believe that certain disciplines are being omitted. If this is the dominant sentiment in a community, it may be wise to begin first with a subject-area block or unified studies program. Success with one of these, coupled with continuing efforts to acquaint the entire community with the values of a core approach, may pave the way for eventual introduction of a core curriculum.

The Principal and Guidance

Guidance is an attempt to assist each pupil in realizing his individual worth. Individual worth can be centered in many fields; the individual should understand his social, emotional, physical, and mental abilities. An important aspect of the guidance program is the study of the individual in order to help him to understand himself and to deal with his needs and problems.

The very nature of the core class lends itself to guidance. The core class usually consists of two or more class periods, so the teacher has opportunity to know each pupil better than the traditional teacher, who sees the child for only one class period per day. Many years ago Strang called attention to the guidance opportunities of the core class in this statement:

The core curriculum provides for an ideal fusion of guidance and instruction. Under the core curriculum form of organization, one of the core teachers has major responsibility for knowing each student in the class and helping each to get the experiences he needs. The person in charge of a core group of thirty or forty pupils is appropriately called "teacher-counselor." He might well be called "teacher-counselor-curriculum reviser" because he is constantly getting suggestions for changes in the curriculum as he gains understanding of individual pupils.[3]

Whenever possible, a wise principal will employ core teachers who have educational background in guidance. In addition, regular in-service training meetings should be organized by the principal to discuss and to develop definitions, aims, objectives, and procedures for guidance in the core class. An example of what can be accomplished when the principal and core teachers work together is the following outline of guidance objectives developed by core teachers in the Shawnee Mission, Kansas, Schools.

Guidance Objectives

I. Satisfying Emotional and Social Needs
    A. Achieving secure relations with other people.
        1. Establishing satisfactory individual routines.
        2. Achieving status in group situations.
    B. Making constructive use of emotions.
        1. Achieving constructive expression of emotions.
        2. Securing balanced satisfactions in living.
    C. Achieving self-direction.
        1. Adjusting to personal strengths and weaknesses—emotional, physical, physiological, intellectual.
        2. Dealing with success and failure.
    D. Meeting sex needs.
        1. Establishing appropriate relationships with members of the opposite sex.
        2. Obtaining constructive social regulations with regard to sex.
II. Responsibility for Moral Choices
    A. Determining the nature and extent of individual freedom.
        1. Responding to authority.
        2. Acting upon a personal set of values.
    B. Determining responsibility to self and others.
        1. Preserving integrity in human relationships.
        2. Meeting the needs of others.
        3. Developing and using the potential abilities of self and others.
III. Growth in Social Participation
    A. Establishing effective social relations with others.
        1. Developing friendships and affectionate relationships.
        2. Responding to casual social contacts.
        3. Participating in social activities.

[3] Ruth Strang, *The Role of the Teacher in Personnel Work*, 4th ed. (New York: Bureau of Publications, Teachers College, Columbia University, 1953), pp. 44–45.

 B. Establishing effective working relations with others.
  1. Working with others on a common enterprise.
  2. Working with others in service group enterprises.
  3. Working in situations demanding guidance relationships.
 C. Deciding when to join a group.
  1. Deciding when group activity is desirable.
  2. Deciding on the nature and extent of group participation.
 D. Participating as a group member.
  1. Helping to formulate group policy.
  2. Selecting leaders.
  3. Helping to carry out group policies.
 E. Taking leadership responsibilities.
  1. Outlining preliminary plans needed to carry out leadership responsibilities.
  2. Securing cooperative participation of group members.
 F. Working with racial and religious groups.
  1. Understanding the basic purposes and characteristics of racial and religious groups.
  2. Safeguarding the rights and responsibilities of racial and religious groups.
 G. Working with socioeconomic groups.
  1. Determining the validity of distinctions between socioeconomic groups.
  2. Safeguarding the rights of socioeconomic groups.
 H. Dealing with groups organized for specific action
  1. Deciding when group action is justified.
  2. Securing cooperative interaction among groups. [4]

Such a core-based guidance program, supported and coordinated by a strong guidance department and operating under effective administrative leadership, is a potent force in the education of young people.

The Principal and Evaluation

The principal bears ultimate responsibility for the evaluation of all phases of the program of studies. Evaluation is not effective unless it is done with regularity, honesty and thoroughness.

During the past few years this writer, working with committees of core teachers, has developed the evaluative check list that is reproduced in Appendix E. It is used by each teacher when a unit of study has been completed. It is especially helpful to inexperienced teachers and those who are new to core.

Summaries of these reports are compiled by the principal, who then schedules

[4]"Guidance Objectives for the Unified Studies Class," unpublished curriculum material, Shawnee Mission, Kansas, Schools, 1960.

staff meetings to evaluate the work. The following in-service activities have been stimulated by this procedure:

1. All resource units have been revised.
2. An outstanding film catalogue has been compiled.
3. A teacher's guide for field trips has been written.
4. Many new maps, charts, and other materials have been recommended for purchase.
5. A great many hours have been spent developing techniques for better committee work.
6. Curriculum specialists have been secured to help teachers with subject matter areas.
7. Guidance specialists have been hired to assist core teachers with counseling.
8. A more complete and accurate cumulative pupil record system has been developed.
9. An elective course in beginning speech has been added to the ninth grade curriculum.
10. A great many suggestions have been made for improving instruction in creative writing and critical thinking.

Such are the positive gains that may be made when the principal accepts his responsibility for working with core teachers to develop good evaluative procedures. Without the leadership and enthusiasm of the principal, little can be accomplished. Of course, a check list should be revised often if it is to be most useful.

The greatest problem in using an evaluative tool of this type is the matter of time. Core teachers and principals alike are busy people. They need time to properly evaluate procedures and techniques. The principal should use every means in his power to schedule in-service training and committee meetings at a time when they will produce best results. This does not mean at seven o'clock in the morning or four-thirty in the afternoon. If projects such as these are important enough to be a part of the school program, they should be important enough to schedule during the class day.

The Principal and Public Relations

It is imperative that the principal properly inform and educate the school community about the program of studies offered by the school. Curriculum innovations such as core must be explained thoroughly from year to year. As the old saying goes, people are quite apt to be "down on" the things they are not "up on."

Good public relations, good teaching, and good school administration are inseparable. Public relations has been defined as the planned effort to influence and maintain favorable public opinion through acceptable performance, honestly presented, and with reliance on two-way communication.[5] In its simplest form it is an extension of human relations.

For the school principal, the basic meaning is that of good salesmanship. Education has become big business. A business has to cultivate good will. It has to sell itself and it has to sell its product, or the public will not buy. It also has to keep pace with the rapidly changing times, has to be willing and able to accept more responsibility, and has to be able to defend itself in the face of criticism. The school principal has the same selling job with the school's program of studies. If he is not a good salesman and is not sold on the program himself, little hope can be held for its success.

Understanding the core curriculum can come about only through communication. Good communication, be it person-to-person or through mass media, is the heart of public relations. Language used in communication is a primary tool. The jargon of the educational world too often interferes with the task of presenting the education story. To parody the canard about the Lowells and the Cabots, "Educators can talk only to educators."

Classrooms teachers are the largest group of educators, and their responsibility is great because of their direct line of communication with pupils, parents, and other teachers. Principals can develop enthusiasm and interest in the school's program, but the teacher meeting with the pupils each day is a major public relations agent. Teachers and principals alike should utilize the three keys to successful public relations suggested by the National School Public Relations Association: be interested, be positive, and speak simply.

Conclusion

Curriculum development, guidance, evaluation, and public relations are major responsibilities of the school principal. He also sets the tone of a school. Hopefully he functions like a core teacher in his relations with his staff, using every means at his disposal to liberate and cultivate the full creative potential of each individual. Much of the success of a core program depends upon the principal's ability to both demonstrate and communicate his enthusiasm and understanding of the core concept.

[5] Edwin Emery, Philip H. Ault, and Warren K. Agee, *Introduction to Mass Communications* (New York: Dodd, Mead, 1960), p. 330.

Unit V

The Future of the Core Curriculum

Chapter 13

Core Curriculum
in the Decades Ahead

by Gordon F. Vars

The editor here dusts off his crystal ball and tries to predict the future of the core curriculum concept. Not surprisingly, he concludes that core will continue to be a viable concept in the field of education and then offers some words of advice to those who wish to have a successful core program.

In previous chapters we have seen that the core curriculum approach to common learnings has a long history, as educational concepts go, and that it appears today in many forms. A sizable number of junior high and middle schools have block-time programs, some of them approaching a genuine core curriculum. Other junior and senior high schools are seeking to accomplish some of the objectives of core through interdisciplinary team teaching programs, often under such names as humanities or American studies. Independent study programs, too, whether or not they are directly related to a core class, often utilize procedures closely allied to the core concept. Core has been found to have special relevance in the middle school and to be amenable to at least one form of the nongraded approach. Finally, the stress on student involvement, typical of the core approach, is proving effective in programs for the culturally disadvantaged, whose rejection of the traditional curriculum is apt to be particularly intense.

But what of the future? Is the core curriculum concept likely to have continued relevance for schools in the decades ahead? To answer this question we must examine the core concept in relationship to the major determinants or foundations of the curriculum: the learner and how he learns, society, and the nature of organized knowledge.

The Learner

Human nature changes but slowly, we are told. No matter what shape the world of the future takes, youth of ages 10 through 17 will undoubtedly continue to evidence two major characteristics: vast differences between individuals and rapid changes in physiological and psychological make-up. As in the past, individual differences will reach their peak during the junior high or middle school years, where different rates of maturation lead to classes composed of "men, women and children." Each grows according to his own timetable, which varies from month to month and which is not even the same for all aspects of his development. Teachers quite literally face a different group of children each time they meet a particular class.

Arising in part from internal causes and in part from the demands and expectations of society, young people have identifiable personal-social needs or developmental tasks. Two of these will assume even greater importance in the future: the need for self-understanding and the need for the skills, habits, and attitudes essential for good human relations. Adolescence in our culture frequently brings with it a crisis of identity, and the increasing complexity of our society can only compound the difficulty of establishing a stable self-concept. Human relations, too, become increasingly crucial in a world whose population expands exponentially at the same time that it is rent with conflicts that threaten the extermination of the race. Added to this is the adolescent's traditional preoccupation with peer relations during this life stage, when he is temporarily alienated from both child and adult society. Human relations and self-understanding will be areas of major concern to young people for many years to come.

Learning

Contemporary discussion of learning bristles with such words as discovery, inquiry, critical thinking, and the like. Although they differ to some extent, they all assume that some kind of problem solving is under way. Thus they lend psychological support to the problems approach to instruction that has long been advocated by educators, especially those associated with the core movement. It is difficult to conceive how learning theorists in future decades can avoid continued attention to these processes, although their conceptual tools will no doubt become more refined.

Another concept prominent in some contemporary learning theories has to do with the learner's perceptions of the world. Many psychologists and educators assert that the change in behavior we call learning takes place primarily because the learner's perception has changed, at least at the higher levels of intellectual functioning that are the school's main concern. Direct involvement of the learner in identifying his present perceptions and in evaluating their adequacy are essential to effective learning, according to this view of learning. Even psychologists who place much reliance upon conditioning and reinforcement recognize that whether the stimulus provides positive or negative reinforcement depends upon how it is perceived. It is unlikely that any learning theory developed in the future will minimize the importance of either problem solving or the learner's perceptions.

Society

Predicting the shape of society in the future is extremely presumptuous. Yet we can be reasonably sure that changes brought about by social forces such as technology will continue to accelerate. Likewise, it seems inevitable that society will continue to be beset by major social problems—unless, of course, the millennium arrives. Problems such as the population explosion, war, and human rights seem destined to intensify as the years go by. Complicating mankind's attempts to solve these problems is a plurality of values that is highlighted by population mobility and modern communications media. Disagreements may be trivial or profound, but they will probably intensify as the world's people become more closely linked. The world-wide consensus that may evolve from this interchange seems far in the future, if, indeed, it is possible at all.

Knowledge

Jerome Bruner deserves credit for making it once again respectable to give organized knowledge its rightful place as a basic consideration in curriculum building. Whether or not one accepts his premise that instruction should reveal the structure of the various disciplines, it is true that schools have a responsibility to give students some conception of how man organizes and expands his knowledge. Specialization has proved to be a most powerful tool in the generation of new knowledge, and the decades ahead should be no exception. At the same time, scholars from many disciplines decry the narrow vision that extreme specialization may bring. Marshall McLuhan puts it this way:

> Specialization won't work any more as a means of learning. The only technique today for obtaining depth is by interrelating knowledge, whether it be in physics or anthropology or anything else. When a man attempts to study anything, he crosses the boundaries of that field almost as soon as he begins to look into it.[1]

Needed are both scholars and ordinary citizens who are generalists, who can see life whole. The well-documented knowledge explosion, brought about in part by specialization, also demands the kind of person who can discover the broad principle lurking behind the mountain of detail.

Implications for the Core Curriculum

If the preceding forecast is at all accurate, what kind of curriculum is indicated for the decades ahead? Does the core concept have a role to play in future educational designs?

First, it must be recognized that the schools cannot provide the whole of

[1] Marshall McLuhan, "From Instruction to Discovery," *Media and Methods*, Vol. 3 (October 1966), p. 8.

education. Among the many tasks which the schools could assume for society, the development of intellectual competency has been proposed as their top priority assignment. This should not be misconstrued as the *only* purpose of the institution, but all others should be seen as contributing to this primary function.[2] Considering the current state of mankind, the very best rational thought is demanded if he is to avoid disaster. This "citizenship" application of intellectual competence is matched by the importance of sound thinking in each individual's personal realm. To be fully functioning as an individual demands, among other things, maximum development of intellectual competence.

If intellectual development is accepted as the primary goal of the school, how may it best be accomplished? Since problem solving is vital in the learning process, and problems seldom fall completely within a single subject area, the curriculum must provide some opportunities for students to sharpen their intellectual powers by examining problems "in the round." Such a multifaceted examination of problems also would be ideal for both clarifying and exploiting the relationships among the scholarly disciplines. To date, core appears to be the best curriculum pattern for accomplishing these purposes. Whether students had best examine problems under the guidance of one teacher or several is unsettled at the moment, although Tompkins' experience, reported in Chapter 4, suggests that the mechanics of team operation may get in the way of effective problem-centered teaching.

That the problems examined in core should not be limited exclusively to those of society is indicated by our examination of both learning theory and the nature of the learner. The learner's perceptions must be used as the starting point of rational examination of a problem, and the perceptions of young people are profoundly influenced by their current needs. Young adolescents, especially, must see themselves as making some progress toward self-understanding and effective human relations before they can free much energy for examination of society's problems. The necessity for value clarification, too, permeates both the personal concerns and the social problems youth faces in our contemporary culture.

Since many of the personal problems and concerns of youth also have implications for society as a whole, it does not seem wise to separate the two into a so-called "guidance" class and a "social problems" class, as found in some schools today. A problem-centered curriculum devoted to examination of both the personal and the social dimensions of an issue is what is needed, and these specifications fit the core curriculum to a T.

In summary, certain future dimensions of society, the learner, organized knowledge, and learning theory point to the core curriculum as a most appropriate vehicle for accomplishing the school's primary task of intellectual development. At the same time, emphasis on student involvement and concern for feelings and beliefs, evident at many points throughout this book, reflect a parallel regard for the emotional component of human life. Further arguments for core may be

---

[2] *The Intellectual Responsibility of the Junior High School: A Statement of Position by the Staff of the Junior High School Project*, rev. ed. (Ithaca, N.Y.: School of Education, Cornell University, 1966).

derived from other school purposes such as exploration, guidance, socialization, or development of basic skills, as elaborated in earlier chapters.

It must be made perfectly clear, however, that core is not the whole of the curriculum, nor even the whole of common learnings. Responsibility for intellectual development, for example, must be shared with many other elements of the school program. Nor is problem-centered instruction the most efficient way to acquire specialized knowledge or to discover the basic structure of a discipline. Carefully developed courses outside the core class are required for additional common learnings and for specialized preparation. Nongraded sequences in such fields as mathematics and foreign language are needed to make optimum provision for individual differences and for variable rates of learning in these fields. Individual differences, the need for self-understanding, and social problems such as increased leisure time call for a broad program of exploratory experiences and student activities. In other words, core is conceived as only a part, albeit a very important part, of the school curriculum.

Some Admonitions

As desirable as the core curriculum may be, the development of such a program should not be undertaken lightly. In addition to the many recommendations made throughout this book, the following words of advice may be in order.

1. Do not be satisfied with half-way measures. Block-time, back-to-back scheduling, or interdisciplinary team teaching are merely first steps toward the kind of problem-centered core program required to meet the demands of the future. Educators may need to move slowly, but they must move toward the full-fledged core concept if they are to reap in full the advantages inherent in this curriculum design. Interdisciplinary and combined-subjects approaches have their merits, but they are cursed with the same devotion to mastery of subject matter *per se* that makes much conventional instruction so repelling to students. And for the sake of all who labor in the educational vineyard, do not call it "core" unless it really is!

2. If you would be an educational leader, exert your leadership. Chapters 11 and 12 described how effective leadership can bring about and sustain a core program. Today's educational leader must be neither autocratic nor laissez faire. Instead, he must accept his role as a dynamic change agent, using all the tools of modern administrative theory and research to induce the staff, students, parents, and the community at large to move in the desired direction. Research indicates that teachers who appear at first unwilling to change usually find that they like the new way of doing things after they have tried it a while. Much of the drudgery of administration is being taken over by computers, paraprofessionals, national and regional administrative service groups, and the like. Administrators, be they superintendents, curriculum directors, supervisors, principals, or department heads, may never have a more propitious time to exert their leadership to institute a core program.

3. Core teachers are made, not born, and most of them are made on the job. One vital responsibility of the school administrator is to see that the program is properly staffed, and this requires both careful selection and thorough and continuous in-service education. Whether a teacher bears an elementary or a secondary certificate, comes from a teacher's college or a liberal arts college, is old or young, man or woman, has or has not received special training for core teaching, he must be given constant support and encouragement. Much of this can come from his colleagues, but the support of the administrator is crucial. Schools unwilling to invest heavily in in-service development programs should not attempt core or any other curriculum innovation.

4. Stay on the growing edge of the profession. Core withers and dies if it is cut off from sources of new ideas. Core teachers must do their best to keep informed of major developments in the supporting disciplines: history, sociology, anthropology, economics, political science, geography, literature, linguistics, and so on. Perforce much of this will be through summaries and interpretations provided by curriculum study projects, regional educational laboratories, university extension services, and professional associations. That he chooses to instruct youth by means of the problems approach should not make the core teacher any less a scholar. It does impose upon him the task of searching through the minutiae that frequently concern scholars in the disciplines to locate the big ideas that can illuminate and clarify the great human problems dealt with in a core class.

That core teachers must keep up to the minute in their knowledge of youth goes without saying. They also must keep in touch with developments on another dimension—curriculum and instruction. Curriculum theorists seek to apply insights from many disciplines and applied fields to improve curriculum design and development. As they devise plans that appear to offer advantages, they should be carefully tried out and evaluated in the schools. It is no credit to the profession, for example, that the core-plus-disciplines idea proposed over a decade ago has yet to see a major trial in the schools. It may be that the curriculum design proposed by Broudy, Smith, and Burnett will suffer a similar fate.

Exciting developments in instruction revolve around both theory, as represented by Bruner's *Toward a Theory of Instruction,* and techniques for analyzing the teaching process. Processes such as Flanders' interaction analysis give teachers a tool for profoundly reshaping their classroom behavior, especially when used in conjunction with modern videotaping equipment. Since the interaction between teacher and students is critical in a core class, core teachers should be the first to capitalize on the research and experimentation along this line.

New instructional media, such as 8-mm film loops and various sophisticated forms of programmed instruction, represent another growing edge of the profession with which educators must keep in touch. At the same time a core staff must organize to keep up with the torrent of more conventional materials coming from the publishers.

Conclusion

Just as the core concept is not necessarily passé because it has been around a while, neither must it go on forever simply because it once served a useful purpose. The ultimate test of any idea is its adaptability to changing circumstances. After more than forty years on the educational scene, the core idea still has much to offer. How well it fulfills its promise depends upon the wisdom with which it is applied by members of the educational profession.

Part II

Current Block-Time, Core, and Interdisciplinary Team Programs

Unit I

Block-Time and Core Programs

1

The General Education Program
at Oneida Junior High School,
Schenectady, New York

by Harvey Handel, Principal

The "general education"[1] program was introduced at Oneida Junior High School in 1931. At the time the school housed grades K through 9. Harry Linton and Roy Abbey, two forward-looking educators from Schenectady, working with the faculty and consultants from several colleges, planned this innovation. The stated philosphy was, "We are attempting to discover the needs of our children and then to help them solve the problems which grow out of their needs." Although grades K through 6 moved into a new elementary school building in 1955, and the philosophy has been expanded to keep up with the changing times, the general education program has continued without interruption for thirty-six years.

At first, general education included English, social studies, and arithmetic in grade 7 and English and social studies in grade 8. The primary purpose of the curriculum was to provide a common body of important experiences for all pupils, emphasizing social values and social problems. It continued, for at least one year, the self-contained classroom of grades 6 and below, helping to span the difficult years of early adolescence when the student was poised between the child-centered curriculum of the lower grades and the subject-centered curriculum of the high school. The advantages, as the planners envisioned them, were (1) freedom from subject matter patterns, (2) emphasis upon group problem solving, (3) opportunity for pupil-teacher planning, (4) provision for a daily block-of-time, and (5) greater attention by the teacher to the guidance function.

At present the general education program enrolls the entire seventh grade of 261 students and the entire eighth grade of 266 students. It includes five periods of English per week, five periods of social studies, and two and one-half periods of reading for those who do not take French. Classes are scheduled in successive periods whenever possible. The same teacher has responsibility for two groups of children, one seventh-grade and one eighth-grade. About half the students have the same teacher for two years.

[1] "General education" in this report is used synonymously with "block-time."

193

The reader may be helped to understand the significance of a general education program to this school by a brief description of Oneida Junior High. Nearly 850 students share this facility, which was built in 1923. Current utilization is 98 percent. A major addition and complete renovation has recently been approved by the Board and will be completed in the fall of 1968. The student body is heterogeneous in the classical sense of the definition—dissimilar. The school serves the children of the affluent and the deprived, the educated and the uninformed, the ambitious and the unmotivated. The median IQ of the student body fluctuates between 104 and 108, but has been moving downward in recent years. Oneida is widely recognized for its innovating spirit, its excellent faculty, its community support, and its successful graduates. *Esprit de corps* is apparent in the enthusiasm of the faculty, who give willingly and unselfishly to improve the educational offerings.

My observation of types of general education programs in the decade from 1950 to 1960 indicate that (1) more large schools were making use of this scheduling arrangement than small schools; (2) traditional practices prevailed in about three-fourths of all classes using general education as an administrative device, rather than as a curriculum innovation; (3) there was a better counseling relationship, since the general education teacher was invariably a homeroom teacher responsible for the guidance function; (4) the definite growth in popularity was most marked at the junior high level; it never gained a real foothold in senior high, or even ninth grade; (5) there was some evidence appearing that a block-time or a general education program would become the predominant pattern of organization in most junior high schools.

Three new forces, of which you are all aware, began to appear about this same time: (1) sputnik, with an outcry for intellectualism based on academic excellence, (2) team teaching, bolstered by more flexibility in space utilization and pooling of teacher resources, and (3) the middle school, which began to have an effect on school organization. Sputnik panicking is no longer an essential force. However, the advantages of team teaching and the philosophy of the middle school have had a significant impact on curriculum organization with an increased vitalization of general education and block-of-time.

We are currently using the team-teaching approach with three advanced sections of ninth-graders, representing about one-fourth of that grade. They are taught by an English teacher and a social studies teacher within a double-period block of time.

At Oneida, the community has accepted the philosophy that has been prevalent since 1931. There has never been any strong pressure from either within or without to change, although, a citizens' committee recently recommended that the general education program be abandoned in all Schenectady junior high schools, arguing that it spreads thin the talents of the teachers and is too demanding in outside preparation.

The faculty of the school is carefully selected on a basis of training and commitment to general education. Those who find that teaching their major has more personal appeal move into ninth grade or senior high (if they are competent). Those who are caught up in the excitement of teaching in a general education program take additional training and eventually receive dual certification. Since 1931 not one teacher to my knowledge has been prevented from teaching in the general education program at Oneida School because of certification requirements.

What about the mathematics? It remained in the general education block until quality measurement studies made by the writer indicated that a serious weakness did exist when youngsters were compared on various achievement tests and were found lacking in arithmetic and problem solving skills commensurate with their ability. The nationwide drive to upgrade the training of science and mathematics teachers was having its effect on the quality of teachers who were available for employment. Oneida employed highly skilled mathematics teachers, some of whom were science majors in their undergraduate work. Movement toward discovery-centered teaching, instead of rote learning of both scientific and mathematical concepts, indicated that two distinct types of general education specialists were needed—the English-social studies teacher, and the math-science teacher. Based on the needs of children and the wishes of the teachers, the math-science general education program was created. Unlike English and social studies, it never gained school-wide acceptance. It also was apparent that all teachers in the school had to commit themselves to continuous graduate-level studies in order to keep up with the proliferation of knowledge. A positive financial reward system instituted by a forward-looking Schenectady Board of Education encouraged the continuation of this process.

A report of the observations of the faculty may be of interest. Most indicate that it is a greater challenge to teach fresh material each period rather than to repeat lessons four or five times a day. Teachers find the transitional shock from a child-centered curriculum to a subject centered curriculum is gradual for the students with few, if any, developing psychological resistance to junior high. When it is functioning at optimum, each teacher meets only thirty new students a year and has a total of only sixty different students daily. Teachers who cannot operate on a problem-solving approach may use the class time in a more traditional manner (subject-centered), but those who enjoy the large teaching unit technique find this arrangement to be advantageous. Everyone reports that it reduces the fragmentation of knowledge and is thereby more in keeping with the liberal arts tradition. It also tends to bring about a faculty which willingly and systematically takes cognizance of the impact of education on the learner because of their prolonged association with the child and his parent. The teacher who receives real satisfaction in teaching within a given area (government, social problems, mythology, literature, arts) has an outlet by making a contribution to our humanities program.

Unlike core, we have never attempted complete integration of subject matter based on a problem-solving technique. We take this position consciously because we feel that total integration ignores the fact that each discipline functions subject to its own methods of investigation and syntactical considerations. The master schedule makes it possible to integrate, correlate, plan and execute this plan in the time available. Yes, there is a separate curriculum for each discipline! Teachers are constantly urged to plan in large units and to bring together in every possible way the relatedness of their subjects. They are not, however *forced* to do it.

You may rightfully ask if the organization is achieving its purpose. Quality measurement studies indicate that the school has a higher achievement index than its neighbors, which cannot entirely be explained by a higher potential of intellect. A catalogue of school activities included field trips, visits to industry, the theatre, museums, geological and ecological areas; visits by speakers, debaters, guest assemblies and organized symposiums; involvement in the life of the community by service, financial contributions and personal commitment; leadership-building activities including student government, sports participation and interschool programs; visits to the city, county and state seats of government; participation in prekindergarten observations and discussions; presentations of major works of drama and music, both vocal and instrumental; trips to New York City, Boston, and other places of cultural interest; school-wide functions such as science fair, sports night, fine arts—industrial arts night; writing experiences for the anthology, the student newspaper, and the "famous person's days." When these are added to the countless social and vocational activities and the advanced and enrichment courses, it indicates that the students and the faculty are on the move, participating to the fullest extent in a well-rounded educational experience. All of these activities cut across subject matter lines and conventional single-period time blocks, although the seeds of their origin usually are planted within one subject area. It is the writer's contention that only the general education philosophy and organization, wherein teachers have the time and responsibility for more than one discipline, can offer these enriching experiences, which expose Oneidians to the full spectrum of educational thought and action.

General education programs create problems which may be knotty but not insurmountable. It is true that trained teachers are in short supply. Scheduling is difficult. Searching for scholars for the junior high who are also good teachers is a frustrating experience. The explosion in subject matter makes it extremely difficult for the teachers to keep up with daily discoveries as they appear in the professional literature. The general education teacher is usually not trained to diagnose reading problems. The attraction to lucrative industrial positions of teachers and college graduates who are scholarly in their field is discouraging to all administrators.

Thirty-six years of experimentation? Not really! We don't consider this approach to be experimental. Rather, it is a way of life, and we believe the time and subject-matter arrangement encourages intellectual growth. That is its function and to that end we are truly dedicated.

Are there other ways to arrange the curriculum? The answer is obvious. It behooves professional educators to plan strategy and tactics to capitalize on the advantages and to minimize the disadvantages of any system they devise. In this arrangement, tailored to the needs of the community and attuned to the philosophical position of the faculty, lies one demonstration of the true strength of the American educational system.

2

The Block-of-Time Program
at Hampton Junior High School,
Detroit, Michigan

by Douglas J. Kolb, Block-of-Time Teacher
(Presently Administrator, Irving Elementary School,
Detroit)

The block-of-time program at Hampton included the academic areas of social studies and English in grades 7 and 8. I had three groups of children, who were scheduled to my room each day for two consecutive fifty-minute periods. Two of these groups were what might be termed "honors classes" (students with above average IQ and performance), and one group was what could be called "average." Perhaps the most unique aspect of these groups was the fact that they were predominately Jewish in background. However, each group was racially mixed. Although all students at Hampton participated in block-of-time programs, the number of students scheduled to my room was about 109. At Hampton, as is true in most junior high buildings in Detroit, I, as a teacher, was pretty much on my own to conduct the block-of-time program as I saw fit.

Of utmost importance in beginning my program was informing the parents in the community what I expected to do in the classroom as well as out. To accomplish this, I held a tea at school in which I informed them of my approach to block-of-time, what I expected of their children in school, and what they could expect of me. Primarily I explained that this kind of programming provided a span of time each day for the teacher to be with pupils longer than one period. This afforded more personalized guidance for the student, both educationally and personally. Further, it was my desire that (1) children would share in all decisions affecting the class and their program in my room, (2) children should be actively involved daily, and not just from time to time, and (3) students should learn to help each other cooperatively.

To accomplish these goals, each class set up its own organizational framework, which could be best described as a miniature democracy in action. As the students and I progressed, working committees were established, which included

a social committee, a class council for overall program planning, a trip committee, and an instructional materials committee. These committees met both
before and after school, as well as during class time. Membership on each
committee was by class vote, but it also was regulated so that all class members
had an opportunity to participate on one committee during a given term of the
school year. My role as a teacher was that of a consultant (participating) both to
individuals and to the class.

Two examples of the operation of these committees are worth mentioning.
First, the class council felt it was necessary to arrive at some basic goals for the
term around which the class would function. After many meetings, this committee came up with the following objectives for their program, which were later
reviewed, discussed, and approved by the class.

Social Studies

1. Improve our awareness of responsibility, concern for others, open-
   mindedness, creativeness, and cooperation as desirable values to possess.
2. Study geography as it affects man and his environment.
3. Analyze the growth of our country and its relation to our world today.
4. Discuss and review current local, state, national, and world issues and
   problems.
5. Gain experience in the democratic process.
6. Encourage and help each other achieve a basic understanding of our
   American heritage, thought, attitudes, and values.

English

1. Work with each other in the refinement of our selection of books.
2. Promote a conscious effort to write with understanding and clarity.
3. Provide an opportunity to improve oral expression, discussion techniques, and overall appreciation of reading for enjoyment and for
   improvement.
4. Work toward improving presently acquired skills and knowledge in
   English.
5. Gain proficiency in the use and application of the English language.

Second, the class council, during the city elections, felt it was important to
hear local candidates give their positions in person. After much committee work
and class discussion, this committee set about contacting all of the candidates
running for office or seeking reelection in Detroit, requesting them to come and
speak to the students. They were successful in getting 75 percent participation
from the candidates. The list of speakers was impressive, including such people
as Mayor Cavanaugh, his opponent Walter Shamie, all of the judges seeking
reelection, and a majority of the councilmen such as Mel Ravitz and Nicholas
Hood. Other Committees helped make this venture a success. The *social
committee* made all the arrangements for the speakers while in school, including

a welcoming group, contacts with the staff, a tea, and other amenities. The *trip committee* handled the necessary transportation problems, such as a map of the school location, getting in and out of the school parking facilities, and escort service when necessary. The *instructional materials committee* provided all setups for recording the speeches, making sure of audio (mike) arrangements, speaker's platform, publicity, and student seating. After each speech, total class participation took place in evaluating candidates' and incumbents' positions and manner of presentation. Letters of thanks were written by class members designated by the *social committee.*

Similar procedures were followed in attacking all problem areas. The academic areas of social studies (early American history) and English were never separated into individual disciplines, but rather were considered as elements of a whole—life. For example, one current event, the election, contained many elements of English. How can one discuss candidates and issues without using English to convey ideas, to discuss the topics, to evaluate speakers' presentations? We must know words and their pronunciations as well as their meanings, practice listening skills, and be alert to campaign oratory.

To me, and, more important, to the class, the above process was really what the block-of-time was set up to achieve: (1) A unification of structure in the disciplines without the discipline itself really losing its identity. (2) A "self" approach to learning, with leadership demonstrated by the teacher and the students in the most effective and efficient way possible. For the teacher, leadership was based upon an understanding of the disciplines as well as an awareness of the development of children. Particularly, the teacher must be aware of the incredible amounts of energy, resourcefulness, and ability that junior high students are capable of displaying. (3) A guiding of students toward sharing in the decision-making process both as individuals and collectively. Duties, responsibilities, and working together in groups were emphasized at the same time that individuals were growing in their own independence.

3

Basic Education in the Dade County Public Schools, Miami, Florida

A. The Program at Kinloch Park Junior High School

by Leona Goldweber, Assistant Principal

Basic Education at Kinloch Park includes language arts, social studies (civics, geography, sociology, economics), art, and music organized in a two-hour uninterrupted block of time. The Dade County *Basic Education Guide,* last revised in 1965, lists the following suggested units:

Our Educational Community: Orientation
Our Living Community: Social Foundations
Our Local Community: Miami and Dade County
Our State Community: Florida
Our National Community: The United States
Our World Community: The United Nations

All seventh-grade students are involved. Cubans (non-English speaking) are scheduled in three-hour blocks in a similar program with emphasis on English as a second language.

The program is staffed and organized in the following manner. One teacher handles two two-hour blocks, plus teaching one other subject. All Basic Education teachers have a common planning period. There are eight teachers involved plus our art teacher, music teacher, the seventh-grade guidance counselor, and developmental reading teacher.

The neighborhood around Kinloch is predominantly middle class; about 40 percent are Spanish speaking although about 20 percent of this number are bilingual. Our neighborhood is changing; apartment houses are now common. Many people who pioneered the neighborhood have moved to suburban areas or apartments.

Kinloch Park has had this program in existence for seventeen years. Our plans for the future are to keep the sparks alive. Educators have finally endorsed as good practices what we have been doing all along.

The purpose of the program is to offer the best possible educational experiences for *all* boys and girls. The nature of the program allows for variety of experiences and explorations to meet individual differences. We believe that the advantages are:

1. Children are exposed to an integrated subject-type experience.
2. Grouping is heterogeneous, allowing pupils of all social levels to rub elbows.
3. Teachers plan together and share materials.
4. Pupils learn good study habits.
5. The program does not superimpose an artificial environment but takes into account pupils' physical and mental growth.
6. It allows teachers to know pupils better since they teach fewer pupils.
7. The program is guidance-oriented.
8. Children learn democratic procedures through individual, and group procedures. Many pupils going from this school to high school assume leadership roles.

The disadvantages, in our experience, are:

1. We cannot hold teachers in the program. Last year seven out of eight were new teachers. Most seventh-grade teachers in our program have gone into special programs or into administrative or supervisory positions. The program is excellent for developing teaching leadership but hard on us.
2. Few colleges train core teachers. Unless a school has good leadership to train teachers on-the-job, the program is weak or fails.

B. The Development of Special Curriculum Materials for Language-Disadvantaged Students

by Hy Stanton, Curriculum Writer, and Herbert C. Bloom, Former Project Director

This report describes a project of the Dade County Curriculum Development Laboratory. Funded under P.L. 89-10, Title I, the project produced high interest, low readability level materials, primarily for seventh-grade students classified as educationally disadvantaged in language proficiency. The staff consisted of a director, four teacher-writers drawn from several subject areas, and an illustrator. Consultants to the project included social studies, language arts, science and mathematics supervisors. Feedback from teachers, students, and supervisors helped to shape the final products.

The materials represent an expansion of the objectives for seventh graders of the Dade County Basic Education Bulletin, 10B, and the Language Arts Bulletin, 6a. The concept level of these objectives remains the same, but the readability level has been lowered by using the Dale-Chall readability formula and word list. Instructional objectives are stated in behavioral terms and test suggestions directly reflect the objectives of each lesson.

An essential subsidiary objective of the project was to support the Basic Education Program principle of integrating language arts and social studies in an interdisciplinary approach. This was accomplished by using social studies concepts as a base for listening, speaking, reading and writing.

The student population included in the project met the criteria established to identify Title I schools. Approximately two thousand Dade County students are using the materials at this time, and an in-service course is being conducted to orient new teachers in their use.

The materials consist of three textbooks, each with accompanying teacher's manuals, and a loose-leaf binder which contains twenty-nine activities.

Book I, entitled *No Man Is an Island,* concerns the family and the Community, with chapters such as "Learning from Our Families," "My Family Needs Me," "Give and Take," and "Voices of the Neighborhood."

Book II, entitled *A Corner of the U.S.A.*, consists of five chapters on the topographical, historical, sociological, governmental, and economic aspects of Dade County.

Book III, entitled *The Twenty-Seventh Star*, consists of five chapters on the topographical, historical, governmental and economic aspects of the State of Florida.

Each chapter opens with a brief description of what the chapter is about, with several questions serving as clues to its essence. Next a visual related to the theme of the chapter is presented to stimulate the student's curiosity as well as to guide him to verbalize.

Each textbook contains stories written and developed by the project staff, language exercises using the linguistic approach, additional reading selections, and suggested readings from *Adventures for You*, (Harcourt, Brace & World). The concepts of social studies and language arts are interwoven, and science and mathematics concepts are utilized where applicable.

Original stories developed by the staff center around each chapter's theme. The stories in Book III are continuous, based on a single thread. Major vocabulary for the stories is drawn from the Dale-Chall reading list. All language activities provide varied opportunities for children to speak and write standard English. Appropriate pictures accompany each story, and maps, graphs, and charts provide experiences in interpreting data.

The final page of each chapter, referred to as the "concept discovery" or summary page, may be used for evaluation purposes by the teacher. Each book contains a list of situations and a poem incorporating the concepts of the text, which also may be used as a means of evaluation.

Each teacher's manual contains the rationale, concepts and "instructional intents" (objectives), a bibliography, reproduced pages from the pupils' text, pupil activities, and suggested teaching techniques. Follow-up activities, audio-visual aids, field trips, resource personnel, map skills, and projects also are suggested.

Each of the twenty-nine activities in the loose-leaf binder contains two parts, a teacher's guide and student's pages. The teacher's guide is organized as follows:

Intents. Statements in behavioral terms which express the desired social studies and language arts outcomes.

Description. An overview of the activity.

Materials. A listing of required tangible items.

Prerequisites. A statement of skills or knowledge the student should have before the activity can be effective.

Procedure. Step-by-step development of the activity.

Optional activities. Some additional things to do if interest, resources, and time permit.

Test suggestions. Some suggested multiple-choice test items to asses the accomplishment of the social studies and language arts intents.

Seventh-grade classes in eleven junior high schools were used to test the effectiveness of the new materials. Only seven of the eleven schools had a true Basic Education Program, that is, with the pupils of a class in a two-period time-block with one teacher for both social studies and language arts instruction. Both experimental and control groups consisted of classes that were below grade level academically but above the remedial level in reading skills. The control classes did not use the new materials but were expected to follow a course of study derived from the Basic Education Bulletin, 10B. The classes in the experimental group were exposed to one of three methods of instruction:

1. Exclusive use of the new materials; no other written materials used *except* those specifically listed in the pupil's books.
2. Use of new materials in combination with other materials.
3. Use of new materials in *novel ways* created by individual teachers.

The selection of teachers, the level and number of classes, and the method(s) to be used in each school were left to the discretion of the school principal.

A multiple-choice test was used to compare the achievement of experimental and control classes. It included all of the social studies and language arts concepts and instructional intents found in the first three books. The experimental data is presently being evaluated and the findings may be obtained from the Research and Evaluation Department of the Dade County Public Schools.

The following are some representative comments of individual teachers who used the materials during the experimental phase of the project:

"The materials should be revised in light of the experiment and the materials should be utilized in the schools."

"Very good learning experience for those students low in ability."

"The project was of great value to my students and me. We enjoyed every moment. I plan to use the material as long as I'm in the classroom."

4

The Core Program
in the Jefferson County Public Schools,
Louisville, Kentucky

by Margaret Clayton, Supervisor

The Core Program in the Jefferson County Public Schools was organized in 1952. It continues to be accepted by the community as a sound approach to education for the approximately 13,000 early adolescents in this school system.

Jefferson County has a 6—2—4 organization. Seventh- and eighth-graders are housed in a separate wing of the secondary school, under the supervision of an administrative and couseling staff separate from that of the senior high. All seventh- and eighth-graders spend an average of 2 1/2 hours with one teacher, who is responsible for developing skills, information, and understandings drawn principally from language arts and social studies.

A *Core Guide* structures the curriculum by suggesting topics or problem areas to be explored at grade 7 and grade 8, such as Orientation to the New School, Study of Foreign Cultures, Being Teenagers, Our American Heritage. A *Handbook for Core Teachers* explains the rationale of the program and also indicates some techniques for classroom procedures. Chapters deal with the characteristics of the early adolescent, the role of language arts in the core, techniques of group work, and the like.

Innovations in facilities in some of the new buildings make it easier for core classes to share such activities as films, consultants, and field trips. This is not considered team teaching as commonly described, although team planning is being done. In a few schools an exploratory period outside the core block, based on pupil interest, is provided for seventh-graders.

Each school has a materials center from which teachers may get a variety of supplementary materials for core classes. These are on various reading levels and deal with many topics.

In-service activities for both new and experienced teachers are organized through a system-wide steering committee made up of the chairman of the core department in each school. In-service activities include a two-day preschool conference for new teachers; 15 hours of meetings during the year, which earn

209

credit for salary increment; in-service meetings which receive college credit at a local college; and attendance at various state and national conferences. In addition to a full-time supervisor who coordinates the core program in the eighteen schools, the Board of Education provides a full-time resource teacher who works principally with new teachers.

The Kentucky State Board of Education has recently adopted a program of certification for junior high school teachers. It is anticipated that this will make available teachers whose preparation is oriented toward the early teenager in today's school and society.

An Anthropological Approach to Senior High Core at the P. K. Yonge Laboratory School, Gainesville, Florida

by Joseph R. Huber, Core Teacher, and J. B. Hannum, Dean of Students

Core in grades 10, 11, and 12 at P. K. Yonge Laboratory School is a double-period class that meets five days a week and replaces English and social studies. We are concerned here primarily with the social studies aspects of the program.

The complexity of modern life and the rapidity of change in American society require a special approach to senior high core programs. The question is, however, what kind of approach will produce an awareness of value structure, an objective understanding of the problems of culture, and a cognizance of the possibility of directing social change? The achievement of these goals became the target toward which a new twelfth-grade core program was directed several years ago. The concepts of cultural anthropology were chosen as the basic frame of reference within which students in senior high core classes could study problems of meaning to them.

The following concepts seem to be ones that can be understood and used by high school students in looking at the problems of a culture:

All cultures are ways of solving common human problems.

The diversity of cultures shows that there are many different answers to these problems.

A recognition of the values of a culture is a key to understanding that culture.

The individual is the product of his culture.

Cultures are continually changing.

A culture has a more or less integrated pattern; change in one part of the culture brings about change in the total pattern.

Change is the result of interaction between the individual and his culture.

Cultural change can be directed.

Cultural change can be resisted.

The basic readings for the first unit, in which these concepts were introduced, were *Understanding Other Cultures* by Ina Corrine Brown and *Growing Up in New Guinea* by Margaret Mead. The second source gave students a relatively uncomplex society to which they could apply these concepts. The teachers as well as the brighter students found Ruth Benedict's *Patterns of Culture* to be an invaluable reference.

Reading was supplemented by many discussions and guest speakers, as well as by the following helpful films:

Man and His Culture	
The Pygmies of Africa	Encyclopaedia Britannica Films
American Indians of Long Ago	
Primitive Peoples	United World Films
The Mayas Are People	Instructional Films
Pictures in the Mind	McGraw-Hill Textfilms
New Lives for Old	Educational Testing Service
Courtship and Marriage in Four Cultures	
Four Families	Canadian Film Board

After the introduction of these concepts, a study of primitive cultures gave students an opportunity to see these concepts operating in a simple society. Materials were found to be available for the study of the cultures of the Manus, Samoans, Pueblo Indians, Plains Indians, Northwest Coast Indians, Dobuans, Pygmies, Eskimos, and Australian Aborigines. Through this study, students began to realize the great diversity of cultures and the possibility of other answers than our own to the problems of human existence. Students also saw quite clearly that other cultures have other value systems and that these value systems are expressed in the pattern of the culture. In comparing these simple cultures and their value systems to our own, students developed a new objectivity toward their culture and its values. They also incorporated into their vernacular the terminology peculiar to anthropology. This usage not only gave them status in the eyes of underclassmen, but it also showed that they had become at home with the concepts they had struggled with at the beginning of the unit.

This introductory unit lasted approximately ten weeks. In this time, all the students were able to acquire a set of conceptual tools with which to study our own culture. The balance of the year's work, which was concerned with the problems of our own culture, was cooperatively planned by students and teachers. The students themselves were primarily responsible for defining the following outline for the remaining units.

Question for the Year: What are our values and how are they changing?

Unit I: What is the relationship between the individual and the government?

Unit II: How do institutions in our society attempt to mold the individual?

Unit III: What are the social forces molding the individual and what are their effects?

Unit IV: How does social change come about?

In seeking solutions to the problem of Unit I, students did individual research on such questions as these:

Should the government support parochial schools?

Should the government provide every American with a job?

Should the government compete with private enterprise?

How should the government solve the current farm problem?

Should the government help minority groups to achieve social, political, and economic equality?

What is the relationship between government and religion in the United States?

A number of methods were used to help the students find meaning in the information they collected. Small groups of students studying similar problems met and discussed the information they had found, shared resources, and received assistance in directing their research and forming tentative conclusions. Larger groups including students who had studied a variety of problems related to the unit met for discussion of the total problem. In addition, a panel of students representing different problem areas presented a discussion before the total class. A most valuable aid was found in members of the community who visited the school and spoke to the classes on various aspects of the unit question.

Throughout the unit, anthropological concepts were used as a frame of reference in studying the problem.

Similar methods were used in Unit II, "Institutional Influences." The following are some of the research problems related to this unit:

What effect does the family have on the individual?

Are business values overpowering all other values in America today?

What is the role of education in molding the individual?

In addition to hearing visiting speakers from the community, students visited religious leaders, union officials, political party workers, and businessmen.

Questions studied during Unit III, "Social Forces," included the following:

How does class distinction affect the individual?

What is the influence of prejudice on the individual?

What is the role of the woman in America?

How have our modern means of communication affected the individual?

What influence do living surroundings (urban, suburban, and rural) have on individual values?

Throughout the study of the first three units, the overall question concerning the values of American society had been emphasized. A final unit was devoted to summarizing findings in the other three units and relating them to the question. Unit IV, dealing with social change, used Frederick Lewis Allen's *The Big Change* as a basic reference. It dealt with such topics as:

How has American society changed?
What value changes are represented by the innovations in American life?
What value conflicts have appeared as a result of social change?
In what direction is American society likely to develop in the future?

Speakers in this final unit included two psychologists who discussed the values of the individual in our changing society.

Evaluation by the teachers, except for the use of written evaluations by students, was informal, depending primarily on conversations with students and observation of student behavior. Although this evaluation was subjective, the teachers felt that there was real growth in awareness of our culture and its problems, toleration of differences, and sensitivity to personal and cultural values. In looking at the program in general, teachers concluded that the concepts of social anthropology can be understood by high school students, even those of low ability. The program has special value for terminal students, who will probably have no further education for life in our changing society. A number of the students who entered college after completing this program have reported that it gave them excellent preparation for their college work.

Since the inception of this program several years ago, further revisions have been made. In September 1966 the introductory unit in cultural anthropology was given to the tenth grade students in a modified form. Margaret Mead's *People and Places,* Gene Lizitzky's *Four Ways of Being Human,* and single-concept film loops replaced *Growing Up in New Guinea* and *Patterns of Culture.* In addition, such anthropologically oriented novels as *Light in the Forest* by Conrad Richter, *The Good Earth* by Pearl Buck, and *Return to Laughter* by Elinore Smith Bowen were read and discussed by students. It is planned that this introductory unit will set the stage for teacher-student planned examinations of world societies and problems for a period of three semesters. The last three semesters, culminating at the end of the twelfth grade, emphasize a study of the problems of contemporary American society. It is felt that, by dividing the three years of senior high core into two one and one half year blocks, sufficient time will be available to permit teachers and students to plan in-depth studies of the complexities of modern life.

Unit II

Interdisciplinary Team Programs

Interdisciplinary Team Teaching at La Colina Junior High School, Santa Barbara, California

by Jack Richards, Principal, and Imogene Nair, Assistant Principal

Since the opening of La Colina Junior High School in 1959, team teaching has flourished and mushroomed to the extent that during the school year 1967—68 approximately 80 percent of all the history and English classes were in team programs, operating on all grade and ability levels. Time blocks assigned to these teams vary from two to three class periods, permitting instructors flexibility in crossover of subject matter and control of time. Ninth-grade history and English are taught by a team of six teachers. In the seventh grade, art and music are included with English and history in a "humanities" program, and in the eighth grade, English, history, and science are taught by an interdisciplinary team.

Nestled in the foothills on the outskirts of Santa Barbara, La Colina houses approximately 1,300 students, 71 certificated personnel, and 27 "classified" staff on a college-type campus with all classrooms open to covered walkways. Replacing the traditional auditorium is "Academic Hall," which provides classrooms for large and small group instruction every period of the day. Maximum seating capacity is 500, divisible by folding partitions to house a group of 300 in the main section and 100 in each of two side sections. A projection booth in the center is backed by a small activity room suitable for one to thirty students. Currently under construction is a quadruplex especially designed for team teaching.

Seventh Grade English—Music—History—Art

Here a team of 90 students works with 4 teachers in a three-period block. For certain activities the team divides the students into eight groups according to behavior and ability. There are large-group activities and small-group activities. Students are encouraged to use the library for research and to take advantage of the history lab, English lab, and art studio.

217

The way different subjects contribute to the program is exemplified by the unit on Greece that was taught during the 1967-68 school year.

Music and Drama

All students read and discussed *Oedipus Rex*. They also received instruction in the structure of Greek theater, qualities of the tragic hero, the idea of the Greek chorus, and operas based on Greek myths. The more able groups wrote a Greek tragedy and made a model of a Greek theater.

History

Lectures were given on the geography of ancient and modern Greece, government of ancient Greece, Athens, and Sparta, Greek ways of living and thinking, and their contributions to the world. A student who had visited Greece showed slides he had taken.

English

This included an introduction to Greek mythology and religion. The *Iliad* and *Odyssey* were studied, pertinent films were shown, and students undertook a variety of projects, such as, drawing interpretations of Greek myths, planning a TV interview with a Trojan hero, making a chart of the Greek gods and goddesses, or writing a myth in Greek style.

Art

Lectures were given on archaic Greek art, classical art, and Hellenistic Greek art.

The unit examination covered history, English, music, and art by means of objective and matching questions, an open-notebook test, and questions based on art slides.

Eighth Grade English—History—Science

During 1967—68 two classes of students (lowest academically) read Scott O'Dell's *Island of the Blue Dolphins* for English. The novel is based on the life of the Lost Woman of San Nicholas Island whose remains are buried at the Old Mission in Santa Barbara. After reading and discussing the novel, the group took a field trip to the Old Mission and the Museum of Natural History to see the burial ground and the plaque in memory of the Lost Woman. At the museum students observed sea-life displays and items of interest dealing with the novel they had read. The history teacher presented a short lecture on early California missions and Indian history. The field trip was followed by an extensive history lecture and slides show by the art teacher.

Ninth-Grade History—English

The following description of the ninth-grade program is adapted from the evaluation of team teaching at La Colina submitted by the principal and his staff to the Santa Barbara Board of Education in 1966. The report has since been printed as an official publication and may be obtained from the Santa Barbara High School District. Further refinements of team teaching and other pilot programs in the Santa Barbara schools are described in *Secondary Perspectives,* Vol. 1, 1968, available from the same source.

In the fall of 1964, the entire ninth grade (approximately 400 students) was divided into two classes, each of which met during a double-period block of time. The classes were heterogeneous, including the entire range of student abilities, but within each large class of 200 students, twelve homogeneous groups were formed. Because the teacher was freed from repeating the same information to all groups, the material each group received was appropriate to their educational ability, thereby eliminating endless repetition and waste of time. This also gave to the team a large amount of flexibility.

The following were some of the advantages felt to be present:

1. Tremendous flexibility in the program. Any size group could be pulled together for any purpose at a moment's notice. One could form several groups of similar ability, and teachers could call together a very small group of students or meet with a student on a one-to-one basis for specific purposes.

2. Utilization of community resources. Outside speakers were used frequently by the team. A speaker had only to speak to two groups to reach the entire ninth grade. Speakers were more willing to come to share their experiences with the classes.

3. Large-scale special activities could easily be implemented. For example, during the national elections, the entire process of forming a national government took place in each large class. Political parties were formed; each small group was a state; electoral votes were determined on the basis of population; party primaries were held and candidates selected; and a national campaign and national election took place in which the students chose a President and Vice-President, Senators and Representatives, and state governors. The President then appointed his cabinet, some ambassadors, and the members of the Supreme Court, all of whom were approved by the Senate. In effect, there were two complete functioning national governments in the ninth grade at La Colina, both established in the same way as our own national government.

It became obvious that the students were identifying with their national government when in one class the state of Texas threatened to secede from the union. The other states asked the President to call an emergency session of the Congress. Congress voted to send an ambassador to the state of Texas informing them that, on the basis of the policies arising from the Civil War, if they actually seceded, a state of war would exist between Texas and the United States. Crisis was avoided when Texas and the Congress settled their difficulties, and Texas returned to the fold. It was felt by both the teachers and the students that the students learned more by experiencing both the establishment and the structure of our government than they would have learned in an entire year of reading textbooks.

4. Crossover of subject matter when needed. Although the ninth-grade program was not a core program, and crossover in subject matter between American government and the ninth-grade English curriculum was not feasible most of the time, there were occasions when such crossover was utilized to mutual benefit. American government was based upon a unit approach, with a major lecture at the beginning of each unit. Therefore, each student had to develop his skills at note-taking. The English teachers gave special lectures and small-group workshops on note-taking procedures, and a noticeable difference was apparent in the ability of the students, even those of low ability, to take notes and remember material for examinations. In addition, the top groups worked on research papers in special areas of depth study in government. The English teachers taught them the form they were to follow and graded them on structure, while the government teachers worked with them on content and research techniques and graded them on content.

5. Due to the team organization, there was more opportunity for teacher preparation. With two preparation periods, the team teachers were able to spend more time preparing for their classes, and the students were able to reap the advantages of better-prepared lessons.

6. Teacher aides lessened the clerical load of the teacher, also enabling him to do more research and preparation for his classes.

7. There was a constant exchange of ideas among the team members. If there is any single item that spells the success or defeat of a team program it is the rapport and flexibility of the members of the team. If the team members get along well together and can freely exchange their ideas with each other, the team will do well. However, if one or two of the members are not "in the swing" of the fast-moving, flexible program that must exist in team teaching, the team project will in all probability fail or become seriously hampered. In our ninth-grade program there was constant exchange of communication and tremendous rapport among the four members of the team. Therefore, in spite of the problems the team faced that particular year, they were able to resolve many of their difficulties.

8. Team teaching affords one of the best training grounds for student teachers available. The training given to student teachers in the year under discussion was varied, so that the student teacher was forced to meet flexible situations involving not only the regular class-size group, but also very small groups and very large groups. They were given training in leading discussions, working with remedial problem cases, discussing difficult areas with top-level students, lecturing to large groups, working with students on a one-to-one basis, and the varied situations arising from working with different faculty members.

9. The team was able to standardize or coordinate subject areas on one grade level and yet retain the individuality of each teacher. Even though the teachers involved handled their presentations in ways unique to themselves, and though each was free to give assignments peculiar to his presentation, the assignments, tests, and general course outlines for an entire grade in two subjects were coordinated to the extent that a student's individual homework load for any given night was not too overwhelming.

In the first year of the two-subject team involving an entire grade level there were many accomplishments, and students and faculty alike felt a good learning situation had taken place. The students by a 90 to 1 ratio felt that the team program, even with its problems of that year, was far superior to a regular classroom situation.

For the 1965–66 school year the 400 ninth-grade students again were divided into two classes of 200 each, but six teachers were scheduled to the team, three history teachers and three English teachers. In the beginning of the year, the students were grouped in regular-size classes of 25 to 35, assigned to a history teacher and an English teacher. They remained in regular-size classes for approximately a month in order to give them a feeling of security and identification. The teacher to whom they were assigned for each subject continued to be the teacher who graded them and answered their questions regarding assignments and other class work.

Following the month of orientation, the regular class-size groups were subdivided into two smaller groups of approximately fifteen students each, and a more flexible program called "Operation Education" was used for a breakdown schedule. In "Operation Education" the students alternated in a small group of 15 and in a larger group of 45. In the small group, two of the three days were used for discussion and one of the three was used for independent study. The three days in the 45-student group were used for lecture, films, tests, and, to some extent, for discussion. Large groups of 100 or 200 were used to introduce units, view audio-visual or lecture presentations, take unit examinations, and listen to guest speakers.

In addition to the advantages listed for the 1964–65 program, the following advantages emerged:

1. By grouping the students in regular classes and assigning them to a particular teacher for a certain length of time, the students were given a sense of identification and security not present in the previous year's program. Orientation to team teaching and a gradual weaning of the student from dependence upon a traditional classroom situation were accomplished with greater ease and efficiency, as well as a minimum of student frustration.

2. By assigning six teachers to the team instead of four, the problems of excessive load, excessive paper-grading and evaluating, and excessive dependence upon student teachers and teacher aides all but disappeared.

3. Because one of the team members was appointed ninth-grade class adviser, the special activity of electing a complete national government within the ninth grade was given additional meaning and relevancy by the fact that the "President of the United States," elected through the same kind of political institutions as we experience on a national level, became the ninth-grade class president. Congress was the ninth-grade legislative body, and the state governors served as homeroom presidents.
4. Because of the lower teacher-pupil ratio, the team was able to retain students in smaller groups a large part of the time. It is the feeling of this team that the small discussion and activity group is the key to any truly successful team teaching program.

The school year 1965-66 gave to the American Government and English Ninth Grade team as close to an ideal team situation as they had expected to experience. Problems were few, and all the team members were highly enthused about the situation. The program in subsequent years has retained this basic pattern.

7

The Little-School Core Program at Abraham Lincoln Junior High School, Park Ridge, Illinois

by Clifford H. Sweat, Principal

The terms "little school," "core curriculum," and "team teaching" are not usually applied to the program which has been in effect in the Abraham Lincoln Junior High School, Park Ridge, Illinois, for more than twenty years. However, all of these terms might be applied to the program as it has developed in this building, which houses 890 seventh- and eighth-grade boys and girls.

The "little-school core" is a type of program in which the basic subjects, taught by three cooperating teachers, become the center around which and in which about ninety boys and girls work for the two years they are in this school.

More than twenty years ago three teachers decided that they wanted to offer a type of program which they believed would be better than the traditional subject-orientated and lock-step schedule allowed. These teachers combined their skills and knowledge in the subject areas of language arts, mathematics, science, and social studies by presenting a team teaching approach to a correlated or unified curriculum. This program for preadolescents and early adolescents became known as "core." After two years the entire building was organized on this concept.

The following are some of the units which are presented to our pupils: (1) Careers, (2) Illinois, (3) Westward Expansion, (4) Colonial Period, (5) Patriotism. Each does not necessarily involve all four subject areas. However, the Illinois unit is one in which all subject areas participate and the teachers work as a team in its presentation. For example:

Science—geology of Illinois
Mathematics—graphs, charts, and tables on population, area, mileage
Language arts—literature, Illinois writers
Social studies—history, geography, people

Today we have ten little-school core groups or sections, each consisting of three homerooms. The team of three teachers work together for two years with about ninety pupils. We believe that this type of program is right for young adolescents, who need consistent and skillful direction in their academic, social, and emotional development. These pupils spend two-thirds of their time with these three basic-subject teachers and have the opportunity to practice some of the language arts skills in social studies and science classes. The pupils spend one-third of their time in art, home economics, industrial arts, French, music, and physical education. The basic-subject core teachers spend this time in planning, sometimes as individuals and sometimes as a team, meeting with other staff members, or conferring with pupils and/or their parents.

The little-school core team staff is not only responsible for the academic growth of the pupils but has the task of giving guidance and direction to individuals and the group. We have no guidance personnel, as such, in our district. A school social worker does spend time with those individuals who have severe personal or social problems.

Three department chairmen, under the direction of the principal and the curriculum director, serve to help direct instruction and coordinate activities between the ten little-school cores. These chairmen serve on the district curriculum committee and participate in attempts to articulate programs between our elementary, junior high, and senior high schools.

We feel that our little-school core offers the following advantages to our upper-middle-class Chicago suburban community:

1. The pupil has a sense of belonging because of the personal relationship between the teachers and pupils.
2. The pupil has fewer adjustments than in the departmentalized, traditional schedule.
3. The needs of the slow learner and the rapid learner can be met through regrouping within the little-school core without disrupting the schedule or causing the pupil to be shifted away from the pupils and teachers who are well acquainted with him and his needs.
4. The pupil has an opportunity for leadership within the homeroom, the core, and the school.
5. The pupils and teachers have opportunity for closer cooperation in providing for practice in meeting democratic ways of living.
6. The homeroom basic-subject teacher has much opportunity for guidance.
7. The teacher has more specialized training in the subject area taught.
8. The teachers have opportunities to get together and plan before making demands of pupils.
9. The teachers and pupils can save time by presenting related materials at one time.
10. The teachers and pupils have many opportunities to study, use, and strengthen skills presented and planned cooperatively.
11. The pupils and teachers gain approximately one month in the two years because they know each other and what is expected in their relationships.

12. A substitute teacher can be given direction and guidance and be made to feel a part of the team with little interruption in the education of the pupils.
13. The little-school core is a good intermediate step between the self-contained sixth-grade classroom and the highly departmentalized program of the ninth grade in the senior high school.

8

A Time-Block Schedule
That Facilitates Personalized Instruction
at North Arvada Junior High School,
Arvada, Colorado

by Carl R. Zerger, Principal

North Arvada Junior High School, Arvada, Colorado, has an enrollment approximating 1200 students almost equally divided among three grade levels—seventh, eighth, and ninth. While not large by contrast to many urban schools, its enrollment was judged by its staff to be too large for optimum educational experiences for individual children if organized in traditional fashion.

A search began for an organizational format that might reduce traditional scheduling rigidity. Many models designed to provide "flexibility" were examined. Too often "flexibility" was assumed to be a synonym for "variability" and many so-called modular schedules seemed to be characterized by rigidity of structure. Also, the inclusion in a child's program of unscheduled time for independent study seemed educationally self-defeating due to the immaturity of the junior high school pupil.

It was believed that personalized instruction could best be provided through an organizational structure that would maximize flexibility through the coordinated planning efforts of the administrative staff, the teachers, and the pupils. The variables of time, space utilization, personnel grouping, staff usage, and allocation of resources and effort, must, it was felt, be capable of frequent modification.

Modification was to be the result of the professional competence and knowledge of the staff conditioned by a sensitivity to the interests, needs, and abilities of the individual child. Those engaged in the teaching-learning situation were considered the proper ones to initiate changes.

It was decided that, if *flexibility* is to occur, the schedule must provide for:

1. The exercise of options in use of time, space, grouping, content, and allocation of teaching effort by the teachers, teams of teachers, and teams of teachers and children.
2. The formation and operation of a great variety of teams and models of team procedure.

3. The establishment of concurrent planning periods and meetings of classes in the same and related fields to allow for coordinated efforts of teachers and variable groupings of children.
4. The possibility of rescheduling a student without the traumatic experience created by his assignment to a completely unfamiliar complement of teachers and classmates.

Other characteristics that should be incorporated into the organizational pattern are:

1. Procedures for permitting a more intimate association between pupils and staff:
    (a) A well-organized counseling program involving trained counselors available for service to students and available as consultants to teachers and teaching teams.
    (b) A group-guidance program in which children are associated with a guidance advisor.
    (c) The association of a group of children and a group of teachers for the year using the "school within a school" concept to permit a cooperatively designed educational program.
2. Procedures for individualizing instruction to better serve the student:
    (a) Homogeneous groupings in some subject-matter areas (mathematics and foreign language).
    (b) The establishment of learning laboratories (resource centers, open laboratories and independent study areas) equipped and staffed to permit remedial assistance and enrichment experiences to individuals.
    (c) The establishment of scheduling mobility for each child.
3. Procedures related to content structure:
    (a) The block-of-time concept to permit better subject-matter articulation between the disciplines and variability in usage of time, staff, space, and personnel grouping.
    (b) Other variations related to nongradedness and continuous progress.

The Evolution of a Schedule Building Block

The search for a schedule model that would meet these criteria was in reality a search for some basic scheduling unit. Such a unit, if it could be developed, could be used in a variety of combinations to create a suitable master schedule even though enrollment varied from year to year.

We settled upon a building block consisting of a group of 60 children (two traditional classroom groups) and two teachers (the latter representing different, but possibly related, disciplines) associated together for a block of time equivalent to two normal class periods. The internal structure of this unit was to be left to the discretion of the personnel involved. Their decisions would be conditioned by the district's curriculum, the subject matter structure, the capabilities of the teachers, and the needs, interests, and abilities of the pupils.

Schematically, the schedule building block is structured as follows:

Time Block I

Period	1	2
Class	A1	B2
Sections	B1	A2

The symbols A1, A2, B1, and B2 represent class sections of two disciplinary areas (i.e., two classes of mathematics and two classes of science). Personnel scheduled into such a block consist of 60 children and two teachers.

Within the two-period time block the associated personnel can utilize the time completely independent of other classes. The lengthening or shortening of instructional, study, and laboratory sessions provides the needed time flexibility.

Not only is time usage flexible, but the composition of subgroups of pupils can be altered to serve individual needs, interests and capabilities. Subject matter from the two areas can be articulated and the teachers can coordinate their efforts, thus combining the advantages of block-time and team teaching.

Incorporation of the Block into a Full Schedule

The time block unit may be combined with others to create the full schedule. The daily schedule of a single student consists of a combination of four such time blocks, each 90 minutes in length. The combination of twelve such time blocks constitutes the schedule for 180 students. The time blocks are sequentially arranged into the equivalent of an eight-period day. Unstructured time is not formally scheduled but is provided as an option within the block-of-time format.

Of the four blocks of time in which each student is involved, three are devoted to academic areas of instruction while the other is reserved for "activity" classes, guidance activities, and lunch. The time-block arrangement for 180 students creates a "school within a school." The structure depicted below suggests a possible arrangement of time blocks:

I	II	III	IV
A1 | B2 B1 | A2	ACT | L&G ACT | L&G	A3 | B4 B3 | A4	A5 | B6 B5 | A6
C1 | D2 D1 | C2	ACT | L&G ACT | L&G	C3 | D4 D3 | C4	C5 | D6 D5 | C6
E1 | F2 F1 | E2	ACT | L&G ACT | L&G	E3 | F4 F3 | E4	E5 | F6 F5 | E6

Each roman numeral indicates a block of time and the rectangles represent scheduling units. The internal structure of each unit is indicated by dotted lines to suggest the possibilities for variation.

Subject-matter classes, identified by letters, could represent any of the following combinations: science and mathematics, language arts and social studies, or foreign language and practical arts. The latter combination is used at North Arvada because flexibility of time usage is needed for laboratory activities. The symbols ACT and L&G represent "activity" classes (physical education, art, and music) and lunch and guidance. The letter symbols are associated with numbers, and a full sequence of letters; such as A1, through A6, represents the teaching load of one teacher. Thus six academic teachers assisted by needed activity teachers can handle the educational program for 180 students.

Advantages of Schedule Structure

A number of advantages are to be found in this type of structure:

1. Individualizing the schedule:
   (a) Predetermination of some time blocks for "advanced placement," "typical," and "improvement" groups will assist in insuring homogeneous classes. This is necessary in our ungraded foreign language classes.
   (b) Teachers can combine and recombine the 60 students into groups of varying sizes, needs, and capabilities depending upon the content and process involved.
   (c) With each child scheduled into three separate academic blocks of time there can be shifting of class membership from block to block.
   (d) Each time block is an entity unto itself. Therefore, teachers can determine specific experiences for one block without affecting other blocks during the day.
   (e) Since the same teachers serve as the faculty for all 180 youngsters in one "school within a school," a child's schedule within this "little school" may be changed without his having to adjust to a new group of teachers.
   (f) The time block can include time for individualized study. This can be supervised by the teacher, or the child can be scheduled into the learning laboratory (resource center) for specialized assistance or challenge. If the nature of the assistance requires such specialization that it is available only at certain times, the child's schedule can be temporarily altered to suit.

2. Providing a greater variety of learning experiences for pupils:
   (a) Variations of time allotment can be created for formal class presentations, individualized instructional experiences, supervised study, and small- or large-group activities.

(b) Through team agreement, time may be scheduled for individual research or remediation in subject areas without requiring the child to sacrifice instruction in other academic areas.

3. Expanding the dimensions of staff utilization:

(a) Common planning periods for people sharing the same block of time assignment permits coordinated planning and cooperative effort in evaluating students, reporting on student progress, and conducting parent conferences.

(b) The teaching team has complete responsibility for an individual child's educational experience, and through coordinated and cooperative planning they can provide for articulation of subject matter and coordination of teaching-learning effort. Our plan involves cross-disciplinary teams which meet periodically for joint planning.

The "School Within a School" Expanded into the Total Master Schedule

If size of enrollment permits, the "school within a school" can be duplicated as many times as necessary. North Arvada Junior High School has six such units, two for each grade level. Each unit is referred to as a team, and each team is identified by a number and letter—thus teams 7A and 7B serve the needs of our seventh-grade students and teachers. Each of the six teams has a separate complement of students and academic subject matter teachers. The teachers of each team have a common planning period to coordinate their instructional program. Academic teams generally share a complement of activity teachers (music, physical education, and art). The assignment of all pupil members of a team to the activity team at the same time frees the academic members of the team for planning.

Since each team is similarly structured, there is considerable concurrent scheduling of similar and related classes. Thus teams 7A and 7B have virtually duplicate schedules. This means that two seventh-grade science-math blocks are operating simultaneously and can be combined across team lines for a variety of team teaching activities.

Concurrent scheduling also occurs across grade-level lines so that both seventh and eighth grade science-math blocks are meeting simultaneously. Classes could conceivably be nongraded if the subject matter recommends it, or cross-graded on the basis of student interests, abilities, and needs.

Administrative Advantages

In addition to individualizing instruction, the above schedule has several general administrative advantages:

1. The teachers of a team constitute a supervisory unit that can provide a variety of general services related to before- and after-school activities.

2. The teaching team can be authorized to make decisions relative to the supervision of field trips—some of the team accompanying the students on the trip and others remaining in the school to supervise nonparticipating student team members.
3. They can serve as a unit in the preparation and scheduling of parent-teacher conferences.
4. They can plan procedures related to assemblies, testing programs, and other activities that are unique to their students without involving the rest of the school faculty.

Conclusion

The schedule described above permits the personalization of instruction to a degree not possible in rigidly structured schedules. It places a premium on a faculty's professional knowledge of learning theory, child growth and development, analysis and evaluation of individual differences, organization of subject-matter content and structure, and evaluation of the effectiveness of instructional strategies.

This emphasis on professional competence has induced changes in role definition for staff members. Decision-making now becomes a function of the teaching corps. Administrators are called upon for different kinds of support. Counseling personnel find increased demand for service in the area of identifying the characteristics of individual children.

The change in staff morale and attitude is evidenced by a team *esprit de corps*. Mutual support and coordinated planning encourage many innovative practices and procedures which individual teachers might hesitate to attempt. Content orientation changes to process orientation as a predominant objective.

Pupil participants profit from the kinds of experiences that can be facilitated under this organizational plan. They develop an identification with teachers and fellow pupils on their team. Collective judgments by the teaching team in the evaluation of individual student's needs and progress supplement the evaluations commonly made by the individual teacher. The increased sensitivity coming from a common concern on the part of the team is reflected in differentiated assignments and scheduling mobility. In short, we believe that this schedule fosters the individualization of instruction.

9

American Studies
at O. L. Smith Junior High School,
Dearborn, Michigan

by Frederick Schreiber, Principal
(Presently Principal, Edsel Ford High School, Dearborn)

Our objective was to design a program, using American History as a core, which would embrace learnings in American art and music as they related to themes inherent in American life.

We chose an interdisciplinary approach, teaming an art and music teacher with three members of the social studies staff. These five people rewrote the traditional American history course in a summer workshop.

First, they recognized that a different organizational approach to content was necessary. Thus, they set about identifying several themes that they felt would capture the interest and imagination of their eighth-grade students. They agreed on the following: 1. The Role of Protest in American Society; 2. War as a Solution to American Problems; 3. The Ever-Changing Constitution; 4. Industrialization and You; and 5. Minority groups, Past and Present.

This is really an adaptation of the "integration" or "correlation" of subject matter which all good self-contained elementary classroom teachers practice. The difference in this approach is the inclusion of problem-centered themes and the large-group—small-group instruction, as well as independent study.

Each unit is braced with tapes, both commercially and teacher-prepared; as well as filmstrips for students to view individually. Liberal use is made of paperbacks and community resource people when they are available.

Art and music are interjected in large-group settings, in small discussion groups, and in independent creative projects arising out of the student's interest. One might say we are trying to immerse the student in his American cultural heritage. We can show American art and music as integral parts of the culture. Students begin to understand the arts as a mirror of the cultural period, not created in isolation from the cultural pressures of the particular historical period.

We are enthusiastic about this theme approach because it allows for the inclusion of current materials. When the study of "protest" is begun, current news events are used as a springboard to the past.

The teachers were in general agreement that the 50-minute period, five days a week, would not be a workable unit of time to operate such a program. They settled on 90 minutes every other day as a block of time which would provide the necessary flexibility. Since the building is on an odd-and-even day schedule using twenty-two 18-minute modules per day, it was possible to group five modules together on alternate days.

With 110 people meeting on the even day and an additional 110 on the odd day, the five teachers could handle the entire eighth-grade social studies program. This also enabled them to garner 72 minutes of planning time each day for their team work. In addition, they have 54 minutes of planning time to devote to their two other traditional social studies assignments.

This program is designed to reach each ability group. It includes all of our eighth-grade students with the exception of 15 pupils who are in a remedial block-time program. Materials have been selected and the units written in an open-ended fashion. All units are built around levels of assignments. Levels 1 and 2 are expected of all students. Those who complete these quickly, and this is normally the brighter, more capable children, go on to levels 3 and 4. Level 4 may be inquiry by the student into an area or topic of his own choosing and is done with the consent of the instructor. It could be the writing of a "protest" song or the arranging of a mock protest with banners, and the like. Our feeling is that this levels approach provides opportunity for each child to progress, within reason, at his own pace.

O. L. Smith Junior High contains grades 7, 8, and 9. The children are from families of office, skilled and semiskilled workers. In many homes both parents work to maintain a home in the neighborhood. The average IQ is about 104 for the total 780 students.

The American studies program is in its third year. Plans are now being made to include American literature. Our English department does a great deal of correlation with other subjects but is not at present included on the planning team.

Whenever large groups of children are placed together there are bound to be logistical problems. We have found that careful planning can overcome most of these. Judging from a recently conducted questionnaire study, the students reacted most favorably to the small-group settings where they could share their own ideas. Many expressed a desire for more independent study time, and all said they liked the variety of experiences which were made possible by the organizational pattern. Each staff member must constantly be aware of the possibility that students can and do feel lost in a large-group setting. This need not be a disadvantage of the program, but it certainly is a danger to be guarded against.

No program or organizational pattern is the single answer. However, the chance to create a new offering, develop a different pattern for presenting material, and see children respond positively does wonders for the teachers involved. Certainly any program which results in the increased enthusiasm of both instructor and learners will bring us closer to our ultimate goal of maximizing the amount of learning for each child.

A Humanities Approach to English and American History, Grade Eleven, in Pueblo High School, Tucson, Arizona

by Marjorie Benson, Chairman, Language Arts Department, and Richard Rodgers, Chairman, Social Studies Department

So that students would become more aware of the many facets of American society and become acquainted with the materials and techniques necessary for the study of this society, major curriculum changes were made in the study of American history and English in a number of sections for eleventh-graders at Pueblo High School. The course is not a "humanities" course as the term is usually interpreted. However, a humanistic approach is used since the course involves lectures, field trips, and studies in American music and American art and architecture, along with American literature, language, and history.

Genesis

With the encouragement of Mr. Elbert Brooks, who was then principal of Pueblo High School, staff members interested in breaking barriers between subject-matter fields for students and teachers began a series of meetings in the spring of 1963 to discuss possible approaches to curriculum revision. Members of this informal group were the school librarian, several teachers of social studies, English, art, and music, the assistant principal for student personnel, and the principal.

By the end of that school year, plans had been formulated and a tentative curriculum developed for a course to be offered to eleventh-graders. Since the purpose of the proposed curriculum change was to help students experience for themselves the interrelationships between these areas of the humanities, the art, music, language, literature, and history of the American society, staff members developed a flexible course involving the study of these interrelated areas.

Because it was hoped that the course would be responsive to student needs and interests, a highly structured course outline was avoided. A basic, but flexible, unity among the five areas was achieved through the use of selected historical concepts for the structure of the course.

In the fall of 1964 the course was offered to six sections of juniors. During the year the eight teachers directly involved with the students met frequently to revise the original plans. A definite attempt was made throughout the year to maintain flexibility in the organization and content of the course. Throughout subsequent years, continued revision and evaluation was possible, for all staff members involved met voluntarily at frequent intervals.

At the present time the course is fairly well established and gives students a much greater concept of the interrelationships of American culture. The humanities approach, it is felt, is vastly superior to the traditional separate courses in English and American history.

Organization

These classes at Pueblo consist of six sections totaling approximately 200 students. The students are heterogeneously grouped and are randomly assigned to the course. Students who request the subject are normally granted their preference, but the majority of students registered have expressed no preference one way or the other.

Since students with special reading problems are assigned to "reading emphasis" classes in English and American history, these students are not available for assignment to the humanities sections, but otherwise the classes are filled on exactly the same basis as the conventional junior classes in history and English. Humanities here is not a subject for those of high academic ability only, but is designed deliberately to be suitable for both average and above-average students.

There are eight teachers involved in the program: three each from American history and English, plus one art and one music teacher. The history and English teachers function as teams of two, and are scheduled so that each team has two periods with the same two classes of students. In other words, the teams are block scheduled; teacher A's students one period becoming teacher B's the next, and vice versa. Having two hours and two rooms available, each team has the opportunity to vary class size from two to seventy. Furthermore, each team is assigned the same planning period, which allows a high degree of coordination within each team.

Since one room assigned to the program is a double-sized one, the two sections (generally about 65–70 students) can physically be combined with a minimum of difficulty. Also each team has two successive periods together (i.e., first and second, third and fourth) and it is very easy to vary the arrangement as far as combining and dividing are concerned. What the program actually involves is seventy students, two teachers, and two hours of time, with time, teachers and students divided in the manner most appropriate to the current learning goals. The division of students and class time is left to the judgment of the three teams, and this division has understandably varied to some extent.

The teachers in art and music work with the students as each unit is presented. This contact is sometimes with the total group and sometimes with a small group, or even with one individual who has a specialized interest in a particular subject. In the general presentations extensive use is made of all audio-visual materials and equipment, including tapes, slides, records, filmstrips, reprints of paintings, sculptured articles and original paintings. The art teacher serves as a valuable resource person on field trips to local art museums. In the same manner, music appropriate to the unit is presented.

In this course no single text is used for either English or history purposes; rather, extensive collections of paperback books are utilized. Since this is a fee course, books are purchased for student use with this money. The local district initially provided additional funds, and both NDEA and PL 89-10 monies have been used effectively to secure additional room materials. For the books that all students are asked to read, individual copies have been secured, issued, and later collected. In other cases, class sets of materials are available (approximately 70 per set), and in still other instances books number from one to fifteen copies. In the latter case, books are used for individual or small-group work.

Although the subject-matter distinctions between history and English are reduced, separate grades are issued to students in English and American history.

While planning within a team can be, and is, almost continuous, the coordination among all eight teachers requires meetings in the evenings. This enables the entire group to work on common problems such as selection of materials, course sequence, scheduling of audio-visual materials, course objectives and field trips.

Evaluation

Any realistic evaluation of this program must begin with the fact that the evaluators are by no means disinterested bystanders. Since both were involved in the initial planning and have taught the course for three years, they naturally have certain biases in favor of the program which cannot be avoided. In addition, any new experimental program carries with it, to some extent at least, the Hawthorne effect. Being aware of these factors, the teachers have made an attempt to compensate for them, but how successful this compensation has been is for the individual reader to decide.

Strengths

One of the chief advantages of the humanities approach over conventional courses is the breaking down of artificial barriers between disciplines. Students study a particular topic from historical, literary, art and musical viewpoints concurrently, thus receiving a much more balanced picture than would otherwise be presented. The interdisciplinary approach has obvious advantages, and this is achieved to a greater extent in this program than in other courses. Avoidance of single texts goes a long way toward meeting individual differences in students. Concentration on major ideas and movements eliminates great amounts of useless trivia. This is not nearly as great a sacrifice as teachers, especially history teachers, once thought, for most teachers will readily agree that little of this trivia is retained by the students for any appreciable length of time.

Weaknesses

The course, at least in its first year of operation, tended to concentrate somewhat on historical material at the expense of certain skills in English. Greater stress needed to be given to research writing and technique, and more time allotted for student writing. In certain areas, especially in the earlier period of American history, some additional background needed to be developed. Assignments tended to be class assignments; the need for greater individualization in instruction and in assignments was felt by students and teachers. Hopefully, these weaknesses have been recognized, discussed by the group, and steps taken to correct them.

Changes in Personnel

The teaching teams have not remained stable, as one English teacher left to become a department chairman in another state after the first year, and a second English teacher took a leave of absence the next year. Thus only one of the three teams had its original membership for the third year. This naturally has an effect on the program, though it is only fair to state that the newer teachers have been of especially high ability and interest.

Students

To a limited extent, students have been misassigned to the program; in some cases students should have been in basic sections instead. However, this is a factor which operates in any high school course. No one has yet reached perfection in class assignment, but assignment to the program has been equal to, or perhaps better than, other subject areas. Some schedule changes have been necessary, especially transfer of students into reading emphasis classes. As is true in any class, some pupils had a lack of adequate motivation, though it is felt that this was not especially directed toward this approach but rather toward academic subjects in general. It is further felt that heterogeneous grouping of students was achieved, and is desirable. The course was not intended to be an elite class for those of high ability, nor has it become so. The humanities approach can and does work for average students. This is a fairer test than using only high-ability students, for they will achieve anyway, sometimes even in spite of what is done rather than because of what is presented.

Materials

Considerable wasted motion and time resulted from shortages of classroom material. These shortages were of two types—either not enough copies of a particular title, or gaps where too few books were available on a particular topic.

These shortages resulted from lack of funds or slowness of delivery. In one or two cases, inadequate forethought on the part of the group resulted in failure to anticipate needs far enough in advance to have materials on hand when needed. In all honesty it must be conceded that some inappropriate books were selected, books which either failed to interest students or which proved much too difficult for the majority to understand. The teachers, along with the classes, had to learn quite a bit as the course went along.

More adequate quantities have been made available in recent years, and more titles are appropriate to both the subject and the students. In regard to purchase of materials, a word must be said for two federal programs, NDEA and PL 89-10. These programs have really been of tremendous value and it is difficult to see how adequate stocks of materials and equipment could otherwise have been secured.

Facilities

Plant facilities are good, and large-group–small-group instruction is convenient to arrange. Lack of another large room prevents expansion beyond the present six sections.

Miscellaneous Problems

In any new approach there will be growing pains, and this course was no exception. The most noticeable was the development of more units than it was possible to cover. Two were eliminated during the first year, one during the second. At present the course is organized around the following units: (1) Colonial and Early Federal Period, (2) Immigration, (3) Westward Movement, (4) Regional Culture, (5) Politics in America, and (6) Recent America.

All involved felt to some degree that the pace of the course was too slow. This was due primarily to the fact that lack of individual copies of basic readings required excessive amounts of class time for reading and class exercises. This limited both discussion and writing time. This problem has been mitigated to some extent in recent years.

Student Responses

Students have received the course well, with many asking for it. By the same token, no one, to our knowledge, has requested transfer from the course due to dissatisfaction with the program. The schedule changes which were made were for other reasons, such as jobs, transportation, and program conflicts. On a more intangible basis, the sections seem somehow to develop a special *esprit* of their own. This is difficult to describe or define, but it is definitely there. Briefly, these students like the course, are pleased to be in it, feel it is something special, and act accordingly.

Art and Music Features

During the first year, the two teachers in the fields of art and music presented formal lectures in relation to each unit. Recordings, slides, filmstrips, and art reproductions were integral to the lectures. The material and presentations were fine, but none of the eight team members felt that enough student involvement occurred, for only a few students were other than listeners and observers. Progress was made in several ways the second year: more lectures were given, several field trips were arranged, and students presented panels in several sections on the art aspects of some units. The art teacher assisted students in preparing these panels, working with them in the school library. Successful, too, was the study of cartoon art. Students examined cartoons in current issues of newspapers under the direction of the art instructor.

Not unnaturally, students felt a considerable interest in the historical development of jazz as an American art form and in the presentation of political campaign songs. As a result of the continuous appraisal of the course, the music instructor worked at various intervals with groups of four to six students from each section during the third year.

The bulletin board displays were good, but too few. Part of this problem lay in the fact that the teachers simply did not change these materials often enough. Another part of the problem is common to the use of all bulletin boards: much time is needed to gather and prepare materials for exhibit.

Conclusions

In summarizing the first three years of Pueblo's humanities approach to the teaching of American history and English, several salient facts emerge. The program now has sufficient materials to provide the individual students with a range of sources, and the units have been reduced to allow adequate development of vital topics. It has proved popular with both teachers and students and it has successfully combined English and history instruction. Furthermore, this approach has encountered no unsolvable problems in spite of its various unusual features. Team teaching, block scheduling, large-group—small-group instruction, avoidance of single texts, and interdisciplinary teaching have all been successfully achieved.

Each year indicates more clearly just what materials are appropriate. Such works as *The Autobiography of Benjamin Franklin* and *The Oregon Trail* are not good choices for these groups. Materials such as *The Crucible, Fiddler on the Roof,* and *Vanguards of the Frontier* are more suitable. The integration of art and music would be more successful if the teaching teams were skilled and knowledgeable enough to handle this instruction themselves, using the art and music instructors as additional staff and resource persons. The entire teaching group needs to have periods of time during the school year for such pursuits as evaluation of unit plans and preparation of materials; evening meetings are just not sufficient.

It is hoped that our attempt to stabilize the course of instruction will not result in deadening class work or ignoring students' individual needs and interests, but rather that teachers will continue to avoid an overly rigid approach and to capitalize on the special aptitudes of the students.

Unit III

Other Innovations

In - Service Education
for Core Teachers
in Michigan City, Indiana

by Robert Raisor, Assistant Superintendent
for Secondary Schools

The core curriculum in the junior high schools in Michigan City is the oldest in the state of Indiana. It began at Elston Junior High School in 1946 under the leadership of the principal, Mr. A. K. Smith, who is presently Superintendent of Schools. Since that time, the core curriculum has been expanded into two newer junior high schools and is presently operating in all three junior high schools in grades seven and eight. It includes the English Language Arts, social science, and personal guidance, operating in a two-hour block of time. It is required of all pupils and groups are arranged heterogeneously.

A fundamental problem from the very beginning has been to secure trained teachers. Since few institutions of higher learning prepare teachers for the core curriculum, in-service training is necessary. This has taken a variety of forms. Teachers have frequent meetings with their fellow core teachers, with the building principal, and with the assistant superintendent to discuss problems relating to the core curriculum. In 1967, a number of core teachers requested a more detailed in-service education program. Officials at Ball State University in Muncie, Indiana, were contacted and a team of people from Ball State came to Michigan City several times to plan a program with our committee.

A unique feature of the in-service workshop was that it was operated as a core class would operate. Twelve weekly meetings were held, each of four hours duration—two hours before dinner in the evening and two hours afterwards.

The twenty-five participants helped in planning the workshop so that specific problems of the teachers were considered. Several professors from Ball State participated in the workshop. Sometimes a meeting was conducted by two or three people, but in most instances the teachers themselves developed the activities of the course. Credit was granted by Ball State University, and the school corporation paid half of the tuition of the participants.

A variety of techniques were utilized. One of the teachers taught a lesson to a

245

group of eighth-grade core students. This lesson was observed by the workshop group on a television monitor in another room, and also videotaped. Following this session, the group made a very careful analysis of the lesson, and the tape was filed for further reference. Philosophical as well as practical points were discussed and the workshop was concluded by a dinner, at which time committees reported on their investigations.

As a result of this in-service program, there has been a general improvement of teachers' understanding of the core curriculum. It has enhanced the understanding of noncore teachers, also, because some noncore teachers participated in the workshop, including some high school staff members. A few lay people were included too, thus enhancing community understanding of core. All in all, we feel the workshop was a success and that it would also be effective in other subject areas.

12

The Transition Class Program
in the Cleveland, Ohio, Public Schools

Adapted from Seventh Grade Transition Class Curriculum
Guide (Cleveland Public Schools, 1966), pp. vi–x.

The increasing prevalence of that group of persons whom we call "culturally disadvantaged" offers a great challenge to educators. Statistics show that in the large urban communities today, one out of three children is classified as "culturally disadvantaged." Continuing at its present rate, this group will include one of every two children in the large cities by 1970.

Some of the characteristics of culturally disadvantaged children are:

- They come from the rural South and Appalachia.
- They are non-English-speaking people.
- They have not had the benefits of sustained quality educational opportunity.
- They are members of a subculture which is not fully assimilated into the mainstream of American society.
- They suffer in varying degrees from poor self-images.
- They have low levels of aspiration.
- They are transient in school and community.
- They are looked upon as nonachievers by their teachers and by themselves.

As children from culturally and educationally disadvantaged groups enter the schools of the big cities in greater numbers, the problem of effectively and meaningfully escalating them, socially, culturally, academically, and psychologically has greatly increased and has, in some instances, become critical.

The Cleveland School System has recognized the critical need for new and dynamic approaches, organizational as well as methodological, in more effectively meeting the educational needs of this group. Since many of the children entering junior high school from elementary grades are "not ready" to assume the minimum responsibilities connected with secondary school life, it was felt that something had to be done to help bridge the gap between elementary school and junior high school. The Cleveland Public School System's answer was the

Transition Class, which was originally established at Addison Junior High School in 1960 as a part of the Hough Community Project.

The Hough Project demonstrated many promising practices in experimental approaches to teaching the basic skills and in the utilization of nontraditional teaching materials (i.e. telephone directory, the newspaper, mail-order catalogs). It was further shown that many positive educational advantages are made possible with highly flexible scheduling.

Careful consideration was given to the needs of the pupils for whom this curriculum was written. It was felt that the Integrated, Fused, or Theme Approach in teaching would be best suited for these pupils. In this approach, two or more subjects are replaced by units which usually cut across former subject-matter boundaries. Part of the time may be spent on subject matter skills separately, but a significant portion of time is used in studying an integrated area such as "Our Community."

The guide developed for this curriculum includes the following units:

Grade 7B

Unit I	Becoming Acquainted with Our School
Unit II	Helping in Our Homes
Unit III	Knowing Our Community
Unit IV	Living in Our City

Grade 7A

Unit V	Understanding Our Country
Unit VI	Learning About Our World
Unit VII	Improving Our Skills

The scope and sequence of all units to be covered have been included in the Transition Class Curriculum Guide, but the teacher is to use his own creative ability in the development of each.

The transition class should include pupils who

- Are two or more years retarded in reading skills.
- Are two or more years retarded in mathematical skills.
- Are emotionally and/or socially unready for the traditional junior high school organization and program.
- Are greatly in need of close supervision.

The objective, then, of the Transition Class Program is to help these pupils to overcome their unreadiness. To reach this goal a number of accomplishments must be achieved. These include

- Providing the pupil with an understanding of the organization and function of the school.
- Developing a pride of accomplishment within the child (a taste of success) thereby raising his level of aspiration.

- Developing a sense of respect for himself, his classmates, his school, and his community.
- Broadening and enriching his cultural experience.
- Upgrading the child in the basic skills, such as reading, arithmetic, oral, and written expression.
- Providing an atmosphere that will permit the child to grow and develop according to his unique needs, interests, and abilities.
- Demonstrating a practical relationship between school and everyday living activities.
- Eliminating the tensions and frustrations frequently associated with school and education.
- Developing a curriculum that will indicate to the pupil the interrelationship among various subjects.

The experiences of the professionals who have worked in this program have clearly demonstrated that those who work successfully in this program are those who

- Are highly dedicated teachers.
- Have empathy with the slow, reluctant, and/or deprived child.
- Have a great deal of patience and compassion.
- Have an experimental attitude.
- Are willing to utilize innovative teaching methods, materials, and equipment.
- Are willing and able to adapt both methods and materials to meet the needs of the pupils.
- Select materials and activities that have a high degree of relevancy for the "unready" junior high school pupil.
- Can "show" the pupils how they will benefit from that which is being taught.
- Are firm but fair.
- Maintain reasonable standards of discipline and control.

Operational Strategy
of the
Transition Program

1. Transition classes will be organized on a team basis.
2. Each school will have a project leader reporting to the principal. The project leader will serve in a capacity similar to department chairmen.
3. A team leader and a teacher assistant will compose an instructional team serving a class of approximately twenty-five pupils.
4. The team leader and teacher assistant will work with a transition class during the self-contained instruction time.

5. A supportive group of resource teachers will be assigned as members of the team to provide instruction in science, mathematics, music, art, and counseling. Resource teachers will be assigned to transition classes as a portion of their total teaching load.

6. Team leaders will be assigned to four transition periods, one team-planning period and one class within the regular class schedule of the school.

7. Flexibility in scheduling and organizing instruction suitable to individual needs of pupils will characterize the planning and operation of transition classes.

8. Essentially, transition classes are conceived as a team teaching effort. Homeroom teachers will remain with each class through the multi-period block of time. Subject specialists in the team will be available as resource persons to provide specific instruction in various subject areas. As an example, science will not be considered as a subject to be offered each day for a given period of time. Rather, as a unit of work is developed which requires a demonstration or instruction in science relevant to the unit, an appropriate member of the team will be scheduled by the team leader to participate in the class. It is possible, depending upon interest and readiness of pupils, that a majority of the block of time can be science oriented.

9. The reinforcement of study skills and communication skills will be emphasized throughout the instructional program.

10. Likewise, other subject areas such as art, music, and mathematics will be integrated into the program in such a way that the approach will capitalize on the interests that have been generated through the particular unit of instruction.

11. During the remaining periods of the school day, the pupils will attend classes in industrial arts, home economics, music, art, and physical education. Every effort will be made to keep the transition class intact for instruction in these subjects. For certain laboratory type classes, the pupils will move to appropriate facilities.

12. All transition class pupils will be part of the total school program. They will attend assemblies, be eligible for sports and extracurricular activities, and will have representatives in the student government.

13. Unit scheduling will insure maximum coordination of subject areas through a team effort of all the teachers of transition class pupils.

14. Each transition class will participate in group-guidance sessions. The guidance counselor assigned to the transition class will direct the group-guidance activities and will provide individual counseling through regularly scheduled conferences.

15. A teacher's assistant will facilitate the growth of mutual understanding between home and school by developing and maintaining the channels of reciprocal communication.

16. Boys and girls will be separated for instruction in transition classes.
17. Transition classes will have a maximum enrollment of twenty-five.
18. Class-to-class mobility and the number of teacher contacts will be minimized by operating each transition class as a self-contained unit. The pupils in a given unit will remain in one classroom for a multi-period block of time.
19. Each pupil will be evaluated regularly by the transition team. When sufficient growth and readiness has been demonstrated, reassignment to regular classes will be arranged.

English–Social Studies

There is no basal textbook in the field of English–social studies for the transition classes. The teacher should fully utilize a variety of suggested texts, magazines, pamphlets, newspapers, and other supplementary materials. Map study will comprise a large portion of both the 7B and 7A curriculum.

The English–social studies curriculum of the Transition Program is fused and is designed to improve the pupil's skills in four areas of communication: speaking, listening, reading, and writing. The topics listed in the guide are arbitrary. The teacher should develop the topic according to the needs of the pupils. These topics should be correlated, whenever possible, with the units covered by the resource team.

The English–social studies resource teacher, with the help of the reading specialist and the librarian, should develop a list of suitable reading materials to accommodate the various reading levels within the class. Much of the team leader's class time should be spent in developing reading skills and reinforcing the instruction of the resource team. Book reports, both written and oral, can and should often be related to the topics studied in the other subject areas.

It is suggested that a vocabulary notebook be kept. The weekly vocabulary list will be composed of vocabulary from all subjects. The English-Social Studies teacher should allow ample time for discussion, drill, and review of vocabulary words presented in all areas.

Guidance Counselors

Many topics usually covered by the guidance counselor will be studied under the direction of the team leader and resource personnel. The counselor will reinforce their work as he serves as a member of the team.

Many pupils are handicapped by their attitudes toward themselves, their school, their home, and their community. Children from low socioeconomic groups often have the problem of conforming to the standards of the dominant culture. Herein lies an important function of the counselor in the Transition Program. He will look toward establishing more positive attitudes so that pupils are better able to take full advantage of their opportunity for learning.

Group counseling is suggested as the primary technique because of limited time (as compared with individual counseling) and because at this age pupils are more easily influenced by their peer group than by adults. Individual and small-group counseling may be scheduled as required.

A central theme will be used in the classes in order to coordinate the work of all departments. The counselor will attempt to guide his discussion into channels related to these general topics. His program must be flexible, however, and the focal point must be the immediate needs of the pupils and not limited to the central theme.

The topics for discussion may be initiated by the counselor or by the pupils. Pupils hopefully will feel free to bring their problems to the group and to discuss them. This is the place where their hostilities, their anxieties, their personal experiences, their fears, and their needs for understanding can come forth and be given the dignity of having some value and of being worthy of attention.

Pupils must also be given an opportunity to have conferences with the counselor. If they have problems which they feel cannot be discussed with the group, the counselor should honor requests for private conferences.

The counselor must be alert to the developmental progress (educational and emotional) of the individual pupils. He will confer with the resource teachers, make recommendations, and administer tests when needed.

As a part of the team he should be consulted relative to a pupil's readiness for sectional changes. Such changes must be approved by the principal or the administrator in charge of the program.

The counselor will work closely with the teachers to assist them to better understand each pupil's conduct, attitudes, and needs. Teachers should then be able to more effectively help the pupils.

The counselor's knowledge of individual pupils will be of major importance in evaluation of the total Transition Program. He will work with pupils who are ready to be moved out of these classes and will recommend that certain pupils from regular classes be scheduled into the transition classes. The counselor should be in a position to evaluate each pupil's adjustment. He should keep and encourage teachers to keep anecdotal records of pupils. Keeping a record of the number of pupils enrolled in these classes, those transferred to regular classes or to other schools, and the number added to the classes will also be the counselor's responsibility.

Mathematics

Since pupils are usually grouped according to reading scores rather than according to arithmetic scores, the mathematics classes will be more heterogeneous with reference to the pupils' mathematical ability levels. Therefore, the math teacher should give the pupils diagnostic tests and should divide the class into groups based on the results of these tests. This necessitates the use of individual work for most classes. Those at the upper level will be able to use more seventh-grade content material. *Basic Modern Mathematics* (First Course)[1] is recommended for lower and middle groups within a class. The

[1] Reading, Mass.: Addison-Wesley Publishing Co. Inc.

teacher must be selective so that all pupils are given material commensurate with their arithmetic ability levels.

The main topics of the transition classes may not at all times coincide with the skills and concepts being taught in the math class. Although mathematics is a sequential subject, the math teacher will often be able to relate the mathematical skills to the unit of work being covered by the team leader. Close cooperation and team planning among the teachers involved will provide much useful and unique material that will be meaningful to the children.

Upgrading in basic skills is felt to be a basic need for these pupils; therefore, considerable emphasis has been placed on fundamental concepts and operations. Certain geometric concepts are important for these children and have been included in the 7A section of the guide. It may be that a supplementary unit on intuitive geometry can be introduced. This will be left to the discretion of the individual teacher.

Science

As in other subjects, there is an absence of a basal textbook in science. Teachers are at liberty to use a variety of supplementary materials, but they must keep instruction at the level of the pupils' comprehension and continually work to improve the basic skills. The science curriculum is designed to be flexible, creative, and motivational. Science, health education, and home economics are highly correlated.

Industrial Arts

Industrial arts projects are to be kept on the pupils' level. Children should be given the freedom to choose from several projects. These projects should have several operations in common that will cover the same basic skills needed in this field of study. Correlation of industrial arts work with that of other subject areas is desirable and can be effected through team planning. The 7A home mechanics course is designed to introduce the pupils to some of the many small house repair jobs that can be done quickly, simply, and inexpensively. It is not intended to make master craftsmen of the pupils, but rather to encourage them to do some of the jobs themselves in the hope that they will develop a pride in their accomplishments.

Home Economics

The home economics teacher should correlate her subject with the topics covered by the team leader. During the 7A semester the emphasis will be placed on nutrition. The home economics teacher will be expected to aid the team leader in the development of the unit on nutrition for the boys as well as girls.

Each home economics teacher will choose the projects desired. The projects should, if possible, meet the objectives of both the transitional program and the home economics program. In order to achieve a feeling of freedom, the children should have a choice of several projects.

Reading

Although all resource teachers have the responsibilty of teaching skills as a part of their respective areas, it is the reading specialists who will give the in-depth remedial reading instruction. By using worksheets and phonics charts, the reading specialist will cover the 20 topics listed below.

The alphabet	The bossy R
Initial consonant sounds	Prefixes
	Suffixes
Consonant blends	Syllabication
Rhyming ends	The G and C sounds
Short vowel sounds	Word endings
Long vowel sounds	Compound words
Vowel rule I	Contractions
Vowel rule II	Vocabulary and comprehension skills
Vowel rule III	
Letter teams	

Generally these topics will be developed in the order presented. However, the teacher should use his knowledge of the pupils' weaknesses in deciding which to emphasize. It is the responsibility of the reading specialist to keep the other members of the team informed regarding pupils' progress in reading. The reading specialist is expected, whenever possible, to correlate his lessons with the unit being studied by the other teachers of the team.

Though one teacher may be designated as the master reading teacher, *all* teachers must share the responsibility of providing reading instruction in their respective subject areas.

Art

During the 7A semester, art will be offered to the transition pupils. The art teacher should correlate his units with the topics studied in the other subject matter areas. Some suggestions for possible correlation are: the drawing of contemporary life after a study of historical American art; lessons on portraiture which could be followed by a lesson on recognizing and portraying our President, the use of contemporary events in social studies for the development of political cartoons, the study of maps (population locations, climatic conditions, physical features) could be used along with studies of contemporary art styles. The art teacher may also help the student to design covers and draw pictures for notebooks made in other subject areas.

Music

The music teacher should correlate as much as possible with other subject areas and provide special instruction upon request from the team leader.

13

The Use of Closed-Circuit Television in Block-of-Time Classes for Disadvantaged Students in Spain Junior High School, Detroit, Michigan

by Leonard J. Dazer, Block-of-Time Teacher and CCTV Coordinator (Presently Sixth-Grade Teacher, Burger Middle School, Garden City, Michigan)

The core program in the Detroit Public Schools is called block-of-time. In 1959, the block-of-time program was recommended by the Board of Education for all the junior high schools of the city. Our block program at Spain Junior High School involves grades 7B through 9A. The subject matter is a fusion of English and social studies. One teacher meets with the same group of students for a double period of time, five days a week. Curriculum policy limits the block to specific subject content but encourages the problem-solving approach. A flexible teacher applying a liberal interpretation of this policy has no difficulty in dealing with problems meaningful to his class regardless of the topic under study.

Charles L. Spain Junior High School is located in the heart of Target Area Number One, as designated to the Total Action Against Poverty (TAAP) Program of the City of Detroit. The community and students possess all of the socioeconomic characteristics associated with depressed areas. Of the 1,100 students in grades 7 through 9, 99.9 percent are Negro. Average class size is 29.5.

A major concern in Spain Junior High School is the enhancement of our students' self-images. Because we are in a disadvantaged area, our students come to us with an all-too-negative view of self. This is detrimental to learning. We try to build self-confidence through the problem-solving approach in a democratically oriented classroom. We place strong emphasis on the dignity and worth of the individual. We feel that everyone has something worthwhile to contribute. Our closed-circuit television system is an excellent tool in helping us to reach our ultimate goal.

257

We believe that a unimedium (print) approach to education fails to meet the needs of disadvantaged youngsters. There is, however, one thing that exists in almost every deprived home—television. If there is no TV, then almost certainly there is a transistor radio or a record player. The disadvantaged child's preschool orientation to learning involves audio-visual media rather than print. The CCTV program at Spain builds on this fact.

Closed-circuit television also can be a motivational force for our students. We believe that the majority of our students will not progress to the level of establishing their own educational purposes until each has strengthened his concept of self-worth. Operating upon this philosophy, we have constructed the following objectives for our CCTV program:

1. To help each student develop a more positive self-image.
2. To provide an opportunity for our students to see themselves and their peers performing in a constructive manner.
3. To create awareness of the necessity of mastering the communication skills, especially the oral and aural, combined with the realization that observation is a vital part of education.
4. To present the same lesson to many classes at the same time, resulting in a greater coordination of teaching effort.
5. To present lessons and units which could not be handled in the conventional classroom because of their uniqueness or the time necessary to prepare them.
6. To share a teacher's specialties with the entire school rather than limit his or her talent to just the five classes he teaches.
7. To encourage and improve school-community relations.
8. To encourage the staff to view our CCTV facilities as their teaching tool.
9. To expose students more frequently to our administrative officials, thus establishing a warmer rapport between them and the administrators.
10. To experiment with the concept of pupil-pupil learning.

The CCTV facilities at Spain Junior High School are utilized in many ways by our block-of-time classes. As an individual teaching tool, CCTV may be used by a single class for the specific purposes of that class. For example, during orientation week, class members conduct their person-to-person interviews on camera. This provides a first exposure to TV while at the same time it allows the students to see themselves on the monitor screen. This usually is the first time the students have seen themselves as others see them. Needless to say, most are quite surprised.

Block classes use CCTV to practice their presentations prior to live telecast. This allows the groups to attain a high level of performance. The final presentations of a unit also are given on CCTV, which provides these advantages:

1. Models, pictures, and objects which are too small for clear observation in a normal classroom setting can be used.

2. The speakers are brought closer to the listeners by camera close-ups.
3. Every listener has the impression that the speaker is directly addressing him. TV is one of the few media that make it possible for the speaker to look directly at each listener. This helps hold attention.
4. If videotape is available, the presentations can be taped and the class can watch them as a whole. This provides an opportunity for the group that made the presentation to watch along with the class. This makes answering postpresentation questions easier to handle. Also, the teacher can have the tape run back to point out highlights or to clarify misconceptions.
5. Students have the opportunity to see themselves and their peers performing in a constructive manner.
6. Self-evaluation becomes easier and more valid as the students see and hear themselves and their material.
7. Tapes can be preserved so that each student can evaluate the progress he or she has made since his first presentation early in the semester or year.

CCTV can be used to help in guidance. This simply means that once the camera has been set up, students gradually become accustomed to its presence and eventually ignore it. In the meantime their classroom behavior is being taped. Various behavior patterns can then be shown to the students who have behaviorial peculiarities. It is remarkable what happens when a student sees himself in action.

Classes may invite other classes to tune in on their presentations if they so desire. This helps students boost their self-confidence. Parents, too, have an opportunity to see their children perform in a constructive manner by viewing videotapes on PTA night.

But what is probably most important is the fact that the student has the opportunity to see himself in a way that he has never before experienced. He realizes for the first time that he is somebody, that he can achieve. The cultural limitations and handicaps of the ghetto are not insurmountable. Life does have meaning and education does have purpose. And what is more, he realizes that he is entitled to the dignity of sharing these privileges because of the simple fact that he, too, is a member of the human race.

14

The Secondary Continuous Advancement Program (SCAP) at Binford Junior High School, Bloomington, Indiana

by Martha A. Lee, Director

The Secondary Continuous Advancement Program is an ungraded interdisciplinary approach to instruction in social studies and language arts. Random selection is used in assigning students to the program, although requests for entry are honored whenever possible. In the program a flexible organization of learning experiences is adapted to individual differences in pupil ability, interest, and rate of progress.

Without major concern for chronological age or grade level, pupils are assigned to variant instructional groups in which they may advance as rapidly as their capabilities permit. This concept of ungradedness is designed to accommodate differentiated rates of growth and to allow for exploration of subject matter in varied depths of study according to the interests and abilities of pupils. In an ungraded SCAP classroom, pupils work at their own pace without having to wait several years to learn what they are capable of learning now, or without having to be in classes that concentrate on learning experiences beyond their comprehension.

Four teachers, two in language arts and two in social studies, teach 200 students representing grades 7, 8, and 9. There is a morning and an afternoon two-period block with approximately 100 students assigned to each. The four social studies classes and four language arts classes in each block of time sometimes meet separately, sometimes in larger or smaller groups.

Large-group—small-group instruction allows a SCAP teacher with special competence in delivering large-group presentations to specialize in this direction. A SCAP teacher with special talents in dealing with small groups can concentrate with smaller, more intimate groups and with individual students.

Area studies, arranged in a three-year cycle, provide the focus of instruction in language arts and social studies. One semester is spent examining each of the following areas: the Soviet Union, Europe, China, Southeast Asia, Africa, and South and Southwest Asia. Each pupil in SCAP studies the same topic at the same time but at his individual level of understanding, without regard to his chronological age or grade level. The team of teachers works with the same pupils for three years. This keeps learning experiences for each pupil on a continuum, since each team member knows what the pupil has been taught while in the program.

Instead of a single textbook, multiple materials are assigned to students according to different ability levels. Paperbacks are used as much as possible. In this way, students are introduced to many different points of view and are taught to arrive at their own conclusions. An example of social studies materials used at various levels for Cycle III, Semester I, Africa, is as follows:

Social Studies Materials for the Study of Africa

Level I (Reading Grade
   Equivalent: 3.0—6.9)
My First World Atlas (Hammond)
Africa (Allen)
How People Live (Greig)
Book I: Workbook (Benton)
Africa (Fideler)
Handouts prepared by
   teachers

Level II (Reading Grade
   Equivalent: 7.0—9.5)
Emerging Africa (Scholastic)
Africa (Allen)
Story of East Africa (Wiles)
Story of West Africa (Wiles)
Africa: World Today (Rosberg)
Africa (Nielsen)
Map Skills (AEP)
Southwest Asia and North Africa (Allen)
The New Africa (Cambridge)
Comparative World Atlas (Hammond)
Handouts prepared by
   teachers

Level III (Reading Grade
   Equivalent: 9.0—12.9)
Africa (Nielsen)
Africa: World Today (Rosberg)
Emerging Africa (Scholastic)
Comparative World Atlas (Hammond)
Map Skills, Today's Geography
   (AEP)
Handouts prepared by teachers
Current newspapers, magazines

Level IV (Reading Grade
   Equivalent: 10.5—12.9)
Contemporary Africa (Wallbank)
Africa (Hapgood)
Emerging Africa (Scholastic)
Comparative World Atlas (Hammond)
Africa and The World Today (Rosberg)
Physical Geography (AEP)
Handouts prepared by teachers
Current newspapers, magazines

The literature used in the language arts classes is correlated with the area of study. The following titles illustrate this correlation in the Africa study.

Literature for the Study of Africa

Level I
Tales
   Hat Shaking Dance (Courlander)
   Drummer Boy (Ekwensi)
   Sons of the Desert (Gidal)

Level II
Tales
   Lion's Whiskers (Davis)

Novel
Jamie (Bennett)
Short Stories
Calvacade (Robinson)
On the Threshhold (Humphreville)
Stories to Remember (Lyons)
Treasure Gold (Witty)
Silver Webb (Witty)
Level III
Tales
African Myths, Tales
   (Feldman)
Novel
Things Fall Apart (Achebe)

Return to Laughter (Bowen)
Short Stories
African Treasury (Hughes)
Great Short Works (Conrad)
Adventures in Reading (Lodge)
Poetry
Handouts prepared by
   teachers

Novel
Boy Ten Feet Tall (Canaway)
Short Stories
Wide Wide World (Pooley)
Poetry
Handouts prepared by teachers

Level IV
Tales
African Myths, Tales
   (Feldman)
Novel
Cry the Beloved Country
   (Paton)
Return to Laughter (Bowen)
Short Stories
African Treasury (Hughes)
Great Short Works (Conrad)

Poetry
Handouts prepared by
   teachers

At the beginning of each year the language arts teachers cooperatively outline the year's study. This determines when the skills suggested in the SCAP Language Arts Curriculum Guide for each level of the cycle will be taught. The teachers at this time decide which skills they feel they are most capable of teaching.

English grammar is taught for a minimum of six weeks each semester. This includes a two-week introductory unit which is taught at the beginning of each school year. Otherwise, grammar is interspersed with the study of literature and other language skills. The theories of "new" grammar are incorporated in the curriculum whenever possible. Placement of students in one of the following classes is determined by performance on an achievement test and on a grammar pretest. Some attention is given to grade level and/or former group placement.

General Course Outlines: Grammar

Class A: Seventh-grade students scoring above average on pretest
   Review parts of speech. Review basic parts of a sentence. Review action and linking verbs with emphasis on the latter. Introduce prepositional phases. Introduce completers: objects, predicate nouns, and adjectives.
Class B: Seventh-grade students scoring below average on pretest
   Review basic parts of a sentence: nouns and verbs. Discuss types of nouns and verbs. Introduce four basic sentence types.

Class C: Eighth- and ninth-grade students in Level I
        Review basic parts of a sentence: nouns and verbs. Review particular material covered in depth during previous cycle.

Class D: Eighth- and ninth-grade students in Level II
        Review all parts of speech briefly. Review the basic parts of a sentence: nouns, verbs as simple subject and predicate. Review particular material covered in depth during previous cycle.

Class E: Eighth- and ninth-grade students in Level III
        Review all of the parts of speech. Review basic sentence structure and four types of sentences. Review particular parts of speech and usage covered in previous cycle. Short writing assignments may be effective here to check usage.

Class F: Eighth- and ninth-grade students in Level IV
        Review all of the parts of speech briefly. Review basic sentence structure briefly. Review parts of speech and sentence structure covered in depth during previous cycle. Short writing assignments may be given.

Schedule (Two-Hour Block Divided into Four Class Periods)

Teacher*	1	2	3	4
Field	(Social Studies)	(Social Studies)	(English)	(English)
	Large Group	English	English	English
Period A	Classes D-E-F			
(25 min.)	studying social studies	Class A	Class B	Class C
Period B	Classes A-B-C			
(25 min.)	studying social studies	Class D	Class E	Class F

		Break		
Teacher	3	4	1	2
Field	(English)	(English)	(Social Studies)	(Social Studies)
	Large Group		Social Studies	Social Studies
Period C	Classes III–IV			
(25 min.)	studying English		Class I	Class II
Period D	Classes I–II			
(25 min.)	studying English		Class III	Class IV

Note. Teacher 2 has the greatest amount of preparation. Therefore the other three teachers involved must help teacher 2 with mimeographing, paper marking, etc.

    Spelling is taught in the language arts classes, with many of the words drawn from social studies materials. Effective oral and written expression also is taught throughout each semester of the three-year curriculum. Goals and instructional procedures are varied for the different ability levels.

    Flexible scheduling within SCAP permits varying arrangements of instructional time, class organization, and staff. Schedule modifications within the two-hour block of time include variable period length, variable sequence or rotation of classes, variable grouping of students, variable staffing, variable meeting patterns, and variable total time spent on each subject. SCAP teachers reap many of the benefits of team teaching that have been described earlier in this book.

SCAP teachers do not assume that pupils must all learn the same material at the same age. The SCAP team assumes responsibility for grouping and continuously regrouping pupils in order to give each student the best possible learning advantage. Factors considered are physical maturity, social and emotional maturity, special needs, interests, readiness for skills, ability in reflective thinking, reading skills, and language skills.

From time to time both student and parent questionnaires have been used in the continuing evaluation of SCAP. Parent questionnaires have indicated the following: (1) Parents feel that their child's attitude toward school has improved as a result of his being in SCAP; (2) Parent-teacher conferences would *not* be of greater value than the present report-card method of showing student progress; (3) Parents overwhelmingly approve of their child being with older and/or younger children in the classroom; (4) Parents feel that the child's academic progress has improved as a result of his being in SCAP; and (5) Parents feel that the child's academic progress would have been less if he had not been selected for SCAP.

The following are findings from student questionaires: (1) students feel that they receive enough attention in large groups; (2) students feel that they receive enough attention in small groups and more attention than in regular classes; (3) students dislike the lecture technique; (4) students enjoy meeting in large groups for individual assignments and all other activities except lectures; (5) students prefer grades that indicate an individual's performance as compared with what he is capable of doing rather than those that compare him with friends and classmates; (6) students feel freer to participate in SCAP classes than in regular classes; (7) students enjoy using multiple materials and are generally not bothered by not having their own individual SCAP books to take out of class each day; (8) students feel that reading related materials in literature helps them to understand social studies and that the study of social-studies materials helps them to understand literature; (9) no matter how low or high the letter grades received, students feel that they have not worked as hard as they could.

Additional data on the value of the Secondary Continuous Advancement Program may be found in the writer's doctoral study, "Development of Inquiry Skills in Ungraded Social Studies Classes in a Junior High School" (Indiana University, 1967). It was found that, although intelligence and reading may be factors affecting the degree to which problem-solving skills are learned and applied, the difference in ages and grade levels of pupils within the same class is not a significant factor in the proficiency and utilization of inquiry skills. The level of pupil maturity, however, apparently is related to pupil ability to apply skills in problem solving.

Teachers participating in the program report that the flexible nature of the program: (1) allows students to move within or among groups, (2) allows teachers at any given time to deal with a smaller range of abilities than normally found in a regular classroom, (3) tends to encourage wide pupil participation in small groups, (4) offers pupils more opportunities for success, (5) permits a variety of activities, such as large-group—small-group instruction, independent study, team teaching, (6) leads to a correlation between two disciplines, (7) encourages the use of materials at different levels of ability, (8) eliminates needless duplication and repetition of teacher tasks, (9) forces teachers to evaluate each student as an individual, (10) provides for effective use of teacher time and talents, and (11) provides teachers with opportunities to teach pupils of varied age and ability levels.

Relatively few problems have been encountered throughout the four years of this program. At times, however, there have been unusual demands on teacher time connected with the location and selection of appropriate materials, the development or construction of multiple materials, and the testing and place-ment of 200 pupils. Also, the traditional building design, without flexible walls and without several large-group instructional areas, has at times restricted the flexibility of the program.

15

The Component Curriculum at
Roosevelt School,
Eastern Michigan University, Ypsilanti

by Gerald V. Sharp, Assistant Professor

For the past two years the staff at Roosevelt School, Eastern Michigan University's Laboratory School, has been developing a reorganized general education program. During the 1965–66 school year, portions of the program replaced core, mathematics, and science classes in grade 7. The success of this pilot led to continued development and expansion. Grades 6, 7, and 8 were involved in a more comprehensive program during 1966–67, and now grades 4 through 8 are included.

Like most education programs in the United States, the Component Curriculum Project aims to develop thinking citizens for a democratic society. But unlike most previous general education projects, it stresses the following four factors: (1) It is necessary to humanize education during the current technological revolution, while taking advantage of technological innovations. (2) Progress in transportation and communication has made it necessary to consider the world as the student's society and to train for world citizenship. (3) Man is a generalist in his citizenship role. Current educational systems address their primary efforts toward developing the specialized qualities of man. The conventional school's skill-content organization reflects this emphasis. The Laboratory School's new program reverses the emphasis. Since it is the general qualities in man that allow him to become a thinking citizen, the primary effort is addressed to developing the essential general skills, knowledge, and experiences. (4) Change is recognized as a permanent condition in society. To cope with such a society, an individual needs extended margins of tolerance for indecision, tentative solutions, dilemma, error, variety, disagreement, and nonpermanent absolutes.

Our school's evolving educational organization is based on the learning process in which the student is engaged, rather than on the student's age and/or the content area involved. The program provides:

267

1. The opportunity for all students to acquire a general information base and a common experience base which provide both the media and the content of communication within the social setting of the school.
2. The opportunity for each individual to examine, develop, refine, and pursue his own needs, interests, and desires.
3. The opportunity for groups to apply, share, and assess development in chosen areas.
4. The opportunity for individuals to express, explore, examine, and amend ideas.

The Educational Program

To provide the four opportunities described above, Roosevelt School developed a four-part program, each part corresponding to one of the necessary opportunities.

The program currently utilizes team-teaching, nongraded organization, flexible-modular scheduling, descriptive performance and evaluation criteria, workshops, block-of-time, seminars, and programmed materials.

1. Social Assessment Component

The goal of this component is to provide a common base of experience for a group while expanding and enriching individual differences. The experiences serve as the base for future action either by the group or by an individual. In this component students observe, examine, experience, plan and evaluate activities which concern man's impact upon himself, upon others, and upon the environment.

Currently the Social Assessment Component utilizes 1 1/2 to 2 1/2 hours per day in the following manner:

(a) A short presentation of an idea, skill, experience, or small portion of knowledge is made by a resource person or an audio-visual device. The purpose is exposure, motivation, and stimulation. The subject matter of the presentations over time will hopefully mirror the knowledge and thinking of society.

(b) The students choose fields of exploration and then form groups to plan and carry out exploring activities. The range of exploration is limited only by legal and reasonable possibilities. Students are encouraged to explore new fields in a group to assure common experiences for communication.

(c) Students meet regularly to deal with total group concerns. Total group activities and self-government are encouraged.

The particular nature and organization of these activities is worked out by each group and therefore is unique to each group. This is basically a group-center block-of-time activity.

2. Individual Development Component

The goal of this component is individualized depth study, often growing out of experiences in the Social Assessment Component. Using materials and equipment which are designed to implement self-pacing and self-selection, individual students develop and refine skills and enrich and expand knowledge. The selection of materials, equipment, skill areas, and interest areas is worked out in student-teacher conferences.

Each student's program is influenced by: (1) the student's felt needs, (2) his interests, (3) diagnostic test scores of skills, experience, and knowledge (which are shared with the student), (4) the individual's learning pattern, (5) materials available, and (6) the need for balance with other activities in the student's total program.

The areas of study are restricted only by the availability of instructional materials, staff, and facilities. Students may be practicing arithmetic or handwriting, working with clay or scientific apparatus constructing a bibliography, reading, studying grammar or Spanish vocabulary, doing geometric constructions, or other diversified individual activities.

The Learning Laboratory, a room especially equipped for individualized instruction, is available to all students at all times to implement their particular individual study programs. The amount of time each student spends in the Learning Laboratory is determined by his own needs, interests, and tolerances.

3. Applied Learnings Component

The goal of this component is to give social meaning to individual endeavors. Individuals with common interests form a group in order to apply, practice, refine, enrich, and study a specific topic. This process serves to reinforce and enrich interests and motivation.

Usually a small group meets with an instructor or other knowledgeable person to work in a specified interest area. These groups usually operate on a workshop basis, since the sequential development of content or skills is not the primary concern, as it is in the Individual Development Component. A student is able to enter and leave these classes according to his own unique tolerances and satiation levels. For example, he may enter a French-conversation workshop, stay 3 weeks, leave for 1 week and return for 5 weeks.

Specific classes come into and go out of existence continually. The process is as follows:

(a) Students, parents, and staff members recommend that a topic be added to the list.

(b) Interested staff members write a proposed syllabus.

(c) The syllabus is reviewed by interested students, parents, staff members, and consultants and revised as necessary.

(d) Students are polled to ascertain interest.

(e) If interest is evident, the class is scheduled as best suits the learning process and activities involved.

(f) Students are made aware of the class and allowed to elect it. (Some classes carry prerequisites which bar some students.)

(g) If an adequate number of students (usually a minimum of five), elect the class, it begins at the first convenient opportunity.

(h) The class continues to meet until it reaches a logical conclusion or until so many students have dropped the class that it can no longer function, in which case students still interested usually continue to pursue the topic as an individual study project.

4. Integrative Component

Although integration can take place at any time in any place, it is important that the resulting generalizations be verbalized in order for the individual to receive feedback. Therefore, time is set aside each day for small-group seminars, composed of students with different backgrounds, values, and experiences, to discuss topics of current member interest. The seminars are an attempt to explore how individuals, groups, and societies validate observations, facts, beliefs, and opinions. It is hoped that isolated facts, detailed knowledge, personal experience, and opinion will be woven into broader operational concepts, and, most important, that the individual will understand the validity limits of each concept.

The seminars are usually open to students desiring to attend either on a scheduled basis or, with permission, on an unscheduled (impulse) basis.

Scheduling

Since man is both a social and an individual being, most students are required to spend some time each week in a Social Assessment activity and in the Individual Study Program. For scheduling purposes, each student is assigned to, or elects, a Social Assessment group or activity. The final decision is usually mutually agreed upon by the student, the group, and the student's staff advisor. The decision is usually based upon the student's ability to meet the demands of the activity and the group. For example, a group planning to camp out in the woods of Northern Michigan will place demands of a different magnitude on an individual as compared with a group planning to visit the local banks. The camp-out will be attractive to most individuals, but not all who are interested will be able to tolerate the time interval between the initial brainstorming and the actual activation of the plan. Not all will be able to tolerate the complexity of planning required in order to account for all the individuals in the group for prolonged periods and diverse activities. Therefore, in selecting a Social Assessment group an individual and advisor must consider the activity and its complexity in relation to the student's interest, previous experiences, and maturity.

The remaining time in each student's schedule is assigned to the Learning Laboratory. In the Learning Laboratory the student and his advisor work out, not only an individual study program, but a completely individualized schedule. An attempt is made to balance Applied Learning Classes, Integrative Seminars, and Individual Study activities so as to correspond with the individual's learning pattern, needs, and interests. Each individual's schedule is reviewed and revised as necessary by the student and his advisor during a counseling session at least every two weeks.

Diverse patterns are common. Among the students electing Introduction to Algebra, an Applied Learnings class, some use programmed materials in the Learning Laboratory to reinforce the class work, some use the class to clarify or enrich the programmed materials studied in the Learning Laboratory, some take no other mathematics concurrently, and some use the Learning Laboratory to refine basic skills. Other mathematics-oriented Applied Learnings classes also are available, such as Introduction to Geometry, Computer Mathematics, and Common Fractions. The same pattern prevails for all skill, content, and interest areas. When sequence in skill or content development is necessary, such sequences are usually preserved in the Individualized Development Component, often using programmed materials which present sequential material efficiently and effectively.

A balance of components within the daily diet of each student is necessary. Since each student has unique needs, interests, and tolerance levels, the correct balance for each student will be unique. Program diversity and flexibility are essential for each student to maintain a balanced schedule. Therefore, the program currently uses a modular schedule in order to gain the required flexibility for constructing diverse, balanced, and appropriate individual schedules and in order to provide the appropriate time blocks for each activity. However, it does not sufficiently allow for day-to-day differences of student needs. As a result, a fluid schedule, which will be more flexible without sacrificing continuity and ease of administration, is currently evolving within the program.

Staff

The Component Curriculum project is currently staffed by a seven-member team. Each member of the team assumes responsibility for all students within the program and all aspects of the program. Although the team delegates specific responsibilities to specific individuals, as a matter of policy each member is involved in as many aspects of the project as possible in order to maintain the team effort at a meaningful level. Each team member has a project-related responsibility, a responsibility working in each of the components, is advisor to a group of students representing the total age range, and must remain informed regarding all aspects of the project. For example, the team member primarily responsible for the testing and data collecting dimension of the project also is working in a Social Assessment group with the team member responsible for attendance, and each will teach various Applied Learnings, meet with Integrative Seminars, and assist in the Learning Laboratory during each semester.

The seven-member team is assisted by specialized staff on a voluntary and assigned basis, as well as by resource people from the community. The assistance is usually in the form of teaching an Applied Learnings Class or Workshop, or serving as a resource person to a Social Assessment group.

Student Population

Students in the Component Curriculum Project at this time generally range in between age 10 and 14, but extend from age 9 to 16. The population is representative of the community, economically and racially. Academically the population has a relatively large number of underachievers, a relatively large number of academically talented students, and a relatively low number of average students.

Currently the project is concentrating on the Middle School section of Roosevelt School. Students enter the program upon leaving the third grade and leave the program upon entering high school. The transition from the program to the high school unit is usually gradual. Students in the Component Curriculum project are able to elect high school classes with the approval of their advisor and the potential high school instructor. The practice of electing one or two high school classes before shifting to the high school is becoming quite common.

In a few years it is hoped that sufficient experience will have been gained to begin a longitudinal research study in which students are exposed to the Component Curriculum as their total school experience. Students will enter the program on the basis of specified entrance criteria and exit by growing out of the program into community service, a job, or college, in a manner similar to the way students currently grow out of the middle school into the high school.

The Component Curriculum is intended to begin with initial formal school contact and extend throughout one's entire adult life. The organization can be applied to university and adult education programs as well as elementary and secondary school programs. It is intended to dissolve the age, content, and achievement barriers which currently divide education. Such an organization does not imply a terminal level of achievement or age, but suggests continuous education for all in varied time patterns. The Component Curriculum is designed to be the total school experience.

Appendixes

Appendix A

Selected Resources for
Secondary School Humanities*

1. Robert O'Neal, *Teachers Guide to World Literature for the High School.*
   National Council of Teachers of English, Champaign, Ill., 1966. An excellent
   reference book for teachers. A thematic and comparative study of more than
   two hundred classics in translation, along with some British and American
   works. From this guide the tenth- and twelfth-grade literature teacher may
   make suitable selections for the class.

2. Anthologies in paperback:
   (a) Laurel Masterpieces of World Literature. Classical, Medieval, Renais-
       sance, Age of Reason, and Romantic. Dell paperbacks.

   (b) Viking Portables. Greek, Roman, Medieval, Renaissance. Viking Press.

3. American studies materials designed to promote discovery learning:
   (a) New Dimensions in American History series. Paperbacks developed by
       the Committee on the Study of History, Amherst College. For students
       of average ability. D. C. Heath and Company.

   (b) Problems in American History series. Paperbacks for the college-bound
       student. Scott, Foresman and Company.

   (c) Basic Concepts in History and the Social Sciences. Paperbacks that offer
       important topics to be studied in depth from sources. D. C. Heath and
       Company.

4. Enrichment material for American studies courses:
   (a) *The Life History of the United States,* in 12 volumes. There are also
       available 12 recordings, *The Sounds of History,* which present docu-
       ments, literature, and a good selection of music related to each volume
       in the series.

Note: See Chapter 6 for the criteria applied in selecting these materials.

(b) *Folk Songs in American History.* A series of 12 filmstrips with accompanying records. For junior or senior high school. Can be used for group singing in class. Warren Schloat Productions, Pleasantville, New York.

5. Enrichment material for tenth- or twelfth-grade humanities:

(a) *Great Ages of Man.* Time-Life Books.

6. Sources of slides and filmstrips:

(a) National Gallery of Art
Extension Service
Washington, D.C. 20565

Excellent slides, lectures, and filmstrips free of charge.

(b) Shorewood Publishers, Inc.
Catalogue of Fine Art Reproductions
724 Fifth Avenue
New York, N.Y. 10019

Good selection for classroom use.

(c) Universal Color Slide Company
426 East 89th Street
New York, N.Y. 10028

Color slide library of art through the ages.

(d) The McGraw-Hill Color Slide Program of the World's Art, 12 volumes. Excellent representative slides with adequate discussion guides. May be used by a classroom teacher who is not an art specialist.

(e) Life Filmstrips
9 Rockefeller Plaza
New York, N.Y. 10020

Filmstrips in color of art work, including that of Matisse, Gauguin, Renoir, Rouault, van Gogh.

(f) Warren Schloat Productions
Pleasantville, N.Y.

Color sound filmstrips on U.S. history, American minority groups, artists and their works, and many other topics.

7. *The Schwann Long Playing Record Catalog* is a complete listing of available recordings of all types of music and literature, including full names and life dates of composers. An indispensable aid in locating, selecting, and ordering records. Issued monthly. Available for about 60 cents in most record shops.

8. Books in the humanities area useful for reading or reference by either student or teacher:

Apel, Willi, and Ralph T. Daniel. *The Harvard Brief Dictionary of Music* (Washington Square Press, paperback)

Chase, Gilbert, *America's Music* (McGraw-Hill)

Christensen, Erwin O. *The History of Western Art* (Mentor, paperback)

Copland, Aaron. *What to Listen for in Music* (Mentor, paperback)

Fleming, William, and Abraham Veinus. *Understanding Music* (Holt)

Ghiselin, Brewster. *The Creative Process* (Mentor, paperback)

Janson, H. W. *History of Art* (Prentice-Hall)

Machlis, Joseph. *The Enjoyment of Music* (Norton)

Machlis, Joseph. *Introduction to Contemporary Music* (Norton)

Rodman, Selden. *Conversations with Artists* (Capricorn, paperback)

9. Miscellaneous books for teacher reference:

Deiulio, Anthony M. "Youth Education: A Literary Perspective." In: *Youth Education,* Raymond H. Muessig, editor. Association for Supervision and Curriculum Development, NEA, Washington, D.C., 1968. A discussion of works of literature which deal with the problems of adolescence.

Langer, Susanne K. (ed.). *Reflections on Art.* A source book of writings by artists, critics, and philosophers. Oxford University Press, New York, 1961 (Galaxy paperback).

McGinn, Donald J., and George Howerton. *Literature as a Fine Art.* Harper & Row, 1959. Selections from literature, particularly poetry, arranged chronologically by stylistic periods. Each section is preceded by a helpful introduction and followed by lists of parallel examples of art and music.

Meyer, Leonard B. *Music, the Arts, and Ideas.* University of Chicago Press, 1967. "This book is an attempt to understand the present—to discover some pattern and rationale in the perplexing, fragmented world of twentieth-century culture."

Phenix, Philip H. *Realms of Meaning.* A Philosophy of the Curriculum for General Education. McGraw-Hill, New York, 1964.

Santayana, George, *The Sense of Beauty.* Being the Outline of Aesthetic Theory. Dover Publications, New York, 1955. A paperback republication of the first edition published in 1896.

Appendix B

WEST IRÓNDEQUOIT SCHOOLS   COMBINED SUBJECTS CURRICULUM
UNIT III: NEW FORCES CREATE   GRADE 6
              CHANGES DURING THE
              MIDDLE AGES
SECTION A: SOCIAL STUDIES CONTENT AND
            REFERENCES

Content	References
Part I: The Rise of Islam and the Effects of the Crusades	INITIATORY TIME LINE* BAF 218-22, 232-6‡
A. A new religious force appears	BAF 218-22‡ BOW 211-15‡ HEP 172-7‡
1. Mohammed, leader of a new religion	(B) Reading† BAF 218-9‡
(a) Background of Mohammed	BAF 218‡ SKIT*
(b) Mohammed's debt to the religions of the Jews and Christians	BAF 218‡ BOW 211‡ REPORT*
(c) The Koran, Mohammed's teachings in written form	BOW 212‡ BAF 219‡
(d) Mohammed's conquest of Arabia	BAF 219-20‡
2. The growth of Islam	(7) Panel† (8) Koran† (D) Map†

*ACTIVITIES described in the *Manual for Teachers.*
†ACTIVITIES described in the Activities section of this unit guide.
‡SOCIAL studies textbook references: initials of book title and relevant pages.

279

Appendix C

WEST IRONDEQUOIT SCHOOLS   COMBINED SUBJECTS CURRICULUM
UNIT V: GRADE 6
SECTION B: LANGUAGE ARTS SKILLS AND REFERENCES
NOTE TO TEACHER: Skills listed below are a review of fifth grade material except when marked with an ᵃ. Skills so marked are new skills to be introduced in this unit.

Skills	References
Part I: Speaking Skills	
A. He is able to give a solo recitation from memory of a *short* selection of prose or poetry.	POETRY*
1. He does not *recite* in a monotone.	
2. He attempts the use of dramatic gestures or movements during his recitation.	
Part II: Writing Skills	
A. The student writes in complete sentences to express his ideas.	NEWSPAPER* REPORT* SPECIALTY*
1. He uses and can identify commands.	
ᵃ2. He can identify *imperative* sentences.	
ᵃ3. He writes sentences with direct objects used correctly.	
B. The student groups related sentences in a visual form of a paragraph.	NEWSPAPER*
1. He indents at the beginning of each new paragraph he writes.	(15) Worksheet†

*ACTIVITIES described in the *Manual for Teachers.*
†ACTIVITIES described in the Activities section of this unit guide.

Suggested Content for a
Junior High School Block-Time Program
That Replaces Language Arts,
Social Studies, Science, and Health

Language Arts

I. Giving Ideas
  A. Oral expression
    1. Formal and informal discussions
      (a) Class situations
         (i) Phrasing a point of view
         (ii) Holding interest of the group
         (iii) Committee reports
         (iv) Panels
      (b) Club meetings
         (i) Student council meetings
         (ii) Presiding
      (c) School elections, parties, dinners, etc.
         (i) Acting as host or hostess
         (ii) Campaign speeches
      (d) Telling stories
      (e) Reading aloud effectively
      (f) Conversation
    2. Speech, dramatics, debate
      (a) Choral reading
      (b) Telephone etiquette
      (c) Interviews
  B. Written expression
    1. Writing letters of various kinds
      (a) Sympathy
      (b) Friendly
      (c) Thank you
      (d) Application

       (e) Business
       (f) Invitation
   2. Writing stories
   3. Writing poetry
   4. Making summaries
       (a) Reports
       (b) Materials read
       (c) Films
   5. Reporting
   6. Taking notes
       (a) Spelling words correctly
       (b) Getting essential ideas
   7. Taking minutes
   8. Outlining
   9. Preparing scripts
  10. Making bibliographies
  C. Other forms of expression
   1. Illustrations
   2. Cartoons
   3. Murals
   4. Maps, tables, graphs, diagrams
   5. Aesthetic expression
       (a) Dramatizing
       (b) Singing
II. Getting Ideas
  A. Reading and understanding written material
   1. Resource materials
       (a) Source books
          (i) Comparing viewpoints of different authors
         (ii) Using footnotes
       (b) Newspapers
          (i) Judging information for truth
         (ii) Judging information for propaganda
       (c) Using films
       (d) Understanding directions
       (e) Using the dictionary and the encyclopedia
   2. Free reading for enjoyment
  B. Listening
   1. Speakers
       (a) Conversation
       (b) Church
       (c) Assembly
       (d) Social gatherings

       (e) Minutes of a meeting
       (f) Panel discussions
       (g) Lectures
    2. Radio and TV programs
       (a) News commentators
       (b) Panels
       (c) Inspirational shows
       (d) Dramatic productions
       (e) Documentaries
    3. Respect for facts
    4. Value of opinion
III. Mechanics of Communication
    A. Spelling
    B. Sentence structure
    C. Paragraphing
    D. Parts of speech
    E. Capitalization
    F. Punctuation
    G. Words and phrases
    H. Proofreading

Social Studies

I. Earning a Living
    A. Dignity of work
    B. Standards of living
    C. What my interests and abilities suit me for
    D. My place in the family work at home
II. Securing Goods and Services
    A. Production of goods and services
    B. Making the world's goods and services available
       1. Reciprocal trade relations
       2. Adequate and effective distribution
    C. Buying and selling the world's goods and services
       1. Getting your money's worth—being an intelligent consumer
       2. Dealing with people of other countries
    D. Managing Money
       1. Budgeting income
       2. Investing savings
       3. Borrowing money
    E. Agencies of communication and transportation
III. Providing for Social Well-Being
    A. Working in and through the family group
    B. Participating in community provisions for group well-being

   C. Using government as a means to guarantee well-being
       1. Adequate public services
       2. Legal protection
       3. Controlling the use of natural resources
  IV. How Public Opinion is Formed
       A. Participating in organized education
       B. Working with educative agencies other than schools
       C. Using instruments for disseminating information
           1. Interpreting information
           2. Influencing group thinking
           3. Understanding propaganda
   V. Participating in Local, State, and National Government
       A. Electing governmental representatives
       B. Securing effective organization for government
           1. Finding how government groups are organized
           2. Understanding major issues
       C. Making and enforcing laws
           1. Understanding
           2. Cooperating
           3. Enforcing
           4. Making
           5. Respecting
       D. Providing adequate financial support for government
           1. Taxes
           2. How the tax money is used
       E. Realizing the responsibilities of citizenship
  VI. Understanding the World in Which We Live
       A. Maps, globes, other references
       B. International relations
           1. The United Nations
           2. Other forms of government as compared to our own
       C. Geography and history of the Old World with emphasis on key countries
           in modern world affairs
       D. Our American neighbors
       E. Regions
 VII. American History and Geography
       A. Colonization
       B. Struggle for independence and establishment of a new nation
       C. Development of our democracy
       D. America as a world power

General Science

   I. Understanding the Globe

   A. Surface features
      1. Rocks
      2. Soil
      3. Volcanoes, geysers, hot springs
      4. Atmosphere
      5. Water
      6. Weather

II. Solar System
   A. Planets
   B. Beyond the solar system

III. Continuity of Life
   A. Plants and animals
   B. Life cycles
   C. Balance of nature
   D. Man as an animal
   E. Vertebrates and invertebrates

IV. Energy
   A. Energy for the world at work
      1. Magnetism and electricity
      2. Work and energy
      3. Gravity
      4. Centrifugal force
      5. Friction
      6. Engines and motors
      7. Simple machines
   B. Energy for transportation
      1. Muscular
      2. Mechanical—land, air, water
   C. Energy for communication
      1. Sound
      2. Light
      3. Electricity
      4. Instruments for measuring

V. Modern Science
   A. Jet propulsion
   B. Electronics
   C. Atomic energy
   D. Medicine

VI. Man and His Environment
   A. Inventions and discoveries
   B. Use of power

V. Modern Science
   A. Jet propulsion
   B. Electronics

    C. Atomic energy

    D. Medicine

VI. Man and His Environment

    A. Inventions and discoveries

    B. Use of power

    C. Minerals

    D. Conquest of space

    E. Conservation

    F. Relation to health and safety

    G. Control of environment for sake of health and happiness

Health Education

I. The Meaning of Good Health

    A. Physical

        1. Growth periods

        2. Muscular development

        3. Exercise

        4. Rest

    B. Mental

        1. Habits

        2. Attitudes

        3. Responsibilities

    C. Emotional well-being

        1. Satisfactory relations with others

        2. Satisfactory relations with self

    D. Social

        1. Relationships with opposite sex

        2. Getting along with the peer group

II. How Food is Changed to Fuel

    A. Quality and quantity of food supplies

    B. How the body works

III. The Work of the Blood

    A. Organs of circulation

    B. How and where the blood circulates

    C. Heart and your responsibility

IV. The Air We Breathe

    A. Care of the respiratory tract

    B. Diseases of the respiratory tract

    C. Ventilation and lighting

V. Watchtower Controls

    A. Voluntary and involuntary controls

    B. Nervous system

    C. Work of the nerves

VI. Personal Appearance and Grooming
    A. Skin
        1. Structure
        2. Function
    B. Clothing
        1. Regulation of body heat
        2. Body protection
VII. Family Relationships
    A. Behavior problems
        1. Prevention
        2. Cure
    B. Promoting mental health through family living
VIII. Health and Safety
    A. Routines necessary to well-being
    B. Disease control
        1. Home
        2. Community
    C. Avoiding accidents
        1. Home
        2. Community
    D. Physical defects and injuries
        1. Administering first aid
        2. Procedures for seeking help

A Check List
for Evaluating a Core Unit*

A. General Information
1. Was the resource unit well written?
2. What suggestions would you make for improving the unit?
3. What suggestions did the pupils make for changes and additions to the unit?
4. Should we continue using the unit?
5. Does the unit need revising?

B. Committee Work
1. Did you use committee work?
2. Why or why not?
3. What are some methods you used to get committees into action?
4. How many members did you use on a committee?
5. How were committees chosen?
6. What kind of person does very poor committee work?
7. What percent of the class fit into this group?
8. Do you see an improvement in committee work as compared to the last unit?
9. Do you have any particular methods for getting people into committee work?
10. How do you work different people into the role of leader?
11. How do you keep one person from being chairman each time?
12. Do you use any evaluative methods to guide your class in their development of good committee habits?
13. When a committee has completed its work, how does it present its findings?
14. Do you have some people who refuse to work on committees?

C. Reading and Library Habits
1. How did you use the school library with this unit?
2. How did you use the room library?
3. To what extent did you use the literature books which are supplied you?

*Note: See Chapter 12 for an explanation of how this may be used.

4. Did you use other books and stories to develop an interest in reading? Can you name some of them?
5. What are some methods you used to encourage good reading habits?
6. Did you set aside any time for reading each day?
7. Did you have any required readings?
8. How did you check required readings?
9. Did you allow the pupils to do research in the library?
10. Did you use any new methods for helping pupils find resource materials?

D. Oral Communication Skills
1. What opportunities did you provide for pupils to gain experience in oral communication skills?
2. What are some methods you found successful in teaching oral communication skills?
3. Did you have the opportunity to give individual help to those people who had difficulty in expressing themselves orally?
4. What were some methods you used to help these people?
5. Did the group work experience help in the development of oral communication skills?

E. Creative Writing and Critical Thinking
1. Did you find opportunities to encourage creative writing?
2. What were some of the techniques you used to encourage creative writing?
3. Did you talk with pupils individually about suggestions for improvement?
4. Did you have special class assignments in creative writing?
5. Were the assignments based on materials in the resource units?
6. Can you recall instances in which you felt you helped your class to think critically?
7. Did the unit give ample opportunity to develop critical thinking?
8. Did you find the opportunity to use discussion groups or debate?

F. Listening Habits
1. Did you find opportunities to stress the importance of good listening habits?
2. What methods have you found effective in developing good listening habits?

G. Mechanics of Communication
1. Did you find it difficult to teach the mechanics of expression in relation to the unit of work? What were some methods you used to include them?
2. What are some procedures you used in teaching capitalization and punctuation?
3. Did you emphasize spelling in this unit of work?

4. Did you develop a spelling list? If so, what were the words?
5. Was the spelling list pupil-teacher planned?
6. Did you have opportunity to discuss such things as definitions, contractions, plurals, homonyms, antonyms, and synonyms in your spelling work?
7. If the pupils had difficulty expressing themselves correctly in either written or oral work, did you stop the unit work and discuss these problems?
8. Do you ever spend several days or even a week or more working out these problems and then return to the unit?

H. Social Studies Content
1. What social studies content did you teach directly, instead of relying on student committee work?
2. Did your study of maps and globes include such terms as latitude, longitude, time belts, weather and wind systems?
3. What teaching procedures have you found effective in teaching geographical concepts?
4. Did you have occasion to discuss anything about how our world has changed or how we can move from place to place in short periods of time?

I. Guidance
1. Did you discuss work-study habits?
2. How was this emphasized in your teaching?
3. Were you able to handle discipline problems or did you refer them to the principal or counselor?
4. Did you have any opportunity to offer individual guidance to any of the students?
5. Was there any opportunity to discuss such things as attitudes, interests, appreciations, or social skills?
6. Did you attempt to help any of the pupils with self-evaluation techniques?

J. Use of Films, Field Trips, and Related Activities
1. What films did you use?
2. What filmstrips did you use?
3. What slides did you use?
4. Did you use any resource people? Name them and give a confidential evaluation of their performance.
5. Did you take any field trips? How did you prepare for them and what was your follow-up?

Selected Bibliography

Books

Alexander, William M., and others. *The Emergent Middle School.* New York: Holt, Rinehart and Winston, 1968.

Numerous block-time and interdisciplinary programs are described in this monograph.

Alexander, William M., Vynce A. Hines, and others. *Independent Study in Secondary Schools.* New York: Holt, Rinehart and Winston, 1967.

A comprehensive investigation of independent study programs in 36 schools is reported in this volume.

Anderson, Robert H. *Teaching in a World of Change.* New York: Harcourt, Brace & World, 1966.

Essentially an introduction to education text, this book gives considerable attention to nongraded and team teaching patterns.

Association for Supervision and Curriculum Development. *Perceiving, Behaving, Becoming: A New Focus for Education.* Yearbook 1962. Washington, D.C.: The Association, 1962.

Learning that stresses growth and development of the fully-functioning individual is the focus of this volume.

Beggs, David W., III. (ed.). *Team Teaching: Bold New Venture.* Bloomington: Indiana University Press, 1964.

Many aspects of team teaching are explored in this collected work.

———, and Edward G. Buffie (eds.). *Independent Study: Bold New Venture.* Bloomington: Indiana University Press, 1965.

This book describes several models of school organization that facilitate independent study.

——————————. *Nongraded Schools in Action: Bold New Venture.* Bloomington: Indiana University Press, 1967.

295

As in previous volumes in this series, chapters discussing the general theory of nongrading are followed by descriptions of several current elementary and secondary programs.

Berman, Louise M. (ed.). *The Humanities and the Curriculum.* Washington: Association for Supervision and Curriculum Development, 1967.

These papers from a conference sponsored by ASCD discuss the contributions of various academic disciplines to a study of the humanities. Major papers deal with: (1) the social studies, (2) fine arts and music, (3) language and literature, and (4) philosophy, logic, ethics, and values.

Broudy, Harry S., B. Othanel Smith, and Joe R. Burnett. *Democracy and Excellence in American Secondary Education.* Chicago: Rand, McNally, 1964.

These authors would defer examination of what they call "molar problems" until students have acquired a solid grounding in the content and methodology of various disciplines.

Brown, B. Frank. *The Appropriate Placement School.* West Nyack, New York: Parker Publishing Company, 1965.

———. *The Nongraded High School.* Englewood Cliffs, New Jersey: Prentice-Hall, 1963.

Both the above books describe Brown's conception of the nongraded curriculum.

Butterweck, Joseph S., and Katherine H. Spessard. *The Unified Curriculum: A Case Study, Grades 7–8.* New York: Holt, Rinehart and Winston, 1960.

This pamphlet describes a community study, conducted over a two-year period, that involved teachers of separate subjects as well as the core teacher. The study culminated in the planning of an "ideal" community.

Faunce, Roland C., and Nelson L. Bossing. *Developing the Core Curriculum.* 2nd ed.; Englewood Cliffs, New Jersey: Prentice-Hall, 1958.

This comprehensive text covers all aspects of core theory and practice.

Goodlad, John I. and Robert H. Anderson. *The Nongraded Elementary School.* Rev. ed.; New York: Harcourt, Brace, and World, 1963.

This book is a major source of arguments for the nongraded approach.

Hanna, Lavone A., Gladys L. Potter, and Neva Hagaman. *Unit Teaching in the Elementary School.* Rev. ed.; New York: Holt, Rinehart and Winston, 1963.

Many parallels may be found between the approach to unit teaching described here and the methods employed by block-time and core teachers.

Hock, Louise E. *Using Committees in the Classroom.* New York: Holt, Rinehart and Winston, 1958.

This brief pamphlet contains many practical suggestions.

————, and Thomas J. Hill. *The General Education Class in the Secondary School.* New York: Holt, Rinehart and Winston, 1960.

Methods of teaching a block-time class receive considerable attention in this book.

Hunt, Maurice P. and Lawrence E. Metcalf. *Teaching High School Social Studies.* 2nd ed.; New York: Harper & Row, 1968.

The "reflectively oriented teaching" and "problematic areas" recommended by these authors closely resemble the problem-centered methods and curriculum organization of core.

Lurry, Lucile L. and Elsie J. Alberty. *Developing a High School Core Program.* New York: Macmillan, 1957.

How to structure a core program around problem areas is thoroughly explored in this book.

Marckwardt, Albert H. (ed). *Literature in the Humanities Program.* Champaign, Ill.: National Council of Teachers of English, 1967.

Implications for elementary, junior high, and senior high school education are considered in these papers from a humanities conference sponsored by the NCTE in 1966.

Massialas, Byron G., and C. Benjamin Cox. *Inquiry in Social Studies.* New York: McGraw-Hill, 1966.

A focus on student inquiry and critical thinking as applied to social problems brings this social studies methods text into harmony with the core concept.

New York State Education Department. *The Humanities: A Planning Guide for Teachers.* Albany: Bureau of Secondary Curriculum Development, 1966.

Objectives, methods, and instructional materials are suggested for three alternative ways of organizing a humanities course: (1) The Functions Approach (Man and Self, Man and Society, etc.), (2) The Elements Approach (Form, Reality, Purpose, etc.), and (3) The Chronological Approach.

Oliver, Donald E., and James P. Shaver. *Teaching Public Issues in the High School.* Boston: Houghton Mifflin, 1966.

With its emphasis on values and focus on social problems, the approach to social studies described in this book closely resembles the problems approach typical of core.

Parrish, Louise and Yvonne Waskin. *Teacher-Pupil Planning for Better Classroom Learning.* New York: Harper & Row, 1958. Reprinted 1967 by Pitman Publishing Corp., New York.

Various aspects of cooperative planning are explored, with many illustrations from core classes.

Pennsylvania Humanities Commission. *Universal Issues in Human Life.* Harrisburg, Pa.: Pennsylvania Department of Public Instruction, 1965.

This curriculum guide is designed "to incorporate a non-sectarian moral element into the curriculum and to provide a thread for the proper integration of the separate subjects." Included are the following resource units: (1) Man's Search for Truth, (2) Man's Search for Freedom, (3) Man's Search for Beauty, (4) Man's Relationship with the Natural World, (5) Man and Society, and (6) Man's Relation to God.

Petrequin, Gaynor. *Individualizing Learning Through Modular-Flexible Programming.* New York: McGraw-Hill, 1968.

A ninth-grade combined English and social studies program is included in this detailed and candid report on team teaching at John Marshall High School, Portland, Oregon.

Raths, Louis E., Merrill Harmin, and Sidney B. Simon. *Values and Teaching.* Columbus, Ohio: Charles E. Merrill, 1966.

Core teachers will find here many valuable techniques for helping young people examine and clarify their values.

Rollins, Sidney P. *Developing Nongraded Schools.* Itasca, Illinois: F. E. Peacock Publishers, Inc., 1968.

This monograph describes the rationale, curriculum, role of the teacher, administration, physical environment, and teacher preparation.

Selakovich, Daniel. *Problems in Secondary Social Studies.* Englewood Cliffs, New Jersey: Prentice-Hall, 1965.

The problems approach to social studies content, elaborated here, is equally applicable in a core program.

Shaplin, Judson T., and Henry F. Olds, Jr. (eds.). *Team Teaching.* New York. Harper & Row, 1964.

Team-teaching theory is thoroughly examined in this volume.

Stafford, James L. *An Exploration into Team Teaching in English and the Humanities.* Champaign, Ill.: National Council of Teachers of English, 1963.

This brief case study describes a tenth-grade literature and world history program.

Stoddard George D. *The Dual Progress Plan.* New York: Harper & Row, 1961.

Stoddard's rationale for dual progress is supplemented with brief reports of early experiments with the plan.

Taba, Hilda and Deborah Elkins. *Teaching Strategies for the Culturally Disadvantaged.* Chicago: Rand McNally, 1966.

A personalized approach to instruction, reminiscent of core teaching, permeates this book.

Trump, J. Lloyd, and Dorsey Baynham. *Focus on Change: Guide to Better Schools.* Chicago: Rand McNally, 1961.

Interdisciplinary team teaching is described as one useful variant of the plans developed by the Staff Utilization Commission of the National Association of Secondary-School Principals.

U.S. Office of Education. *Block-Time Classes and the Core Program in the Junior High School,* by Grace S. Wright. Bulletin 1958, No. 6. Washington D.C.: Government Printing Office, 1958.

The most comprehensive survey of block-time practices available, this study was made just before Sputnik.

———. *The Core Program: Abstracts of Unpublished Research, 1946-1955,* by Grace S. Wright. Circular No. 485. Washington, D.C.: Government Printing Office, 1956.

———, *The Core Program: Unpublished Research, 1956-1962,* by Grace S. Wright. Circular No. 713. Washington, D.C.: Government Printing Office, 1963.

These extremely useful monographs deal with the history and theory of core, status and trends, initiation and development, characteristics and preparation of core teachers, core content, instructional practices, and evaluation of program effectiveness.

Van Til, William, Gordon F. Vars, and John H. Lounsbury. *Modern Education for the Junior High School Years.* 2nd ed.; Indianapolis: Bobbs-Merrill, 1967.

Several chapters in this text are devoted to the rationale and methods of teaching in block-time and core programs.

Vars, Gordon F. *Teaching in Teams.* Cornell Curriculuum and Instruction Series, No. 2 Ithaca, N.Y.: Department of Education, Cornell University, 1966..

This pamphlet describes an elementary nongraded team teaching program and a high school plan that emphasizes independent study.

Willey, Roy DeV. and W. Melvin Strong. *Group Procedures in Guidance.* New York: Harper & Row, 1958.

The authors give specific attention to group guidance in the core course.

Zapf, Rosalind M. *Democratic Processes in the Secondary Classroom.* Englewood Cliffs, N.J.: Prentice-Hall, 1959.

Methods for teaching an unstructured core program are detailed in this comprehensive text.

Periodicals

Two newsletters provide the latest information on developments in core and related concepts. *The Core Teacher* is published quarterly as a membership service of the National Association for Core Curriculum, Inc., with editorial offices at 404F Education Building, Kent State University, Kent, Ohio 44240. In addition to news about national, regional, and state core teachers' conferences, it carries reviews of pertinent research studies, professional publications, and instructional materials. Feature articles describe new developments in core theory, school programs in operation in various parts of the nation, suggested teaching methods, and the like. The cost is $2.00 per year.

Teaching Core is published periodically during the school year by the General Education Committee of the Metropolitan Detroit Bureau of School Studies, Fairmont Bldg., 680 Merrick Ave., Wayne State University, Detroit, Michigan 48202. Besides news of core conferences in Michigan and in the Detroit area, *Teaching Core* carries teachers' reports of successful practices, student creative writing, and other suggestions.

Since a bibliography of periodical articles is apt to be out of date before it is published, *Education Index* should be consulted for current information in the professional education journals. Articles specifically dealing with block-time and core programs are listed under "Curriculum—Core Program." As popular attention has shifted to other approaches to the core idea, the number of articles under this classification has decreased, while citations under "Team Teaching," "Humanities," and "Independent Study" have increased markedly. Often it is necessary to examine the article itself to discover that the program under discussion is interdisciplinary. Nongraded programs are described under "Progress in School." Nearly all the educational magazines carry occasional articles describing programs that reflect the core concept in some form, including the specialized journals dealing with the teaching of art, music, business, industrial arts, English, social studies, science, and similar subjects.

Audio-Visual Materials

A Core Class Tells Its Story. (color filmstrip.) Muncie, Ind.: Ball State Teachers College Library, 1958.

Prepared under the direction of Myrtle Dewey Toops, this filmstrip illustrates many characteristics of core and describes how eighth-graders carried out a unit on interpersonal relations.

Focus on Change. (color filmstrip with record.) Washington, D.C.: National Association of Secondary-School Principals, 1962.

Still one of the best succinct explanations of team teaching, this filmstrip was produced under the direction of J. Lloyd Trump.

The Improbable Form of Master Sturm. (13-minute color film.) Melbourne, Fla.: IDEA Information Service, 1968.

This film explains B. Frank Brown's conception of a nongraded high school program.

Teaching Democratic Processes at the Secondary Level. (4 color filmstrips with records.) Detroit, Mich.: The Jam Handy Organization, 1968.

Problem-centered teaching methods and the wealth of learning resources they may utilize are elaborated in this series, prepared under the guidance of Rosalind Zapf Pickard.

We Plan Together. (20-minute black and white film.) New York: Bureau of Publications, Teachers College, Columbia University, 1948.

Written and produced by students, this old but still inspiring film shows a senior high school core class studying world problems and ideologies.

Index